Peer-to-Peer Computing

Technologies for Sharing and Collaborating on the Net

by

David Barkai
Intel Corporation

INTEL PRESS

ISBN 0-9702846-7-5

This book is printed on acid-free paper. ♾

Publisher: Rich Bowles

Editor: David Spencer

Copyeditors: Victor Chapman, Kathy Warfel, Christian Carmichael

Text Design & Composition: Marianne Phelps

Graphic Art: Donna Lawless (illustrations); Dan Mandish (cover)

Library of Congress Cataloging in Publication Data:

Printed in the United States of America

10 9 8 7 6 5 4 3 2 1

To Barbara,

For the “lost summer” and the walks in the park.

Contents

Figures

Tables

Foreword

Our connected and networked world is transforming. A new phase in the evolution of the Internet landscape is upon us. It is a sign of the pervasiveness of resources and how accustomed we have become to relying on the Internet that we now expect more. Until recently we were content to have our communications mediated by service providers, and we were delighted to find information collected for us by search engines that index web servers. Not anymore. I see people in business and at home wishing for these two things: Direct exchanges between people and relevant sharing of resources on the Net. This book introduces you to technologies that will help bring these about.

Today, the user at the edge of the Internet can easily browse, search, download, or read from the network. In other words, being a recipient has been made simple and convenient. The future Internet will become "writable," enabling uninterrupted two-way communications. Users at the edges of the Net will be able to publish and write back directly from their desktops to the web, and the exchanges will not be mediated by a server, but rather from one person to another. And with the many more connected devices – wireless, handheld, and appliances – the Net will resemble the real world more closely.

The need for a richer experience, focused on direct communications between people and relevant content in all forms, is coincident with the ubiquity of networked computers and the arrival and adoption of broadband and wireless communications. The Internet experience will change from that of reading and receiving data to one where people participate in self-organizing, dynamic, communities built on shared interests, writing and publishing at will and being exposed to customized relevant knowledge bases.

Along the way, the Internet will put more intelligence near the users – and that's where Peer-to-Peer comes in. As we move from today's web to the writable web and to the device-rich Net, Peer-to-Peer becomes the natural computing model. Its conceptual foundations are based on being able to scale to the devices on the outer reaches of the net through node-to-node communications, where huge amounts of resources go unused. This is why the time for Peer-to-Peer is now.

Peer-to-Peer computing is where local and global exchanges between individuals and within communities intersect with technology and vast repositories of information at the edges of the Net. In other words, the ubiquity of resource-rich computers, aided by high-bandwidth networks, enables the direct collaboration and resource sharing that are the hallmarks of Peer-to-Peer. Underutilized resources will be channeled to route communications away from bottlenecks, provide storage, discover the right up-to-date information, deliver relevant content, perform computations, and much more.

Peer-to-Peer is a computing model and a set of technologies that supplement current practices for both consumers and the enterprise. It will become an important tool for applications for e-commerce, novel online collaborations, and entertainment.

I welcome any technology that enhances the Internet and adds relevance and meaning to people's interaction with their peers and participation in online communities. Peer-to-Peer technologies add another building block to the Internet infrastructure.

Peer-to-Peer is much more than sharing music files. But, so far, the buzz about all the possibilities and innovative uses of Peer-to-Peer has been mostly confined to a select and small community of so-called "Peer-to-Peer developers."

This book is an important contribution to spreading the word on the promise of Peer-to-Peer. It tells you of the pioneering work and innovations being created by the Peer-to-Peer developer community and what it means to you, the reader.

I urge you, the user and application developer, to learn more about Peer-to-Peer computing, and take advantage of the technologies described in this book. I also encourage you to join the Peer-to-Peer developer community, a group currently engaged in ongoing work to address the remaining challenges ahead of creating a more seamless and transparent use of Peer-to-Peer throughout our computing fabric.

Patrick Gelsinger
Vice President and Chief Technology Officer
Intel Architecture Group
Intel Corporation

August 2001

Preface

The idea for a book on peer-to-peer (P2P) computing was born out of the explosive interest the public and developers have shown in this new way of using the net and the web. We felt there is a need for a book that will paint the big picture, capture the state-of-the-art of P2P, describe the enabling technologies, compare design and implementation approaches, highlight the challenges, and present an outlook of the future of P2P.

When I started thinking about the concept for the book last year, the central theme was going to be "P2P is not just for swapping music files; it is also good for business and the enterprise." In the following months it became clear that this thesis does not require further promotion; it has been accepted by everyone. And so, I started looking for signs that all the pieces will come together. The possibilities and barriers to interoperability within platforms and applications in a computing model that brings back some of the old and dear features of the Internet's early days.

This is a book about technologies that enable P2P. It is about technologies developed by the P2P innovators outside of the software powerhouses. Not all could be included. I chose representatives from several application areas. What these companies have in common is their focus on P2P applications for the enterprise, and services that support online communities.

Peer-to-peer computing is important

Certain events in the last twenty years have been catalysts of innovation for the computer industry. The major milestones were the arrival of the personal computer in the early 80's, and the invention and introduction of the World Wide Web in the early 90's. It may well be that the adoption of P2P computing will have a similar impact on creating innovative and novel usages for our computers.

P2P hails the decentralization of the Internet: the center of the action moves to the edges of networks. Huge amounts of unused resources get tapped. With P2P, our "cyber lives" resemble real life. We have direct exchanges. We form communities. We create and share our content.

When I started writing this book (in late 2000), the excitement over P2P was at its peak. Many new startup companies were formed; others declared themselves to be "P2P." A few months later, with the bursting of the dot-com bubble, there was some talk about the demise of P2P. Both swings of the pendulum were exaggerated. The irrational exuberance was overdone, as was the gloom and doom that followed.

P2P is alive and well. It is not a product. It is a way of doing things; it is a mindset. It enriches and empowers the individual computer user, and allows us all to make use of resources that have previously been wasted. P2P cannot be put back into the bottle.

Acknowledgements

This project would not have happened without the trust that three people placed in the concept and in me. Bob Knighten, Justin Rattner, and Pat Gelsinger – from my management chain in Intel – supported the book idea and made it possible for me to spend long months on its creation.

One of the most rewarding aspects of writing this book is meeting the people who feel so passionately about the wonderful things that P2P computing brings about. They are the heroes of the P2P story; the people who make it all happen.

These are the people who spent hours patiently telling me about their products and technologies. Without their help the book could not have been written.

From Avaki, Anh Nguyen-Tuong, Andrew Grimshaw and Mark Morgan. From Endeavors Technologies, Art Hitomi, Greg Bolcer, Peter Kammer, Michael Gorlick, Jim Lowrey, Clay Cover, and Brian Morrow. From Engenia, Jeffrey Kay. From Entropia, Karan Bhatia and Andrew Chien. From the Escher Group, Andrew ("Drew") Sutherland. From the Global Grid Forum, Ian Foster and Charlie Catlett. From Groove, Andrew Mahon and Kurt Niska. From Mangosoft, Scott Davis. From NextPage, Tom Ngo. From OpenCola, Cory Doctorow, John Henson, Andy Flinn, and Grad Conn. From United Devices, Jikku Venkat, David McNett, and Ed Hubbard.

I gratefully acknowledge conversations with Brent Gutekunst and Mark Boyns from FirstPeer, Jamie Bernardin from DataSynapse, and Robin Waldman from Oculus.

Many of my Intel colleagues offered me their support and wisdom on numerous occasions. Tim Mattson helped me the history and theory of distributed computing. Carl Klotz, Andrew Henroid, David Grawrock, and Ernie Brickell taught me a lot about security. Henroid also described the P2P trusted library, which he coded. Dermot Honan, Shelby Siegel, and Ivan Harrow told me about P2P projects in Intel.

Scott Robinson, Andy Anderson, Sharad Garg, John Wei, Cedric Yau – all from Intel, and Damien Stolarz from Blue Falcon, did the work on which much of the Communications chapter is based. Anderson also reviewed and clarified NATs and firewalls text in the book.

I am grateful for information and stimulation received through discussions with Andy Anderson, Claude Cruz, Sharad Garg, Bob Knighten, Paul Pierce, Jeff Reinemann, Scott Robinson, and Vijay Tewari.

My gratitude goes to the good people who set aside some of their precious time to review the draft manuscript. The benefit from corrected errors and the many helpful suggestions is invaluable. Whatever is still not clear or not accurate is entirely my fault. My thanks go to: Anh Nguyen-Tuong, Art Hitomi, Jeffrey Kay, Karan Bhatia, Drew Sutherland, Ian Foster, Scott Davis, Tom Ngo, Cory Doctorow, and Jikku Venkat. And my Intel fellow workers were among the reviewers, too: Daven Oswalt, David C Stewart, Dorothy Bowers, Jim Prelack, and Paul Sullivan.

Finally, this book would not have been possible without the support and guidance of the Intel Press team. I am indebted to Stuart Goldstein who managed the project, and David B. Spencer who guided the development of the text. Donna Lawless put up with endless changes to the figures, and Denise Myers who put the word out. And, of course, the editors: Victor Chapman, Kathy Warfel, and Christian Carmichael, who showed me how my prose appears to the reader.

I thank you all.

David Barkai

PART I
PEER-TO-PEER COMPUTING

The premise, the possibilities, and the lessons from the past

"If a million people use a Web site simultaneously, doesn't that mean that we must have a heavy-duty remote server to keep them all happy? No; we could move the site onto a million desktops and use the internet for coordination."

David Gelernter, *The Second Coming – A manifesto*

Chapter 1
A New Computing Model for the Internet

Just when people began to talk about the "end of the PC era," at the beginning of 2000, peer-to-peer (P2P) computing burst onto the scene.

The concept isn't new. What's new is the enthusiasm with which developers and users are embracing peer computing. Napster, a music file-sharing application, brought P2P to the forefront by attracting millions of users, saturating colleges' networks, and raising some fundamental questions about copyrights and digital distribution of content.

Exchanging files, which is what the Napster application enables, is just one way of sharing resources among networked computers. Sharing and collaborating via the Internet today can happen in many other ways as well:

- Dividing the load of performing large computations.
- Collaborating in creating media or software.
- Conversing online and directly.
- Organizing into online communities.

Peer-to-peer computing is evolving into a phenomenon whose impact will be no less than that which we experienced when the graphical-interface browser and, again, when the client-server computing model were introduced.

The excitement around P2P was a catalyst for an important gathering. Over 350 people, representing about 250 companies and organizations, got together on October 12, 2000, in a San Jose hotel, for the first Peer-to-Peer Working Group meeting. This occasion was significant on at least two counts: It was a testament to the fast pace at which the user community embraces various peer-to-peer applications. And it brought together the Corporate and the Start-Up worlds, competitors, and colleagues alike—developers from a whole host of disciplines. The computer industry started to work together on common issues related to P2P computing.

The event was not, by itself, a turning point, but it validated a level of acceptance by the Industry of the significance of P2P. There were other meetings, public and behind closed doors, which advanced P2P computing. And much of what has happened in the computer industry in the last 20-25 years laid the groundwork for widespread use of P2P computing.

This is the story of peer-to-peer computing—from past experimental projects, to the present resurgence, and its future as a computing model for businesses and consumers on the Internet.

This book shows how P2P computing can enrich our net experience in many ways. This promise can best be realized if cross-platform and cross-application interoperability, preferably through a common P2P infrastructure, comes into being.

What is Peer-to-Peer Computing? – First Take

A good starting point is to explain P2P computing in terms of the client-server architecture for network-based computing. In a client-server model, the client (the computer where the user is) makes requests of the server to which it is networked. The server, typically an unattended system in a back room, responds to, and acts on, the requests. The idea behind P2P computing is that each *peer*, i.e., each participating computer, can act both as a client and as a server *in the context of some application*.

Computers in P2P computing are not rigidly defined as either clients or servers. They can be both, to some extent,[1] and "peer" is the word that best expresses the new role and relationship of these computers.[2] So, a peer is a computer that behaves as a client in the client-server model, but also contains an additional layer of software that allows it to perform server functions. The peer computer can respond to requests from other peers. The scope of the requests and responses, and how they are executed are application-specific. Typically, there is a request for access to resources that belong to the other peer. The request may be for a file to be

---

[1] The extent is limited because a desktop computer may have some server functionality, but is not likely to be able to replace a large multi-processor database server, for example.

[2] Deriving from the familiar client-server model some developers call this new type of end-user computer a *servent*, and others call it *clerver*.

read or copied, information on content and files, computations to be performed, a message or a file to be passed on to others, etc.

The client-server duality exhibited by a peer is a central feature of P2P.

The client-server model and the P2P model are not exclusive of each other. The two models can, and do, co-exist. The addition of some server functions to the client, making it a peer, does not diminish its capability to act as a full-fledged client towards servers on the net. Later you will read about the so-called hybrid model of peer computing where servers are used strictly as servers in the client-server sense.

The term *P2P computing* can refer to the model, or it can refer to the action of computing within that framework. Both facets are useful in defining P2P computing.

The P2P framework allows peers to interact with each other directly. An important characteristic of this direct interaction is that the computing environment becomes *decentralized.*[3] Think of the client-server model as a bicycle wheel where the server is at the center, the clients reside on the rim, and the spokes are the communication lines. In the P2P model, the spokes connect peers directly (see Figure 1.1). In reality, there may be connections to the center of the wheel, but not everything needs to go through the central server. As a result, the effect of P2P computing is to take computing to the *edges of the net*.

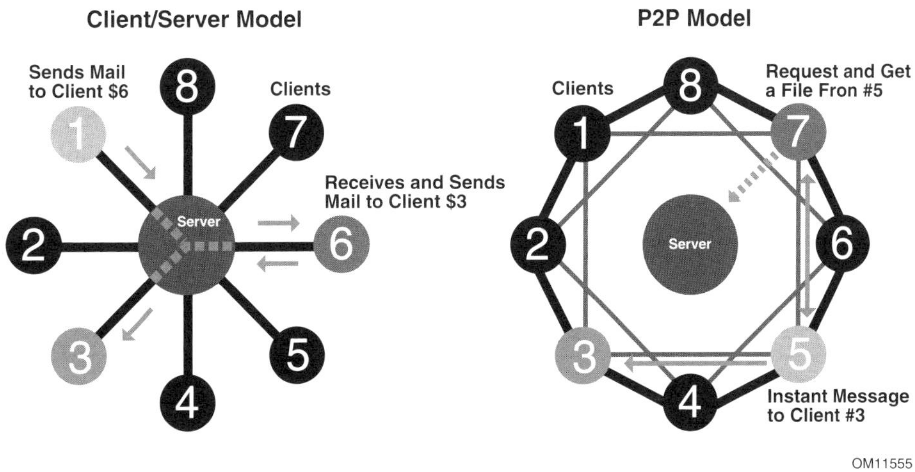

Figure 1.1 P2P computing is decentralized and at the edges of the net

[3] For a thought provoking article on decentralized systems, see Mitchel Resnick's "Beyond the Centralized Mindset" (Resnick, 1996).

When the "computing" in P2P computing is an action, it refers to what we do with the P2P framework. You will read later about many end-user applications that become possible through the P2P services. These applications include storage, computations, messaging, security, distribution, and more. What unifies these application types in the context of P2P is that they involve *sharing* of resources and some form of *collaboration*. Resource sharing and collaboration among peers are the distinguishing properties of P2P applications.

What does P2P computing mean to the user? Direct exchanges with other users, on their peer systems, liberates the users from some of the dependence on central servers. The tools for resource sharing empower users by allowing them to initiate services and provide access to resources under their own control.

From a social viewpoint, P2P computing enables users to organize in groups without the assistance of a central authority. These self-governed communities can share, collaborate, and communicate, or participate in their own private web. The emergence of dynamic online communities at the edges of the net is one of the more exciting phenomenon brought about by P2P computing.[4]

In One Word: Interoperability

Much of the interest surrounding P2P computing is based not so much on what has been demonstrated so far, but on its potential. P2P empowers users. It enables them to accomplish tasks previously done only by some remote server that someone else is managing. P2P allows you and your friends, or you and your family, to create your own virtual world of exchanges and communications. This is what P2P means for the consumer.

P2P also impacts business-to-business interactions as well as business-to-customer interactions. Collaboration and resource sharing take on new dimensions—productivity is increased and costs are cut through the use of huge amounts of resources that previously were unused. P2P computing is a formidable ally in streamlining the business supply chain, and filling the missing links for an effective e-Commerce.

[4] Other terms are also used for "online communities." Examples are "virtual organizations" (Foster et al., 2001), or "coalitions," or "federations," or just "groups."

The potential for benefits from P2P computing is enormous. And we, the Industry and the developer community, can seize this opportunity by enabling *interoperability*. All the uses of P2P so far work as isolated pieces. For each application, the developers create their own underlying services and tools and the applications cannot "talk" to each other.

Interoperability increases the productivity of developers and allows for applications to communicate with each other, but there are other equally important benefits. Interoperability means that P2P computing can span a multitude of platforms, with different hardware architectures running various operating systems, and that different device types can cooperate in the context of P2P computing. Servers, workstations, desktop and mobile PCs, handheld and wireless devices, even sensor-like appliances can all take part in some P2P application.

There are a number of ways to achieve interoperability, but the most effective way is through a *common infrastructure.*[5] Once we have a common infrastructure, or middleware, for P2P computing, the application developers do not need to reinvent the wheel for each new application. The application will run on a variety of hardware and software platforms while communicating with other devices. And users benefit from working in a single environment where applications are integrated to perform more complex tasks or share information and exchange data smoothly.

A number of technical and societal barriers need to be overcome before a broad acceptance of P2P is a reality. A key ingredient for addressing these challenges and assuring a successful adoption of P2P computing is interoperability. In summary:

- Interoperability allows P2P applications to run on a variety of hardware and software platforms.
- Interoperability allows for exchanges between different device types in a P2P computing environment.
- Interoperability allows communication between, and integration of, P2P applications.
- Common services reduce development efforts and improve time-to-market for application developers.

---

[5] Other approaches to interoperability may involve interfaces and bridges among a variety of different infrastructures.

The Popular View of Peer-to-Peer

A great number of computer users, and many developers, first became aware of P2P computing near the beginning of the year 2000. That was when companies like Scour (http://www.scour.com/) and Napster (http://www.napster.com/) became magnets to huge numbers of users for services involving direct swapping of MP3 music files. Napster was a phenomenon. Though it only went live in September 1999, by mid-2001 it had over 50 million users. It had also brought upon itself the wrath of the established record industry because music files were copied and passed on free of charge. The impact of using online MP3 file sharing to distribute music revolutionized what had been a well-established business model. This is a classic example of a "disruptive technology" (Christensen, 1997) in action. This book, however, is confined to the technical aspects of P2P computing. The most basic view of P2P computing, associated with Napster, is that it offers an efficient method for sharing, swapping, and distributing music in digital format. This view is simplistic and incomplete and does not capture the true nature and potential of P2P computing.

Scour[6] actually appeared on the scene before Napster, as early as December 1997. It specialized in sharing media files such as video and photos, in addition to MP3 files. Napster also offers other P2P-related capabilities such as Instant Messaging. You will read more about these capabilities in subsequent chapters of this book.

Other non-music P2P applications are also popular. The Freenet Project asserts that it supports free speech on the net by providing anonymity in direct exchanges among its users. Anonymity here means that it not easy to trace back the source from which a communication originated. Here is how the Freenet Project defines itself:

> *"Freenet is a peer-to-peer network designed to allow the distribution of information over the Internet in an efficient manner, without fear of censorship. Freenet is completely decentralized, meaning that there is no person, computer, or organisation in control of Freenet or essential to its operation."*
>
> (http://freenet.sourceforge.net/ -- Nov. 2000)

---

[6] The Scour technology is now owned by CenterSpan, another company engaged in distribution of digital content over the Internet.

Note the important concept of *decentralization* – this is a recurring theme when we discuss P2P architecture and applications.

You have probably also heard about Gnutella. They define their offering as a "fully-distributed information-sharing technology" (http://gnutella.wego.com/ -- Nov. 2000). The features that characterize the Gnutella framework are any-type file sharing, almost complete anonymity, and the resilience of the service. This last item refers to the fact that the framework of exchanges does not have a single point of failure.

The applications cited so far deal with sharing different types of files and textual exchanges among the participants. Other projects, involving a smaller community of users, entail another type of P2P computing. And this time the term "computing" is even more appropriate. Computers on the net can share more than copies of their files or space for messages and text. They can share their processing power by working together to process data and solve computational tasks of great complexity and magnitude. This is called "*cycle sharing*," and I will describe some fascinating examples in chapter 11.

For now, here is an interesting example of cycle sharing: By October 2000, 2.4 million users from over 200 countries contributed time on their computers to help in a scientific experiment that uses Internet-connected computers in the Search for Extraterrestrial Intelligence (SETI). The users contribute their idle cycles while the guest application runs as a screensaver, and the aggregate performance is bigger than that of the most powerful supercomputer built to date. Each participant gets a chunk of work that takes, typically, several days to complete. The results are then sent in, by the application, to the central database. SETI is a scientific effort to determine whether there is intelligent life out in the universe. The SETI@home project (http://setiathome.ssl.berkeley.edu/) involves analyzing data collected from the billions of radio frequencies that flood the universe, looking for a pattern of signals that indicate the existence of another civilization. This is just one example of the power of P2P-like distributed processing in tackling major computational problems. For an interesting history and case studies of distributed computing for the masses, see *Collective Wisdom* (Hayes, 1998).

Is SETI@home a "true" P2P application? After all, the participants work towards a common goal, but have no communication among themselves, and the computations are controlled by a central server. However, SETI is still P2P because it involves a high degree of collaboration without direct communication between participants. This application is quite common in solving large problems via distributed processing. Peers are cooperating by sharing their resources over the net, and this is yet another manifestation of the possibilities offered by P2P computing.

Many other companies and researchers are engaged in P2P computing while this book is being written. The examples cited here are just a few that received public attention in the early stages of the P2P emergence.

To appreciate the level of activity of P2P computing and the variety of P2P applications, view, for example, the ever-changing list on the PeerProfits site (http://www.peerprofits.com/).

The applications that triggered the emerging P2P computing movement share several salient features:

- The applications span a wide range of application types.
- The applications are decentralized.
- Being decentralized adds resilience against failures and promises a steady and reliable service.
- The application developers emphasize distributed services and distributed processing.

However, each manifestation of a P2P application is self-contained and does not interact with any other P2P application.

As you read on, P2P computing will be defined and described more rigorously, with emphasis on how to take advantage of the strengths of this computing model, and how to deal with its present weaknesses.

Why and Why Now?

What are the factors that came together and allowed and accelerated the emergence of the P2P phenomenon?

First, there was the Internet. Then came the *hyperlink* that allowed easy access and viewing of linked information from within a text document. Multiple protocols drove multiple webs; Telnet, FTP, Gopher, WAIS, and HTTP were the main ones. This was the first generation of the net.

The second generation came about with the advent of the graphical-interface browser, Mosaic, specifically. The functionality built into its graphical interface made the retrieval process transparent to the user. And, through the use of the browser, all the separate webs merged into a single World Wide Web.

And now we are on the threshold of the third generation of the Internet, ushered in by the P2P technology and the computing model it represents. This potent combination will make us members of decentralized, self-organizing online communities. They will change the electronic social landscape and the ways in which e-Commerce and corporate computing are managed and conducted.

Why is P2P computing a good thing and why is it catching on? The P2P model offers several compelling advantages to individual users and large organizations. These advantages can be divided into technical benefits and social appeal.

Technically, P2P provides the opportunity to get back huge amounts of *untapped resources* that go unused without it. The resources include processing power for large scale computations and an enormous storage potential. P2P allows the elimination of the *single source* bottleneck. Data and control can be distributed and requests can be load-balanced across the net. In addition to the performance issue, this mechanism also eliminates the *single point of failure* hazard. Within the enterprise, IT operations may be able to replace some costly data center functions by enabling *distributed services between clients*. Storage, for data and its backup, can be placed on clients. The P2P infrastructure, by allowing access and shared space, improves *remote maintenance* capabilities.

Much of the wide appeal of P2P is due to social and psychological factors. People can create their own online communities easily and run them as they collectively choose. Others like the ability to bypass all centralized control. For better or worse, almost perfect anonymity is possible.

And why now? The concept that underlies the P2P computing model, direct exchanges and sharing of files and cycles between nodes, is not new. Why has the P2P model burst on the scene now?

Several essential developments have reached a stage that makes widespread use of P2P possible. The ubiquity of connected computers has enabled more and more anywhere, anytime access to the net and its resources. There certainly is a critical mass of computer users. The communications bandwidth, still growing fast, makes it possible to move large amounts of data and rich media content from one location to another. The computers have enough processing power and storage capacity to handle the extra services required in a P2P environment.

New technology becomes widely used after it has become viable. It needs to be easy to use by novice users and the tools it requires have to be widely available. In the case of P2P, these tools are today's desktop computers in combination with the net. The average user communicates comfortably on the web, sending and retrieving information, searching, downloading, and even trading. The P2P services are easy to install, and their user interface is simple and familiar.

Another element that accelerates adoption is the emergence of complementary technologies. Three such technologies are noteworthy. The first is *broadband communication*. A mid-February, 2001 report[7] finds some form of broadband for Internet access in 9% of connected households in the U.S., and predicts fast growth rate of subscriptions to DSL and cable modems. Broadband communication makes persistent exchanges and connectivity more palatable to many users. Secondly, the increased popularity of wireless devices adds another dimension to P2P computing and offers opportunities for new applications. Thirdly, advances in software agent technologies provide mechanisms for managing the complexity inherent in P2P computing and avenues for interesting applications. The topic of complexity is noted in Chapter 12, and intelligent agents are discussed in Chapter 7.

These conditions for the introduction of P2P technologies are necessary, but not sufficient. History shows that a *trigger* is needed for a new technology to really take off. In the computer industry this is often referred to as the *killer app*. The PC was embraced in volume when the electronic spreadsheet appeared. Closer and more relevant to P2P is the transformation from the limited use of the Internet into the World Wide Web experience we know today. The trigger was the Mosaic browser. In the year before its introduction, 50 web servers were on the Internet. A year after Mosaic appeared, the Internet had some 10,000 web servers, *and* the first web-based businesses started.

The P2P computing model found its trigger for wide acceptance during the few months spanning the end of 1999 and the beginning of 2000. The trigger was Napster, followed by Gnutella. Not only did their popularity get everyone talking about P2P, it also brought to the fore other uses of P2P. Projects such as Freenet, SETI@home, and GIMPS[8] received

[7] Cahners In-Stat Group (www.instat.com) report dated February 14, 2001.

[8] GIMPS stands for the Great Internet Mersenne Prime Search. See http://www.mersenne.org/prime.htm for more information. Both SETI@home and GIMPS predate Napster.

increased visibility by the public at large. By the fourth quarter of 2000, over 100 companies and numerous research projects were engaged in P2P computing.

What is Peer-to-Peer Computing

So far, there is no agreement on a succinct definition of P2P. People also disagree on the scope of applications that may be "true" P2P applications. Do not be overly concerned with this apparent lack of unity among P2P practitioners. Because this new computing model is rapidly evolving, it is healthy and desirable *not* to be locked down by a rigid definition. The introduction of any new technology introduces surprises, and we need to accommodate them. Also, when P2P stakeholders list the important attributes of a P2P environment, their answers are reasonably consistent.

This variety of opinions regarding the definition of P2P was evident in a meeting, the Peer-to-Peer Summit, called by O'Reilly & Associates a couple of weeks before the first P2P Working Group meeting (Oram, 2000). A few months later, in the mid-February O'Reilly Peer-to-Peer Conference, people were still evolving their personal definitions of P2P computing. You can explore some of these views by browsing the O'Reilly OpenP2P.com site (http://www.openp2p.com/). The same was true at a number of other public gatherings that have taken place recently. The participants in all these meetings were some of the leading proponents of the P2P movement: technologists, researchers, heads of P2P start-ups, and journalists. They did not tell us, collectively, what P2P is. They did point out, individually, what the impact of P2P computing might be, some of the important ingredients to its success, and a number of barriers that need to be overcome to achieve wide acceptance of P2P computing. At least some of the insights expressed at that meeting are reflected, in one form or another, in later chapters of this book.

All that said, a more formal definition sums up this book so far:

Peer-to-peer computing is a network-based computing model for applications where computers share resources via direct exchanges between the participating computers.

This definition highlights two elements that are fundamental to P2P computing – the sharing of resources and direct communication between users. These two together are a common thread in describing P2P applications.

Others may prefer different definitions, perhaps focused on collaboration and moving computing to the edges of the net, or centered on the types of services that support P2P. These are all valid approaches. At this time, it seems more important to agree on the scope of P2P, and that is the discussion that follows.

You can grasp the "spirit" of P2P from Figure 1.2. It provides a visual illustration of how a file is shared in the client-server model, and how it is done using the P2P computing model.

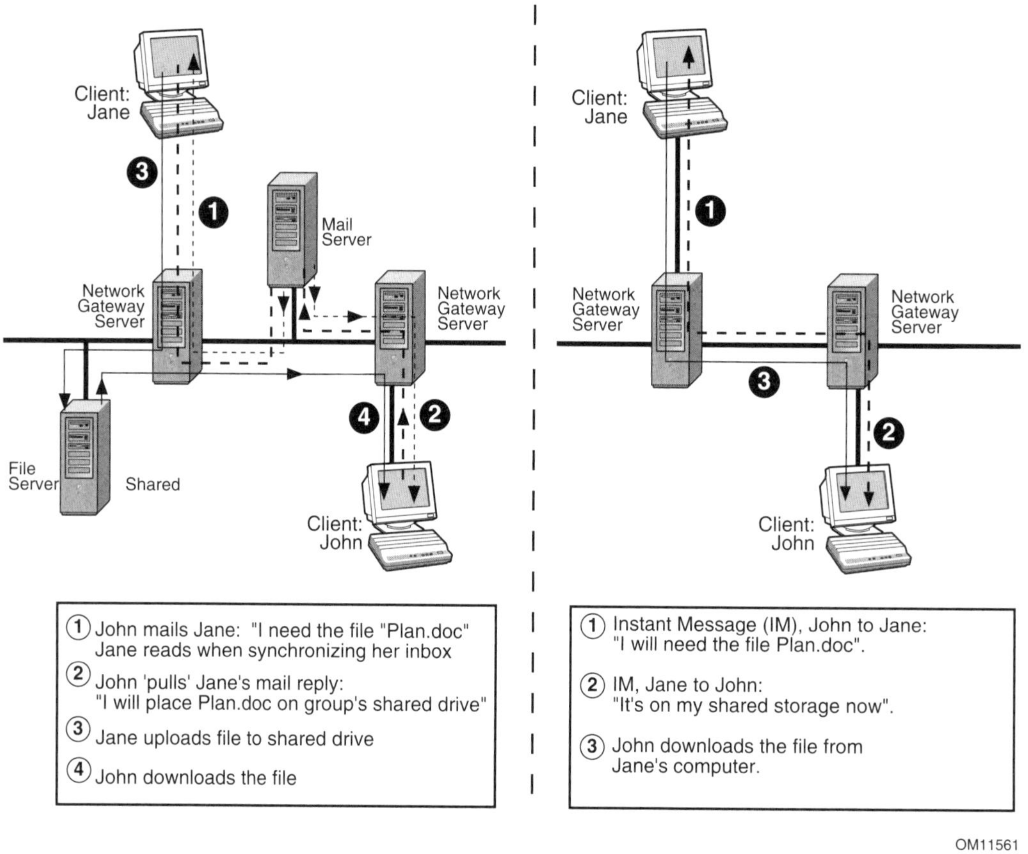

Figure 1.2 Find and download a file: client-server model and P2P model

This is a good spot to address, briefly, an issue of definition that is hotly debated among P2P developers:

Some experts make a distinction between *pure P2P* and *hybrid P2P*. The term *pure P2P computing* refers to an environment where all the participating computers are peers. This definition for pure P2P computing looks reasonable, and a number of developers confine themselves to the pure P2P model. However, on closer look, pure P2P is too restrictive. The most obvious example of an application that does not conform to the pure P2P model is Napster. The Napster file exchange occurs between two peers, but the application relies on a server that contains the directory of all files available for sharing from all the peers. This is hybrid P2P computing, where a P2P application uses a server to enable users to interact with each other. P2P computing in this book includes the hybrid model. The role of servers, if any, will be clear from the discussion.

In pure P2P computing no central system controls, coordinates, or facilitates the exchanges among the peers. Note that one or more servers may be needed. Indeed, there is a server layer in each of the participating clients. You may think of each system as being concurrently a client and a server. The use of server here should not be construed as a replacement for a full-blown server. The server layer contains the functions that the applications require for servicing the requests from, and exchanges with, the other peers. An example of the pure P2P approach is Freenet.

Hybrid P2P computing means that the application relies on a central server to perform some of the functions. The degree of central system involvement varies with the application. Napster, for example, requires the user to connect to the control server, where the directory of all available files is held. Once the information is retrieved from the server, the file exchange takes place without central intervention or involvement.

In spite of what the terms imply, no one method is better than the other. Each has its advantages and drawbacks. Each is the right choice for some applications.

Instead of dwelling on a formal definition of P2P computing, it is more productive to look at the purpose of P2P and the actions it enables. The two fundamental actions that P2P enables users to perform are *share* and *collaborate*.

But share what? And collaborate how? Answering these questions helps us understand the purpose of P2P computing in detail. Note that this detail does not, indeed cannot, spell out all the applications that may be possible through P2P. All we can observe now are the building blocks and the mechanisms that can be used. And, admittedly, future advances may show even more building blocks.

What are the resources that can be shared?

- The previous section showed that files and compute-cycles can be shared. Music, video, or any other type of file can be accessed and downloaded from another peer.
- A peer can perform computations on behalf of an application that originated from, and is controlled by, another peer, as we saw with the SETI@home application.
- Storage space can be shared. A peer may provide storage for files of another peer, or for a community of peers.
- Information can be shared by making it available to peers on one's machine or by transferring it to theirs.
- Services can be shared and managed cooperatively by peers. Messaging and security are two examples of such services.

And what methods are available for P2P-based collaboration? This is an area where innovations are evolving, but here are some techniques now used in P2P collaboration:

- Direct exchange between the peers.
- Transactions taking place with the help of an intermediate (as in Napster).
- Granting access to resources (as in SETI@home).
- Any kind of interaction formed through policies that are implied when a peer joins an online community.

One way to derive a definition of purpose that is more inclusive, flexible, and extensible is this: There are *P2P technologies*, and there is *P2P computing*. The P2P technologies enable peer systems to share resources and collaborate on computational and processing tasks. This implies an abundance of supporting technologies and services, such as security (authentication, authorization, etc.), discovery, remote resource management, and more. Any application that takes advantage of P2P technologies is P2P computing.

Note that an application that employs P2P technologies for sharing resources among peers may also utilize a server for some functions, and it may also have some degree of central control. Distributed computing is a technique where many clients (peers) and non-clients collaborate in solving a computational problem. The participating systems share resources, grant access, and contribute to a common goal. However, they do not have to communicate with each other, and the distributed problem is usually centrally controlled. Yet, distributed computing is one of the cornerstones of P2P computing.

In this book P2P computing is the use of P2P technologies. A resulting phenomenon, highlighted throughout the book, is the creation of online communities that collaborate through resource sharing. This is the immediate result and operational purpose of P2P computing.

Several important characteristics are typical of P2P applications. In the previous section you read about some of the better-known examples and early implementations of P2P applications. They used two basic capabilities:

- File-swapping for exchanging content such as music.
- Cycle-sharing for collaborative, distributed computations.

The attribute of P2P that is highlighted by most of these examples is decentralization. The effect of decentralization is to shift the center of the computation and exchanges to the edge of the net.

But P2P computing is much more. Wonderful environments can be created once we have an infrastructure that provides an easy mechanism for direct and content-rich exchanges between users. Most of the possibilities can be encapsulated by saying that P2P is a tool for creating online communities.

These communities are dynamic. A member may join a group of peers formed with the use of P2P tools for a trial period. Later, that member might invite others, or choose to look elsewhere. In general, the community is *self-organizing*. The group is likely to have no central authority that determines who is a member in the community. Individuals choose to join and to leave. Exceptions to this principle might occur when P2P communities become commonplace inside the corporate world, where membership is more likely to be determined by the associations and functions within the organization. A community may define collectively its acceptable rules of conduct and policies.

The members of any community have a shared interest. This shared interest determines the nature of the exchanges, shared resources, and access between the peers. The principle of *autonomy*, or control of the user over the peer system, should, however, allow each peer to set permissions defining the resources others can access on the peer's computer. For example, an individual may wish to have different permissions for adults and for children.

The online P2P community can also be enduring, in the sense that members can relocate geographically without affecting their contacts and relationships within the online community. As people join such a community it becomes feasible to have an identity that isn't tied in to a physical node and a particular IP address.

The P2P application is particularly *resilient* and *fault-tolerant*, since the P2P application designer needs to assume that peers are not connected all the time. The application has to survive in a very fluid operational environment. In addition, for many P2P applications there is no single point of failure.

Establishing a P2P community is a collaborative endeavor, which creates an environment conducive to collaborative projects and joint activities. These may be structured projects, such as using the P2P environment for software product development by a virtual team. Or, the P2P community may be a looser assembly of participants who engage in online gaming, for example. The possibilities are endless.

Sharing resources across nodes via direct exchanges creates decentralized online communities, operating at the edges of the net. These communities are self-organizing, dynamic, enduring, resilient, and collaborative.

P2P Computing vs. P2P Network and P2P Communications

Sometimes, to understand a concept better, it helps to know what it is *not*. You may be familiar with the terms *peer-to-peer network* and *peer-to-peer communications*. They are not the same as *peer-to-peer computing*. A P2P network allows every computer in the network to act as a server to every other user on the network. Dedicated servers may or may not be present. P2P communication enables both participants to initiate, manage, and terminate the session. P2P network implies P2P communication between computers in the network. But P2P communication can also occur between two computers in a network that is not P2P. How are P2P network and P2P communications related to P2P computing? Unlike P2P networks, P2P computing does not imply that every computer, or node, can be a server to every other computer. In P2P computing the relationship between users is negotiated in some manner. The participating peers, the computers that can be servers to others, may be a part of a P2P network, or may belong to networks with different characteristics. The kind of services offered in P2P computing varies depending on who the other peer is. Computers in P2P computing have software layers that provide server services. The same is true for all members in a P2P network. The peers in P2P computing are likely to exercise P2P communications, i.e., they have equal authority and responsibility regarding the communications with each other. However, the peers may also agree on communication arrangements that are not symmetrical. For P2P computing, communication is only a means to facilitate sharing of resources. In short, P2P network and P2P communications refer to the physical network and a mode of communications. P2P computing defines an end-user application-level environment. The relationships among the three concepts are shown below.

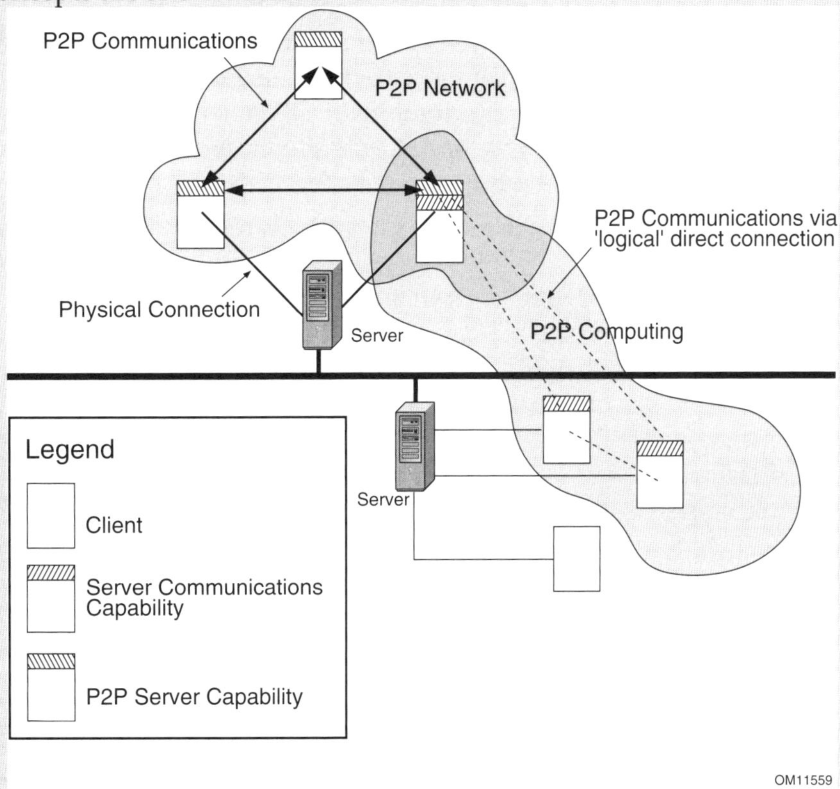

What P2P Computing Can Do for You

Most processing and computing results in interpersonal communication, services, and collaboration. Today the road to this person-to-person interaction travels through many intermediate machines – servers, data centers, and firewalls, to name but a few. Add to this the recent popularity and effectiveness demonstrated by consumer P2P applications, and a question naturally presents itself: Wouldn't these technologies be at least as effective within the enterprise? After all, the enterprise provides a more controlled environment than that found in the World Wide Web. The user community is already defined. There are teams who work jointly all the time. And person-to-person or intra-team exchanges are the norm. Peer-to-peer computing belongs in the enterprise.

Of course, P2P can belong elsewhere, too. Witness the success of various forms of file sharing on the net. In fact, most of the development and innovations in P2P technologies are done outside the enterprise by start-up companies and research institutions. The enterprise has the resources and the environment to test, validate and qualify. It is very appealing to combine the creativity emanating from outside the corporate world with the resources and discipline of the enterprise in order to advance P2P computing.

This line of thinking, the synergy between the corporate-enterprise world and the small teams of entrepreneurs, extends to the opportunities of applying P2P services in the fast-evolving e-Commerce arena. Electronic Business-to-Business (B2B) commerce is augmented by online Business-to-Consumer (B2C) commerce. e-Commerce is maturing to provide more comprehensive two-way exchanges between suppliers and consumers, and variants of e-Business allow for Client-to-Client (C2C) transactions. P2P technologies fit in and offer huge opportunities for e-Commerce and the supply chain on which it relies.

In summary:

- Peer-to-peer computing belongs in the enterprise.
- The entrepreneurial creativity joining forces with the resource-rich, disciplined enterprise is a recipe for success.
- Peer-to-peer computing offers huge opportunities for the advancement of e-Commerce.

Where do P2P applications for business and consumers thrive? Here are some things that become possible with P2P technologies:

- **Community web network:** A group with specific common interests—a family, a village, hobbyists, etc. can expand the idea of lists, shared resources, and a web site and create their own intranet.
- **New capabilities for e-Business:**
  - — Connect and enable all the links that make up a complete supply chain.
  - — Distribute information, content, or software more effectively in a cascading manner. It is akin to turning a single pipe into an ever-expanding network of connections.
  - — Keep details that are needed for e-Commerce but occupy large amounts of storage, or are likely to change in time, on their original node. A central directory or a search capability can refer queries to the source. This is useful for real estate, catalogs, classified advertising, auctions, and many other e-Commerce activities.
- **Gaming:** A P2P infrastructure provides a natural foundation on which to develop online community games that are not centrally controlled. The developers can focus on the game's features, instead of the interface to the communications protocol.
- **Search engines:** Overcome the problems of stale data and a single source for answering inquiries by searching directly across the horizon of the community. The usefulness of this techniques requires that the coverage area is adequate for the item being searched for.
- **Virus protection:** The relationships among the nodes allow the P2P community to collaborate in virus detection and warning, as well as automatically quarantine itself against further attacks (Sandia National Laboratories, 2000).
- **Edge services:** There are instances when it is desirable to locate the data, prior to its use, closer to the client requesting it. For example, such relocation can assure consistent rate of data transmission for video streaming, whether for entertainment or online web-based training. Multiple clients offering storage space can, arguably, provide a more flexible and reliable service compared to that offered by a server, since a server needs to respond to multiple requests simultaneously.

- **Collaborative development:** The scope can range from developing software products, to composing a document, to testing, to rendering graphics, and more.
- **Large-scale computations:** Enterprises and organizations can utilize available computational cycles to solve complex scientific and engineering problems. Such applications may include aircraft simulation, drug design, computational chemistry, climate studies, and many more.

The scope and span of possibilities is exciting and virtually limitless.

The Peer-to-Peer Challenge

For some 20 years now people in academia and research have experimented with aspects of peer-to-peer technologies, mostly in relatively small and controlled environments. There are also some products that enable users to collaborate and share files. And recently we have seen the first applications that caught the imagination of millions of users. The constellations are now aligned. The physical infrastructure of computers and communications is in place, and the concept of P2P in the mainstream of computing has been demonstrated. The time has come to move from the mode of early experimentation to that of a solid computing model.

There are some challenges, however. Today every application or company creates its own basic services, peer plug-ins, and environment.[9] And P2P applications that originate from different sources cannot be integrated and cannot communicate with each other. The application developers do not benefit from existing solutions; they spend time creating the same services instead of developing more interesting and feature-rich applications. The lack of integration results in less than optimal experience for the user. This situation can be resolved when the Industry gets together and works to achieve interoperability between P2P applications.

Interoperability can be accomplished through the use of common protocols. Having agreed on the protocols, there are a number of ways to get to them from the application. First, the application developers can make system calls or employ low-level coding that will exercise the

[9] The only exception to this "one of a kind" is, perhaps, the activity around grid computing for distributed processing. Distributed processing is described in Part II.

protocol's functionality directly. This is hard and is platform dependent. Second, developers can use a common set of Application Program Interfaces (APIs). This option is much easier for application developers, but is still language and environment dependent. Third, developers can use a common set of services that provide the functionality needed for P2P computing above that which is provided by the peer's operating system. This set of common services acts as a *middleware* layer. One of the advantages of a common middleware is that application developers do not need to keep creating the same basic services over and over again. Given that the common middleware runs on multiple platforms, the part of the application that uses the middleware is also portable to other platforms.

Figure 1.3 shows a P2P middleware layer that fits between the peer's local operating system, and the application interfaces that the P2P application can call directly. Note that applications can use different API schemes when calling middleware services, and still be interoperable.

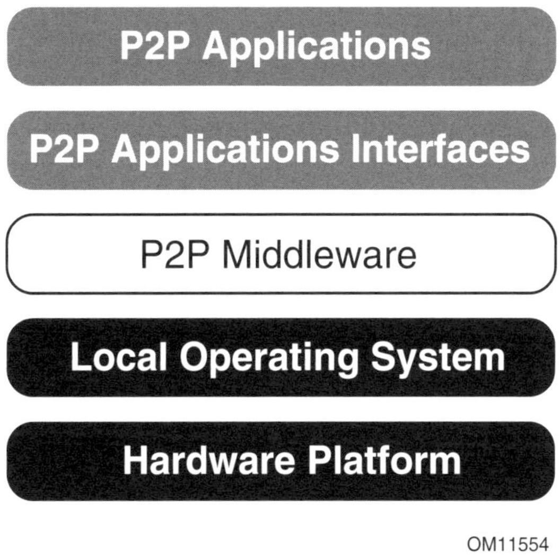

Figure 1.3 P2P Middleware

The challenge, and opportunity, facing the community of P2P advocates is learning to work together in creating an integrated environment where applications can interoperate. The common middleware approach makes it possible to address the P2P infrastructure requirements together. These common functions, some of them quite complex, include security and privacy, access control, fault-tolerance and availability, scalability and extensibility, heterogeneity of operating systems, hardware, policies, and some more you will read about later.

The challenge, then, is to create a framework for solving the common problems together, while allowing plenty of space and flexibility for innovation and creativity.

Chapter 2
Envision the Future

How might P2P computing change the way we use our networked computers? Trying to predict the future is a risky business. New technologies are often adopted in unexpected places or unforeseen applications. Imagining the future, however, is exactly what happens in this chapter.

It helps to have a context in mind when you try to grasp the implications of a technical issue or the possibilities offered by a feature. P2P is not the only way to accomplish many of the tasks described here. It does, however, make their implementation simpler. To make the task easier, we will look only to the near future, the next year or two. This future is described through the use of technologies we already understand. And, no doubt, some projections will be off, others missing altogether. With these words of caution, let us embark on a short journey into the future.

A Day in the Life of a Peer

The term "peer," in this day-in-the-life scenario, is a person, not a computer system. Peer is the name of the character that represents the professional-consumer duality of a typical high-tech user. Peer conducts most professional and personal dealings online. And, typical of the fast pace of life on the Internet, Peer is engaged in many different forms of interactions on an average day. Of course, here the emphasis is on those activities that are relevant to the P2P computing model.

The day's activities for Peer can be divided into these major blocks:

- Morning: starting the day at home.
- At work: desk, online meetings, conference rooms, on the road.
- Evening: back at home.

The following scenarios focus on the capabilities and functions future users will expect or will miss if not there. The implementation of a given function, and how it actually works, may be different than indicated by the hints scattered throughout the narratives below.

Early morning, at home:

What's going on in the world? 6:05 a.m.
With steaming coffee mug in hand, in the family's study, Peer "wakes up" the PC that has been on and connected, via DSL, all night. Two windows are open. One presents a collection of world news headlines from several sources. At the bottom of the screen, a prompt is displayed asking if Peer is ready to view news stories from a personalized list of "interests." Peer clicks and reads. All is well with the world. The second window presents financial news headlines from Europe on high tech and automotive companies, Peer's economic segments of interest. A banner lists opening figures for the U.S. markets. Peer responds to the prompt and opens his portfolio. Note that the world news and financial information is already stored on Peer's computer, in the storage area made available for access by software agents running on computers at information providers' sites.

And the family? 6:20 a.m.
An icon flashes. A communication arrives from a relative, in the private web space shared by the family across the country. Peer clicks the icon and a window opens displaying the text of a message just sent by Mother ("Don't forget your brother's birthday is today").

Start thinking about work. 6:22 a.m.
Peer turns on the work laptop and logs onto the network account, behind the company's firewall. Checks calendar. The 9:00 a.m. meeting notice is highlighted: "Check project space for an urgent message." Peer opens the team's project shared space (to use Groove Network terminology). The meeting needs to be postponed till 11:00 because a participant critical to the meeting has a family emergency.

Notify the team, 6:30 a.m.
Peer sends a single message, announcing a change in the meeting's time, to team member #1. The message cascades to all other eight team members. For those whose systems are not connected, the message looks first for their mobile computers, then for their wireless devices. Peer receives an acknowledgement summarizing where and when the message was delivered in devices of the team members, or whether it is being held for delivery once a team member's system is connected to the net.

Morning at the office:

An instant message, 8:10 a.m.
Peer sends an instant message for rescheduling a meeting with the boss ("Can we meet at 9, instead of 11?"). Both calendars are updated automatically and the administrative assistant is notified.

Meeting with the boss, 9:00 a.m.
Peer meets with the boss to work on a planning document. They both view the file, and can see each other's changes. The boss's boss tries to write to the file, but can only view it. Peer sends a message to the boss's boss ("Numbers will be ready in 20 minutes"). When the planning document is complete, Peer sets the file permissions to allow access by the management team. When a member of the team accesses the file, they will see a note about who updated it last. The file retains a version association; thus the previous version still exists for reference. In addition, the new version is backed up automatically on the distributed backup file system.

IT needs your attention, 9:45 a.m. - 10:45 a.m.
Peer is back at the desk, answering e-mail and phone calls. An instant message from the Information Technology (IT) department flashes: "Is this a good time for us to update the files we backup on your system?" Peer confirms and a background job starts. A portion of the hard drive is used by IT to keep parts of files for backup. The data is striped[1] across a number of systems, so that no one host can view the file, unless authorized. Redundancy algorithms allow reconstruction of the data even when a couple of participating systems are not connected.

Shortly after the cleanup of storage backup is done, Peer receives a message from a colleague: "The software patch from IT is here. I was asked to cascade it down to you. Are you ready to receive?" Peer is. "Here it is. And please upload to your designated target in the other department." The patch is then installed, and Peer cascades the patch to the other department. IT is automatically notified when the task is complete.

[1] Data striping is a technique where by a file is divided into blocks of data that are spread across multiple drives, and possibly across multiple systems.

Collaborating with the project team, 11:00 a.m. - 12:00 p.m.
The project team meets for a working session on schedules and code review of the team's software development project. The eight team members are in three different locations. Files are scattered among the member's computers, but belong to a single hierarchical file structure. All members have access to all files. As soon as the present member is finished editing, the next requestor sees the change of status that indicates the file is available for editing. This allows for a productive flow of aligning project milestones, and efficient code review process.

A quick search, around 12:30 p.m.
Peer needs to see the latest planning document of the division. The document is being edited by the managers. Peer launches a search for a file name that includes "plan" and "2003" to be sorted by time of last modification.

A virus alert, 12:50 p.m.
Peer's screen flashes with a message: "A virus was detected in our plant. Expect slower mail delivery as we're filtering incoming mail. Click here to see what messages you must delete without opening." The virus was detected because somewhere in the facility an engineer noticed a mail from an unfamiliar source, an odd subject line, and with an attachment. She activated a software agent that attached the selected mail message, and pressed "Go." The agent invoked its counterpart at the anti-virus team's system, which confirmed the mail to be a known virus program. The central security agents then alerted all the systems at the facility.

Collaborate across the firewall, 1:00 p.m. - 1:30 p.m.
During an online meeting with a vendor to discuss a Statement of Work (SOW), the vendor views the document on Peer's computer. This is made possible through a setup that, subject to stringent authentication, opens up a "tunnel" through the corporate firewall that leads to the SOW document, and nowhere else.

Take a class, 2:00 - 4:00 p.m.
Peer attends an online class that originates across the country and contains video segments. The course material is uploaded and distributed to Peer and three other participants from the local facility across their own systems. The space taken is cleared when the class ends.

Contribute to a large computation, 4:55 p.m.
Getting ready to finish the day at the office, Peer opens the "I contribute cycles" application on the desktop system, and checks the "My computer is available" box. The company's design team has a queue of parameter-driven simulation runs for some new designs being developed. Before long, Peer's development system is churning away, processing a computational task.

En route, 5:05 p.m.
Walking towards the parking lot, Peer remembers two more small tasks he needs to complete. Peer retrieves the Personal Digital Assistant (PDA) and turns it on. A virtual network connects all of Peer's network-capable devices. First, Peer downloads a file that must be reviewed before morning. Next, Peer sends a signal to the home's oven control to turn it on, and get the temperature up, so cooking can start as soon as Peer gets home.

Evening at home:

The family web:
Peer's cousin runs the family web site. Content, such as stories, pictures, and video clips, is distributed, and each item replicated once, on the half-dozen home systems of family members who keep them always connected. Access to this private web is secure. Only family members and close friends are authorized to participate in the family forum. Peer joins a chat that is in progress, posts a recent photo, and sends an audio greeting to brother Jim.

A group play:
The kids in the household take over two PCs, to resume the online Monopoly game started a couple of days before. The other players are three of their school friends from a nearby neighborhood. All players are alerted, the game is restored, and the next player makes a move.

Meeting the neighbors:
The neighborhood association calls for a vote by the residents. Peer connects to the community's private web, and after being authenticated, casts a vote. The vote is counted and verified as the only vote from the household. Some of the neighbors exchange local news and gossip in a chat room displayed next to the voting tool on the screen.

Local trade:
While connected to the community's private web, Peer spots an item of interest in the local paper's classified section. Peer sends an instant message, and with a few quick exchanges completes the transaction with the seller.

The activities Peer engages in during a typical day are not science fiction. These interactions represent a natural evolution to what we are seeing around us today. In fact, you will recognize that a number of functions are already possible, and you may know of some that are taking place. What will distinguish the future from what you see around you now is that all the exchanges and capabilities exercised by Peer will be commonplace. Any "typical" participant in our business life will interact with the social and business environment just as Peer does, as a matter of course.

The challenge is to bring the full potential of the peer-to-peer paradigm to the mainstream of everyday computing and make it ubiquitous and pervasive. Evolving P2P technologies from early, small scale, experiments to their popular adoption introduces the need for agreed upon interfaces, protocols, and infrastructure. Subtle difficulties and obstacles arise with the widespread embracing of P2P computing. Some serious challenges include trusting other community members sharing your resources, assuring your privacy, guaranteeing the availability of resources you rely on, enabling your identity to migrate among different access points, constructing sufficient bandwidth for communications, and allowing your business application and financial package to share data and analysis. There is more, but you get the idea. A lot is assumed when P2P services are everywhere, all the time.

The scenarios described in this chapter are summarized in Table 2.1, along with the chapter numbers where you will find the topics, or the technologies enabling them, addressed. You will not find a "how to" for implementing a solution for all the scenarios. What you will find is a discussion of technical issues relevant to various aspects of the scenarios, and an attempt to describe what we know and define the challenges corresponding to these technical topics. Most of the discrete functions within the scenarios exist today in some fashion. What we would like P2P computing to bring about is the integration of all these pieces into a consistent, interoperable, and ubiquitous network experience.

Table 2.1 Summary of the P2P user scenarios

Scenario	Technical Issues	Where in this Book
What's going on in the world?	Discovery, distribution of content	Chapters 7, 12
The family	Instant messaging	Chapter 12 (reference only)
Start thinking about work	Collaboration via shared spaces	Chapter 11
Notify the team	Messaging, agents, communications	Chapters 6, 7, 11
An instant massage	Messaging	Chapter 12 (reference only)
Meeting with the boss	Collaboration, file sharing, access control, version control/discovery	Chapters 7, 10, 11
IT needs your attention	Remote maintenance	Chapters 6, 10, 11
Collaborating with the project team	Distributed file system, access control	Chapters 9, 10, 11
A quick search	Search	Chapters 7, 11, 12
A virus alert	Security, agents	Chapter 7, 9, 11
Collaborate across the firewall	Security, authentication, file sharing	Chapters 9, 10, 11
Take a class	Edge services	Chapter 11
Contribute to a large computation	Cycle sharing, resource management	Chapters 10, 11
En route	Wireless P2P	Chapters 4, 5
The family web	Communities, private webs	Chapters 7, 11
A group play	Online gaming	Chapters 7, 11
Meeting the neighbors	Communities, private webs	Chapters 7, 11
Local trade	Commerce, private webs	Chapters 7, 11

The User's Perspective

The scenarios portrayed above articulate the expectations of future net users. These expectations translate into requirements IT operatives and application developers need to meet. This section describes the lessons learned from the scenarios in terms of a framework, saving specification-level details for later.

First, the user changes locations and devices throughout the day. Access to the net might be from home, on the road, from the office desk, via the lab computer, or in a conference room. The devices vary from home computer, to laptop, palm pilot, office desktop, lab server, tablet, and possibly others. The important entity is the person, not the device. The user expects to get to information he or she has permission to access, regardless of which device is being used to connect to the net. The requirement expressed here is that the user has to have an identity that is not tied to a particular physical device or an IP address. The idea of a "net identity" that moves with the person, and not with the device, does not apply only to P2P computing. Nor is P2P impossible without it. It is just that without this mobile net identity much of the power and appeal of various P2P applications is diminished.

Nicholas Negroponte, from the MIT Media Lab, predicted that we are heading into a future where everything will have an IP address. In addition, and perhaps more significant to us, everyone will have a net identity. P2P computing will accelerate reaching that stage.

Second, some of the environments that Peer joined for a period of time during the day imply what content should be available. For example, certain data files should not be accessible from outside the lab or from outside the enterprise. Very different content is presented when communicating with family members. The information and content that are available are a function of the context in which the exchange takes place. In other words, a typical user belongs to multiple communities, and what the user views depends on which community he or she is connected to at the time. Peer's communities are family and friends, work project team, the corporation, neighborhood, and school or college student body.

Another important observation emerges from the association with multiple communities. Any user may have a multitude of *profiles,* the set of parameters and information that defines access permissions, content interests, and other interaction characteristics. Groove Networks (http://www.groove.net) has already implemented the idea of multiple facets of a single person. The Groove framework allows for multiple IDs under a single account. The profiles that augment the user's identity represent facets of that user's life (see Figure 2.1).

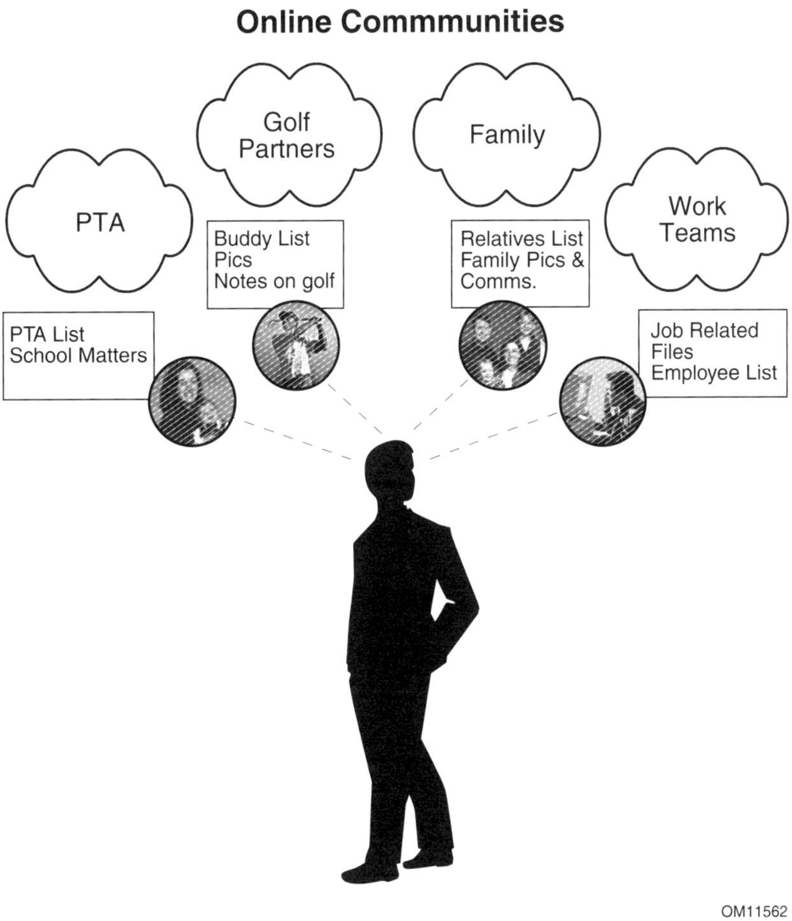

Figure 2.1 Identity, communities, and profiles

Third, as we can see from the identity-profile pairs the user exercises varying degrees of resource sharing depending on the community. Notice that the content and the access permissions vary from one environment to the next. What is shared with others is a function of the relationships. The level of access is a matter of trust. It is important to remember that trust, in the context of peer-to-peer, isn't a two-state variable. The level of trust is defined on a multiple-point scale. The user wants to control what is being accessed, in what way, and when. You can imagine a *trust-space* that encapsulates the relationships between the user and other peers. A trust level can be assigned to a group or to an individual. Central to establishing the appropriate level of trust is confidence in the process of verifying the peer's identity. This verification process is often referred to as *authentication*.

Fourth, associated with the level of trust bestowed by the user, through the peer system, is the equally fundamental attribute of *local autonomy*. It is the user who sets the local policies, the permissions, and access control to his or her peer computer. The scope of usages open to the individual user through P2P computing has expanded in a way that is analogous to the difference between voting in an election and going to the convention to influence the platform. And yet, with all that sharing of resources and direct exchanges, the user expects full autonomy of his or her resources. It is important that no standards of interfaces violate this principle.

Fifth, a by-product of the direct exchanges between peers is that communications are much closer to real-time interactions. This immediacy has significant practical consequences in personal communications and gaming, for example.

Finally, the future user expects to invoke more than one P2P application, switching among them and exchanging data among them, all within the same online session. Providing the ability to participate in multiple P2P applications, within the same software environment is key to a more satisfying experience by the community members. The user's view of interoperable applications provides the impetus for common infrastructure and standard interfaces.

In general, the user desires:

- Online identity that is not attached to a device.
- Community framework with associated user profile definition.
- Mechanism for maintaining local autonomy while entrusting others with one's own resources.
- Applications that are interoperable, or integrated, with each other.

The Implications for IT

The scenarios of online activities that our future high-tech employee, Peer, takes part in, offer both challenges and opportunities to the IT organization. The suggestions here are illustrations only, and many variations and combinations are possible.

Among the most intriguing possibilities that present themselves to IT are taking advantage of the P2P resource sharing and management capability, and using the peers' systems storage area. This may well be the next step in the evolution towards *distributed storage.*

There are a number of operational hurdles to clear before IT planners will entrust enterprise primary data to peer systems. The peers are controlled by individual employees for their own daily tasks. Some are not available on the network at all times, or perform other priority jobs. There are issues of insuring data integrity and access speed. All these can be resolved in time. Until then, the same storage capacity can be used for data backup. The availability requirements are less stringent, and it is simpler to manage the distributed backup data compared to managing distributed primary data.

Distributed computing presents another opportunity for IT to take advantage of available computing power when it is needed. Contrast this approach with having dedicated computing resources standing by to be used on request. The P2P infrastructure makes negotiating for the peers' resources possible and simple. Of course, the computational task needs to be such that it can be divided into chunks of work that are suitable for the desktop and other systems in the P2P network. At Intel, for example, there is an application for running design simulations on peer systems. Distributed applications and techniques for this type of collaborative processing will be discussed in later chapters.

The P2P infrastructure can help some operations that are done online today to be done with greater ease, greater transparency, and more efficiency. Once access control and management exist on peer systems within the enterprise, IT functions can be substantially more automated. A good example of this is the distribution of new software components or code patches for existing software. The automation is introduced through the access control service, where authentication is followed by authorization for access by the IT peer. The process can be made very efficient by using the peers themselves as the source for delivering the software to other peers; the software cascades from one peer to the next. P2P services enable *remote maintenance* to reach new levels.

Of course, any mass distribution of any type of file can use the cascading technique of peers passing on files to other peers "downstream." The single-source bandwidth bottleneck is thus removed. Text of news and large distribution mailings will consume less of the network resources.

As we saw in the online training session part of the day-in-the-life scenario, sharing of storage space by peers provides a means for placing files closer to where they are needed, without having to locate a nearby server. Getting data where it is to be used, when it is needed, is referred to as *edge services*.

The negotiated access and the use of intelligent agents may be combined in defending the enterprise peers from a virus attack. The relevant P2P contribution is the ability to communicate to all peers, automatically and immediately, the virus warning. The environment can take action, when necessary. For example, the agents can shut external communications in case of a denial-of-service attack.

Figure 2.2 illustrates the kind of benefits P2P computing can bring to an IT operation.

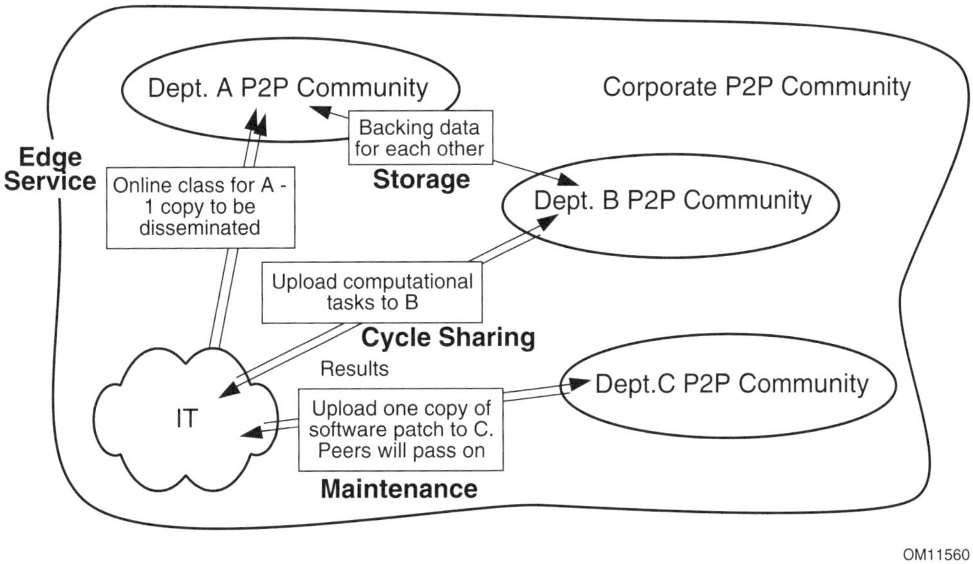

Figure 2.2 IT and P2P: Storage, maintenance, cycle sharing, and edge services

To summarize, P2P offers the following benefits:

- Distributed storage.
- Data backup.
- Distributed computing.
- Remote maintenance.
- Distribution of software and other files.
- Edge services.
- Virus protection.

The Potential for the Application Developer

P2P computing offers many new opportunities to application designers and developers. This section highlights some of the applicable lessons from the scenarios described above. Some are expectations by the user, others represent new ways to think about the behavior of future applications.

The first big requirement is *interoperability*. Interoperability is assumed on several levels. We saw that the application may migrate from one platform to another. Data needs to be read from any one of several file systems. Collaborating peers may be running their piece of the application on different operating systems, while still exchanging data and control information. Applications need to be designed and implemented with interoperability built-in.

The development of such interoperable applications is made simpler and faster by the existence of a common infrastructure with its standard services and interfaces. The application developer can focus on features unique to the applications and on user interface, and not on low-level system software or interfaces among different protocols.

Applications that are adaptable to a dynamically changing configuration will thrive in the P2P environment. A good P2P application is resilient to peers joining and leaving, to data sources migrating during the execution of the applications, and to wide variations in network traffic and effective bandwidth.

The requirements of interoperability and adaptation to dynamically changing configurations will favor object-based and modular programming practices.

More importantly, a P2P application is dependent upon sharing of resources among, potentially, many peers scattered over a wide network. Peer participation is dynamic, and the application has to negotiate access to peer systems as events dictate. The application has to survive network irregularities. The consequence is that security and fault tolerance cannot be an afterthought. They have to be designed into the application.

In summary, the P2P application developer designs for:

- Interoperability.
- Use of common, standard infrastructure.
- Re-configurable environment.
- Secure, fault-tolerant, modular behavior of the application.

Chapter 3
Precursors – A Historical Perspective

The concept of peer-to-peer computing is not new. The emergence of P2P as a new computing model is being fueled by enabling technologies of the Internet infrastructure, and a couple of trigger applications that have captured the user's imagination and enthusiasm. The new P2P applications and services are not just collections of what was done before, but are evolutions of early experiments, cast in the richer environments of Internet-friendly languages and user interface.

This chapter highlights three aspects of past work that is the foundation to P2P infrastructure today. The first one is the direct exchange nature of the Internet as it was originally conceived and used. The second element is distributed computing that provides us with the fundamentals of resource sharing. And the third component is online collaborative work.

The direct exchange, or peer-to-peer, character of the early networks gave way to a client-server model where exchanges became, mostly, indirect. Distributed computing contributed to the development of distributed file systems, but remained confined to scientific and research communities in a small number of large laboratories and universities. Software for online collaborations was also mostly restricted to large corporations and academic institutions.

Note that exchanges, distribution, and collaboration evolved in the past independent of each other. One of the more exciting aspects of P2P computing is the way in which it brings together these seemingly disparate technologies to form a more powerful computing environment.

Today, the profile of peer-to-peer users is evolving to incorporate individuals. In particular, the non-technical home user is beginning to participate in P2P. In addition, financed with venture capital funding, peer-to-peer applications are now being rapidly developed by small, start-up companies.

Application types such as distributed computing and collaborative software have changed over the years. The old-style distributed computing has evolved to grid computing and the cycle-sharing by millions of PCs that we see today. Early document sharing projects have evolved into media-rich and more powerful tools for working together on the net. These "new incarnations" are described in Chapters 5 and 11.

For a brief introduction you may want to read "History of the Internet" (Museum of Science and Industry, Chicago, 1977).

Direct Exchanges – The Beginning

ARPAnet, the network developed by the Advanced Research Projects Agency (ARPA) of the U.S. Department of Defense, was the predecessor to the Internet as we know it. ARPAnet came into being in the late 1960s. Ethernet, the most popular local area network access method, was build in Xerox PARC (Palo Alto Research Center) in the first half of the 1970s. Networks at that time were peer-to-peer. With Ethernet the wire is shared by different messages, but, in those days, computers communicated directly with one another.

Some of the earliest and most important research developments influencing the current distributed computing environment occurred at Xerox PARC in the 1970s. These efforts included research that led to the single-user workstation (Alto), file and print servers, RPC (Remote Procedure Call), and high-speed, resource-sharing local networks (Ethernet). These are the early building blocks of today's computing networks.

The idea of tapping into the potential of unused computer cycles was perhaps first recognized at Xerox PARC by researchers John Shoch and Jon Hupp in the late 1970s (Shoch, Hupp, 1982). Observing the hundred or so idle Alto machines sitting unused at night, the two scientists began experimenting with programs to exploit this resource. With the computers readily hooked together via the first Ethernet network, Shoch and Hupp created "worm" programs that would move, on the network, from one machine to the next, performing a variety of maintenance tasks. Even the risks associated with worm programs are not new – during one of their overnight tests, a worm program malfunctioned, causing dozens of computers to crash. Moreover, every time Shoch and Hupp attempted to restart the computers, the defective worm would reload and reproduce itself, causing the machines to crash again.

The net was designed with direct exchanges in mind. Getting computers to cooperate via intelligent programs is not a new invention.

One-on-one direct communication between users at the edge of the net is emerging with a vengeance through Instant Messaging (IM). As its name indicates, IM is a communications mode that involves instantaneous delivery of short messages between "buddies," other individuals you have previously agreed to communicate with in that manner. IM has become popular in the last few years; the biggest user base is AOL users. IM belongs somewhere in between strictly synchronous communications, such as voice exchanges and conferencing, and asynchronous methods, such as e-mail. It is geared towards immediacy, but allows for an offline mode. There are several popular IM products (AIM, ICQ, Aimster and more). While IM started as a vehicle for short, plain text messages, some IM products are being extended to include attachments, more file types, and other media such as voice, graphics, and video.

IM usage is growing fast, within corporations and at home. Missing, at this time, are open standards for interoperability. Being, as it is, one of the obvious technologies to be incorporated with collaborative P2P, IM will benefit from a common P2P middleware. The issue of openness and standards for IM is a hotly debated topic at this time. The P2P movement can help provide a basis for interoperability between IM products.

Distributed Processing

Distributed computing is a cooperative computation among multiple computers. A single application is broken up into chunks of computations that can be done independent of each other; therefore, they can be done simultaneously, or concurrently. The results from these separate processing are integrated into the final answers from the application. The goal is to perform a large-scale critical task faster than it would have been performed if a single computer system had been used. Distributed computing requires collaboration between processors and sharing of storage and processing cycles between multiple computers. At the beginning, in the 1970s, the computation was distributed among processors that were a part of the same system—multiprocessor computers, such as Cray and massively parallel computers (MPPs).

Programming MPP machines was even harder than programming the multi-processor Cray computers, since the operating system did not provide a single system image. The programmers had to dig in, break their job into pieces, and coordinate the computation on the pieces by hand. The coordination occurred in most systems through the exchange of messages.

There were many early message passing systems, but the one that caught on and enabled the distributed computing we are interested in is the Parallel Virtual Machine (PVM). PVM emerged from a collaboration between computer scientists at Emory University and computational physicists at Oak Ridge National Laboratory. While PVM worked on MPP computers, the real benefit of PVM was its ability to run on clusters of workstations.

PVM was joined by an alphabet soup of message-passing libraries, and it got to be quite confusing for the users of these computers. Fortunately, in the early to mid 1990s, all the message passers got together and agreed on a new API (Application Program Interface) called Message Passing Interface (MPI). Today MPI is by far the most common way to program clusters, though PVM is still in use.

All message-passing libraries suffer from one problem: the programming abstraction is too low-level. It is tied to the hardware and the way the hardware is connected into the cluster. This makes it hard to write adaptive software that responds to changes in the system. It is also hard to write and debug software.

In response to this, in the mid 1980s David Gelernter proposed the Linda concept, and by the late 1980s his student Nick Carriero figured out how to make it all work in a real system. Linda is a coordination language. The elements of Linda comprise a full fledged language with a grammar and syntax all its own specialized to the job of coordinating the execution of concurrent tasks. The concept behind Linda is its associative virtual shared memory called a *tuple space*. The objects placed into memory are called *tuples*. As the name implies, tuples are nothing more than a group of values and objects stuck together. To pull something out of tuple space, you describe what you are looking for, using the rules of Linda, and the system returns the tuple that matches it. This is why the memory in Linda is called associative.

Associative memory lets the needs of the algorithm dictate the way memory is accessed in an algorithm. By divorcing the API from the concept of a physical address, the system can provide the appearance of a shared memory where, physically, none exists. This is why a system using the Linda language is referred to as an *associative, virtual shared memory* system. The operations defined in Linda can be added to any language to create a fully parallel language for parallel or distributed computing.

By 1989, Linda was available on workstation clusters. A user could tell the Linda system how many nodes they wanted to use, and the system would go out onto a network, find available nodes, and run their Linda program on those nodes. A product built as an extension to Linda, called Piranha, uses software agents to detect idle workstations, place a computational load there, and remove it when the owner of the workstation starts using the system. In this way, you can write parallel programs that can extract cycles from a network of desktop workstations.

Why is this important to understanding the history of peer-to-peer computing? Because Linda for networks combined with Piranha was one of the earliest examples of a high-level peer-to-peer infrastructure for distributed computing. Of course, they didn't call it peer-to-peer back then. But many of the elements of a P2P infrastructure were available in Piranha and Linda. Linda supported a location-independent mechanism to share information (the tuple space) with an associative memory detached from the computational agents. By making the tuple space open to multiple programs, an idea first proposed to support heterogeneous computing networks within Linda, diverse collections of programs could interact through Piranha.

Linda and Piranha laid the foundations for the peer-to-peer distributed computing of today.

The tools described above enable heterogeneous computer systems to cooperate in performing distributed computations. Figure 3.1 illustrates a distributed computing scenario within a data center. Control and data are exchanged between shared-memory multiprocessors, massively-parallel processors, and clusters of servers.

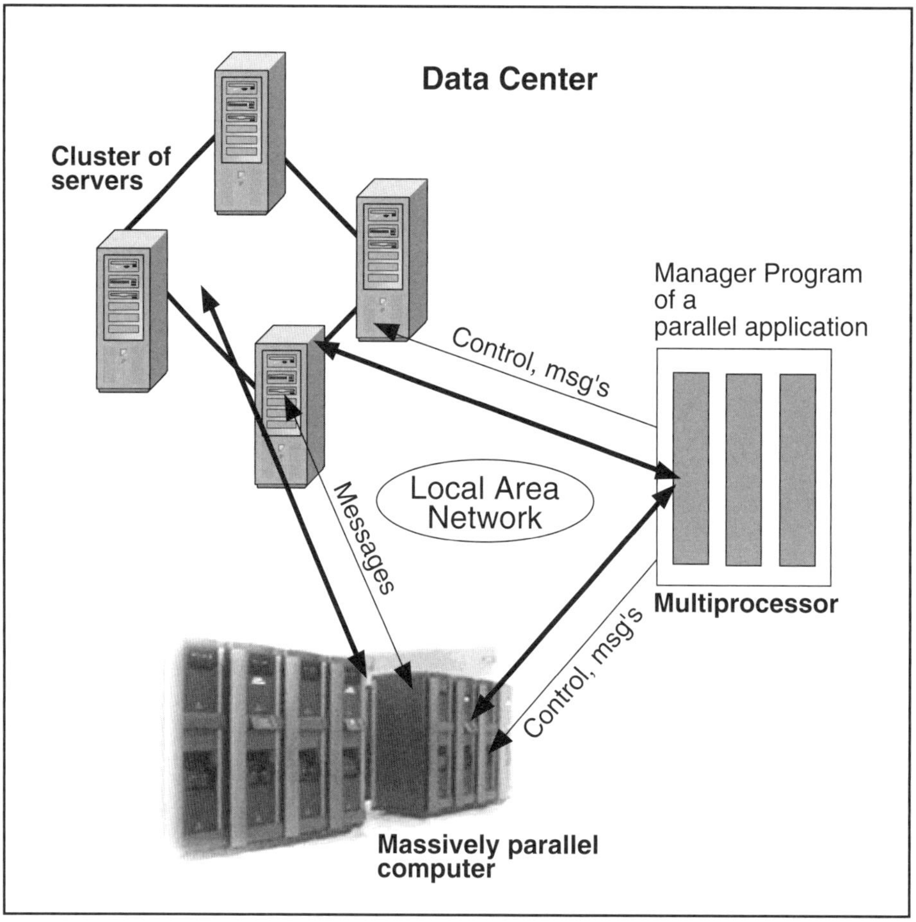

Figure 3.1 Distributed computing the old way

Another trend that contributed to distributed computing as we know it today is a sequence of ever more sophisticated network batch queues. These also came from the "big-iron" supercomputer communities. The Network Queuing System (NQS), from Cray Research and NASA Ames, came first, leading to the Distributed Queuing System (DQS) from Florida State University. Another piece of the puzzle is Utopia, which came from the University of Toronto in the late 1980s. Utopia grew into Load Sharing Facility (LSF), a commercial product from Platform Computing. The availability of network queuing tools increased the distribution span from a tightly connected configuration to parallel applications for distributed computing on a cluster of workstations (sometimes called COW). Examples of the more well-known clusters of workstations are: Network of Workstations (NOW), from the University of California at Berkeley (http://now.cs.berkeley.edu/), and Condor from the University of Wisconsin (http://www.cs.wisc.edu/condor/). A notable example of a commercial use of a large number of idle workstations comes from Pratt & Whitney. Starting in the mid 1990s, the company's IT and engineering organizations joined forces to *parallelize*[1] a structural analysis code and used LSF from Platform Computing to distribute its parts, at night, across thousands of otherwise idle workstations.

Another critical historical thread comes from Grid computing. The Grid was born from work at U.S. national labs. Large supercomputers were deployed around the country, but to get the most from these computers, the supercomputers needed better ways to work together. At the same time, users didn't want to deal with the details of how their supercomputers were spread out around the nation. They wanted to plug their application into a *computational Grid* much like you plug your PC into a power grid. Once the application was submitted to the Grid, it would run somewhere and the results would be returned to the user. Grid computing is discussed in more detail in Chapters 5 and 11.

You can see how the concept of distributed computing, as done in the past, can be extended to the way SETI@home works now. And, along the way, grid computing has also evolved from these ideas of distributed computing. Grid computing started by extending "data center distributed computing" to parallel execution between multiple data centers. When distributed computing is complemented by some of the basic services provided by P2P technologies, the result is a robust, flexible, and more powerful collaboration model for solving computational problems.

In the past, distributed computing was confined to scientific and engineering applications done in research institutes and a few large corporations. P2P companies, such as United Devices, Entropia, Popular Power, and others, bring high performance numerical computations to the homes of millions of users. High performance computing has come out of the labs, and can be found everywhere.

Once people began to use mechanisms for communicating between computers, applications other than distributed computing became

---

[1] To "parallelize" an application is to re-cast it into chunks, or parts, of computations that can be done independently of each other, and, therefore, in parallel.

possible. Distributed storage is one example of such an application, and is an aspect of P2P computing that was developed a long time ago. Xerox PARC can claim Distributed File System (DFS) as another one of many pioneering accomplishments. Xerox DFS was first demonstrated at Xerox PARC in 1977 on a number of Alto workstations. There were many subsequent implementations of techniques for distributing storage, many of them based on DFS. P2P makes us look back to the days before the client-server model dominated the computing scene, and draw on past work to create P2P-style distributed storage.

Early Collaborative Applications

There was online collaboration before we called it peer-to-peer computing. Instant Messaging is an example of a one-to-one direct exchange mechanism. The exchange of short messages between two users is immediate communication that involves a group of users simultaneously, and allows sharing of files and exchanges through other media, such as voice and video.

In the early days of the Internet, group-wide communication took place via bulletin boards and Internet Relay Chat (IRC).

Today, group collaborative software is referred to as *groupware*. The technology allows groups and individuals to work together in a coordinated and collaborative manner. An array of usages, or sub-technologies, are brought in and integrated into typical groupware. These applications include the IM mentioned above, as well as e-mail, bulletin boards, discussion groups, scheduling and calendaring, and so on. In most cases the groupware also provides multiple user access to, and editing of, databases and other complex applications.

There are a number of well-known groupware products, notably Lotus Notes, Microsoft Exchange, and Novell GroupWise. Among these, Notes is the oldest. Its origins can be traced to a mid-to-late 1970s project called Plato at the University of Illinois at Urbana-Champaign. For a short review of Lotus and a general discussion of groupware, see the References list (Groupware and Instant Messaging).

People who use groupware today have a good sense of what it feels like to have a real-time online collaboration. At several places in this book you will read about Groove Networks, a P2P company whose origins are with groupware, in general, and Lotus Notes, a groupware product, in particular.

Another collaborative online activity that has existed for a number of years, independent of P2P, is group online gaming. It requires solutions to some of the challenges faced by P2P, such as intermittent connectivity, authentication, and performance. These issues, and others, are addressed as a specialized solution for the game being played. Online gaming is a collaborative application, and can sit on top of P2P middleware that provides the services the games require.

PART II
LAYING THE FOUNDATIONS

The architecture, the infrastructure, and the basic services that are essential to peer-to-peer computing

"If you have built castles in the air, your work need not be lost; that is where they should be. Now put the foundations under them."

Henry David Thoreau

Chapter 4
Architecture and Infrastructure

In Chapter 2 you read about a number of scenarios envisioned in the life of a near-future professional. The implied interoperability and the expected integrated software interface setup favors a common infrastructure for P2P computing. This common software is the middleware you read about in Chapter 1. The middleware is the layer of software that sits between the local operating system of the peer and the interfaces to the P2P applications that users invoke. Common middleware allows applications developed by one company or organization to communicate with an application from another source, and it makes it easy to present the user with one view of the P2P environment within which all the operations can be performed and all the applications can be invoked.

While it is possible to construct a computing environment where each application is self-contained and stand-alone, this scenario is not desirable. The case for a common, or standard, middleware can be made from a couple of viewpoints.

From the application developer's view, a common platform on which to construct the application allows the developer to focus on features for the application rather than spending time on low-level system interfaces. The middleware also allows the application developer to make use of existing components and libraries, and to interface to other applications. And, most of all, when the application employs a standard programming language, a single version of the application runs on all the hardware and software platforms that support the common infrastructure. The user has the benefit of a familiar interface for P2P computing, though the look-and-feel may vary between applications. The common middleware promotes similar usage patterns of common functions, such as requesting access and authentication.

From the IT organizations' view, the job of providing services and maintenance is much simpler if all P2P applications use a single infrastructure. Common middleware also makes it easier to create P2P applications that communicate between different types of devices, for example, communication between a wireless PDA and a desktop.

At this time, most P2P applications stand on their own by including specially developed services as needed. There are, however, a number of more comprehensive infrastructure and middleware frameworks, in varying degrees of completeness, that are in use or advocated. Some of the ideas conceived by the developers of these early implementations (AVAKI/Applied Meta, Inc., 2000; Foster et al., 2001; Endeavors Technologies, Inc., 2000; FIPA, 2000) are discussed later in this chapter.

There are good reasons to strive for a common middleware for peer-to-peer computing. Much work remains to make this vision a reality. Time will tell if the Industry and all the P2P stakeholders will rally behind a well thought out middleware for P2P computing. This chapter discusses the objectives and the required attributes of a P2P infrastructure.

Nomenclature and Concepts

While current architectures and infrastructures have much in common, there are some areas where different camps are forming. For example, some P2P practitioners focus entirely on what they refer to as pure P2P, with no role for any central control function by a server or any single node. In contrast, others allow for servers, or a node that fulfills a unique function for the application or the environment. SETI@home, described in Chapter 1, is an example of distributed computing. This book assumes that the architecture and its infrastructure (or, middleware) needs to support P2P computing as defined in Chapter 1. That is, the framework is required to support applications that use P2P services for direct exchanges and sharing of resources.

Architecture, Infrastructure, and Middleware

Architecture, in the context of computing, is the manner in which the components of a computer or computer system are organized and integrated. *Software architecture*, the more specific architectural area of interest to P2P, defines the behavior and components of software that incorporate protocols and interfaces for interacting with other programs (*The Tech Encyclopedia*, http://www.techweb.com/encyclopedia/). These other programs might be user applications or other types of system software. *Infrastructure* is the underlying foundation or basic framework of a system or an organization. The infrastructure determines how the system functions and how flexible it is to meet future requirements. P2P computing is tightly related to software layers on top of the local operating system and communication protocols that function with the existing hardware components of the Internet. In this book, *middleware* describes the layer that enables P2P computing and resides between the application, on one side, and the local operating system and communications transports on the other side. *Middleware* is software that functions as a conversion or translation layer. It is also a consolidator and integrator. Custom-programmed middleware solutions have been developed for decades to enable one application to communicate with another that runs on a different platform or comes from a different vendor or both.

Note that delineating where architecture finishes and infrastructure begins is somewhat arbitrary. In this chapter, *infrastructure* at times means *middleware*.

As you read and think about the infrastructure required for P2P computing, it is useful to keep a mental image of the usage environment targeted for its support. Rather than creating a structure of discrete taxonomy components, consider a continuum along three vectors as shown in Figure 4.1. These vectors refer to characteristics of P2P applications and provide a convenient way to classify them. As we move from left to right on the horizontal axis, the applications get less dependent on a central computer, be it a server or a peer. Looking at the vertical axis and moving up, we go from applications with little or no interaction between the peers to those where the cooperation among peers is frequent and ongoing. Of course, even at the bottom of the vertical axis there is a minimal exchange, as the peer has to be asked, and then grant, access by other systems.

The third axis, the one you can visualize coming out towards you, is less familiar. We think of the computers at the edge of the net, the old clients, as being the peers in P2P computing. But the fundamental P2P services that enable direct exchanges, access, and sharing of resources, can also take place between servers or among an ensemble that contains both clients and servers. The applications in a servers-as-peers configuration are different than those with only clients-as-peers. The human interface is not present when only servers are involved. But this does not exclude P2P applications such as distributed storage, for example. That said, the focus of this book is almost entirely on applications that exist in the plane of the horizontal and vertical axes, where people interact with people and content.

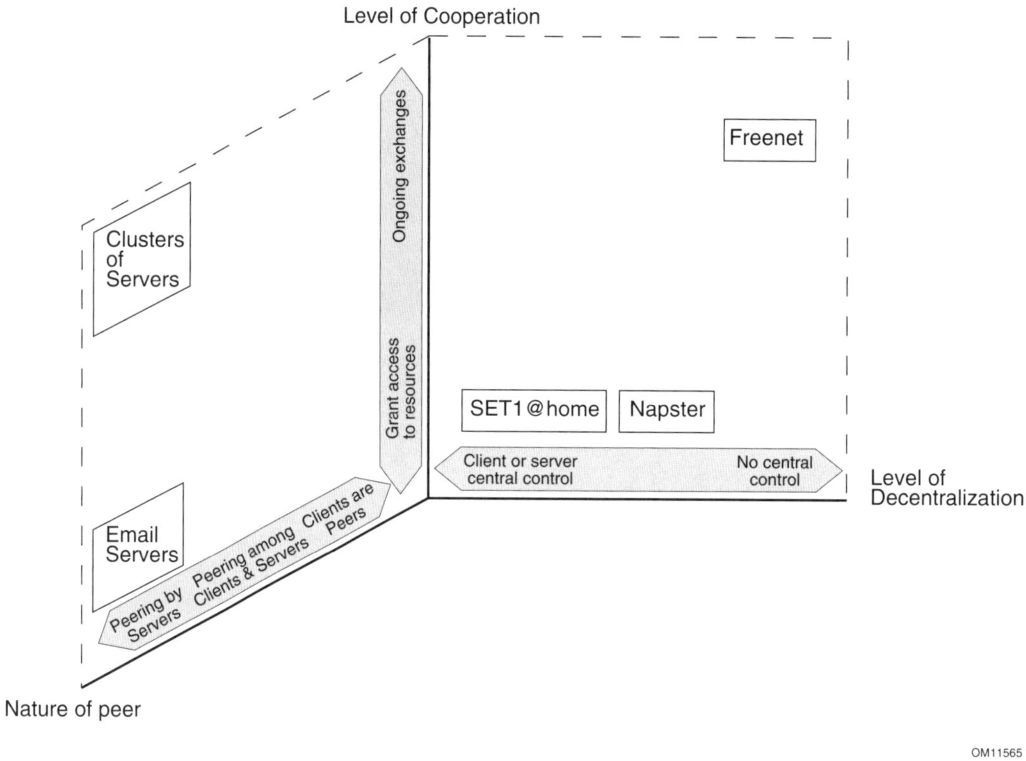

Figure 4.1 The three vectors of P2P computing

The foundations of the architecture are the components, or building blocks, and how they interact with each other. In the case of P2P, this underlying architecture is the Internet with its clients, servers, and network. Abstracting the architecture to a level above that of the building blocks, there are three layers to the P2P environment, as shown in Figure 4.2.

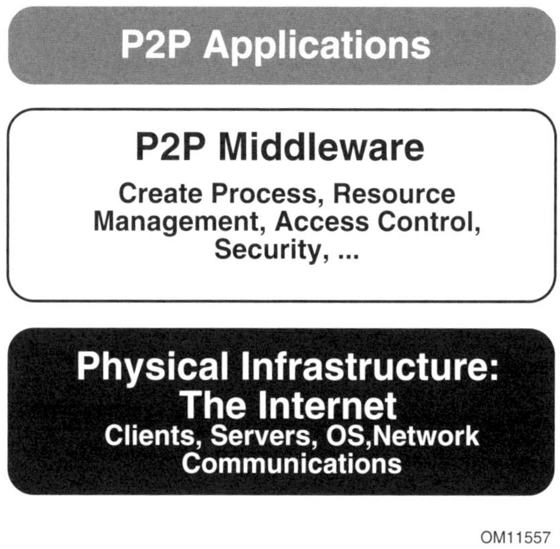

Figure 4.2 High level view of P2P architecture

The first layer is the *physical infrastructure.* In addition to the computers and the networks that connect them, the physical infrastructure also includes the operating systems that run on each node and the communication protocols and mechanism. This layer is, essentially, the World Wide Web as we have known it for the last few years.

The top layer represents end-user P2P applications. Note that Figure 4.2 does not call out the whole universe of useful applications, but only those that make use of P2P services.

The middle layer represents the P2P middleware, and is the subject for all of Part II of this book. The services and technologies listed in the middle layer are the components on which the P2P middleware is based, and from which it is constructed.

When describing middleware that resides between the operating system and the application in a networked environment, *protocols* and *Application Program Interfaces* (APIs) play a role. Protocols, APIs, or a combination of the two, facilitate the communication between P2P applications. In particular, they are related to the issue of interoperability.

Here are some of the salient aspects of APIs and protocols to consider when designing a middleware for P2P.

The protocols of interest here are communication protocols. They define the rules governing transmitting and receiving of data. There may be several layers of protocols that build on each other. The Open System Interconnection (OSI) standard, for example, has seven such layers, ranging from the physical layer of electrical signals to the application layer that defines the type of communication (file transfer, e-mail, etc.). A protocol states how to construct that which is being transmitted. A typical construct defines the protocol analogous of an envelope that contains the command, or action to be performed, accompanying meta-data, and the payload, or content, itself. The crucial insight here is that the use of common protocols provides a basis for interoperability.

API is a language-specific message format used by the application to communicate with the operating system or some other system. APIs are implemented by including function calls in the program. The function calls provide the link to executable routines that are external to application source code. APIs, in the sense used in this book, do not include direct interface between the application and communication protocols as described above. Just as using common protocols provides for interoperability, using common APIs provide compatibility. For example, if a library of routines is implemented on different platforms, an application that runs on one platform can be compiled and run on the other platforms that support the library. And this concept is important to the use of APIs: The actual implementation mechanism and details are abstracted, or hidden, from the application developer.

In the context of P2P, API is an application-level call that allows one peer to communicate with another. Since peer-to-peer communication is a central feature of a P2P application, the implementation of the software invoked by API calls on different peers needs to be compatible. The two implementations need to communicate. In other words, they need to use the same protocols. While the same application running on multiple platforms usually uses the same protocols, it may not do so when one application attempts to have an exchange with another. If we wish to see integration of, and communication between, different P2P applications, they need to share a set of APIs that also employs the same protocols.

What makes a software entity a *service*? A service is a network-enabled entity that provides a specific capability, such as storage allocation management or file transfers. A service, in the sense used here, is defined by the action taken, or the behavior exhibited, in response to messages of the protocol with which it works. Conceptually, we can think of a service as a behavior superimposed on top of a protocol. Note that this view of a service allows developers to implement various API schemes for the same service.

Now that we know some of the key aspects of APIs and protocols, let us explore the goals that need to be set for P2P middleware. These objectives point to components within the middleware, and to attributes and properties of the architecture.

The Net Infrastructure

A closer look at the physical infrastructure helps define the requirements imposed on the P2P infrastructure, so that it can enable P2P applications. Figure 4.3 shows the building blocks of the physical layer.

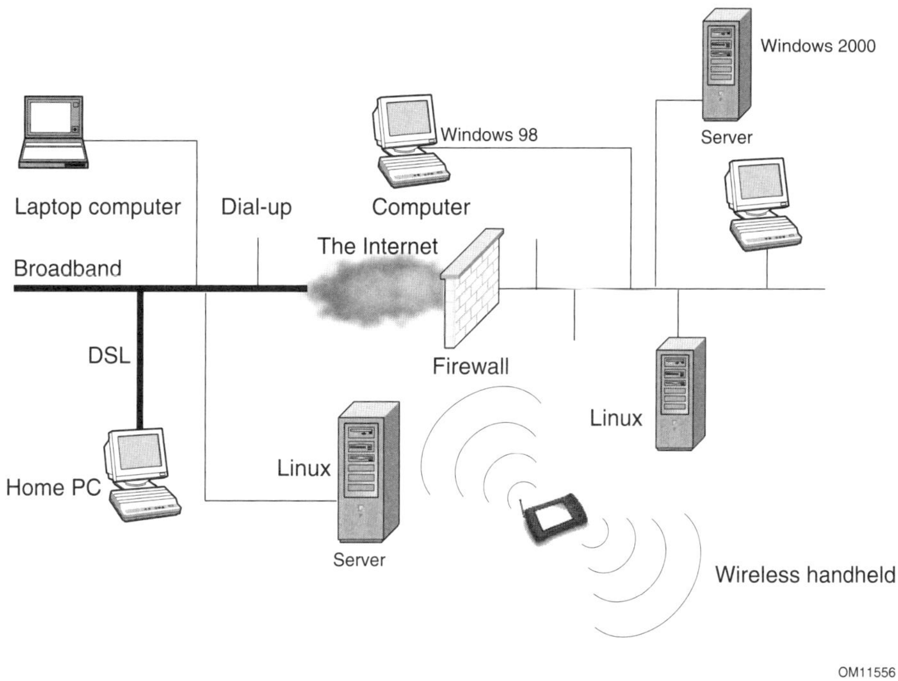

Figure 4.3 Building blocks of the physical infrastructure

The physical domain for peer computing encompasses PCs at home and desktops at work, mobile and handheld devices, and multi-tier server configurations. The physical connections of these devices span the range from broadband and optical fiber to telephone lines and wireless.

Participant users are found on the Internet, or on intranets behind firewalls. A variety of operating systems are encountered on network nodes and servers: Windows†, Unix†, Linux†, or Macintosh†.

While looking at the physical layer, and before moving on to the higher layers, note the communication patterns and paths between peers that are expected when running a P2P application. First, for contrast, here is a typical non-P2P interaction on the web (Figure 4.4). Steps A1-A3 illustrate a search, and steps B1-B3 show an e-mail message being sent:

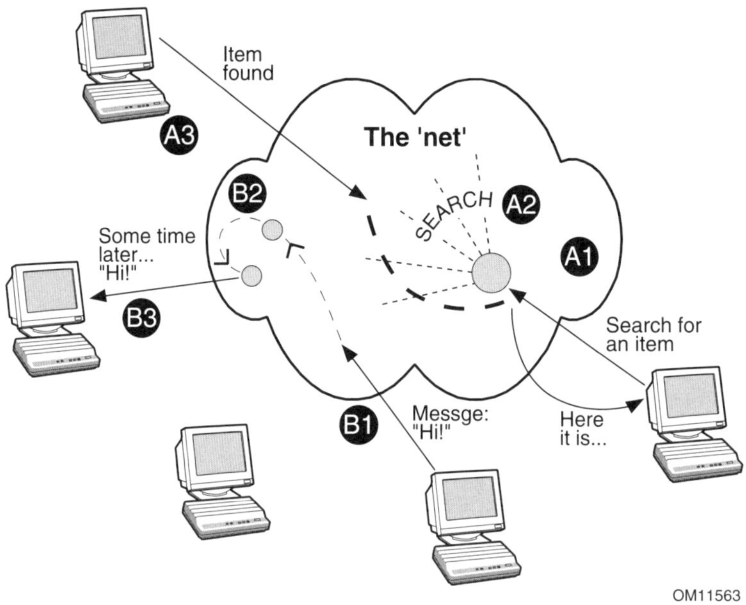

Figure 4.4 On the web without P2P

The communication patterns are centralized. Whether the user visits a web site, conducts a search, or transfers a file, the client needs to contact a server. Even what appears to be a person-to-person communication, such as sending an e-mail message, is really a multi-step operation where a server receives the message and passes it on to the addressee.

In peer computing the users communicate directly with each other, as shown in Figure 4.5. Note that a server may provide directory services, or one of the peers may control and supervise a computational task divided among the peers. Figure 4.5 illustrates distributed computing, instant messaging, and distributed storage. Distributed computing has two steps. In step 1 the user discovers who can perform the computation. In step 2 the computational task is sent over.

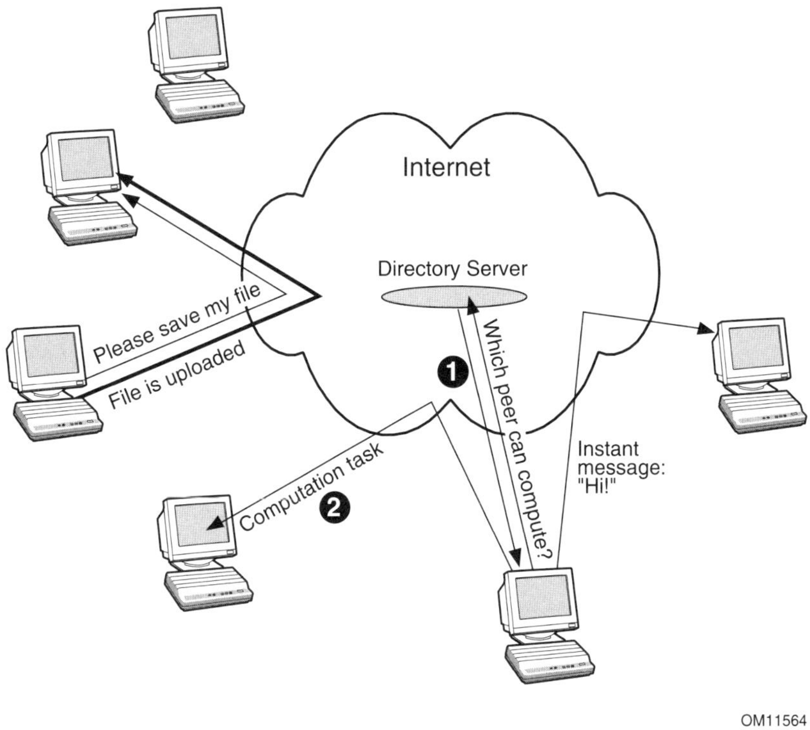

Figure 4.5 Peer computing on the Web

The physical infrastructure layer can be thought of as the client platforms, the peers, and all the ways they are connected with each other. On top of this layer, which may also contain optical and wireless elements, there is a software layer. Device drivers and operating systems, which may not communicate with each other, provide the interfaces through which the P2P services perform their tasks (see Figure 4.6).

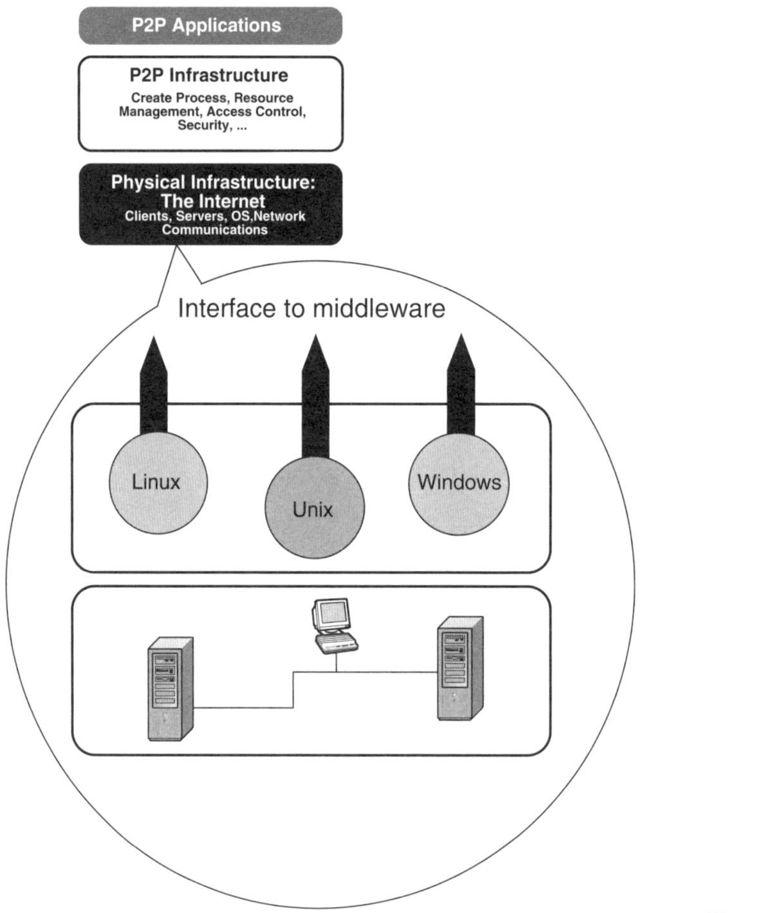

Figure 4.6 Components of the physical infrastructure

Objectives, Attributes, and Requirements of the Middleware

Now that we can identify the building blocks of the architecture or the infrastructure, we need to state the objectives of the P2P computing environment – what it is supposed to accomplish, and how it is expected to behave. These objectives define attributes and principles of operation. Here is where we move from an architecture discussion to a description of the infrastructure.

P2P middleware provides a set of interoperable services, while leaving enough flexibility for the application developers to create specific APIs, or use common ones, when such are available. P2P applications run over the net, and involve direct exchanges and sharing of resources between peers. The foundation to P2P computing is a collection of distributed resources connected by a network. The infrastructure that supports P2P applications must handle challenges not often encountered by traditional computing systems. P2P middleware must provide the tools that will enable effective implementation of P2P applications, freeing the application developers to design cooperative, distributed applications, instead of having to spend time coding system-type functions.

What are the realities and fundamental challenges that must be overcome to make meaningful P2P applications possible? Here are some of the important ones:

- **Lack of trust:** Sharing of resources and access must be granted between peers who are unknown to each other.
- **Hardware heterogeneity:** The whole environment is made up of heterogeneous components. The processors can be from different architectures or generations, with varying sizes of memory, and different peripherals. The computers may range from handheld devices to a supercomputer.
- **Software heterogeneity:** P2P applications are expected to incorporate peers running on any of the commercially available operating systems.
- **Network heterogeneity:** The networks connecting the peers differ in bandwidth and latency by orders of magnitude.
- **Scale:** The number of peers, or nodes, participating in the application can be as few as two or in the millions, and any number in between.

- **Intermittency:** The systems, and configuration, are not fixed and static. Nodes may come and go, not as defined by the P2P application, but due to external interests. The presence of peers is assumed to be intermittent.
- **Location:** Resources, such as files, storage, contributing peers, or executing programs, may move around during the session.
- **Autonomy:** Peers agree to share resources and collaborate while maintaining autonomy and being a final authority over their local system.
- **Local policies:** The application usually spans nodes with different security measures and administrative policies. At times collaborative peers belong to organizations that want to protect information from each other.
- **Distance:** The peers are expected to be geographically separated.

There are environments where some of these issues don't come into play. A P2P application running on dispersed resources within a single facility of an enterprise, for example, does not face a number of the challenges listed above. But, in general, the P2P infrastructure must be resilient in the face of these realities.

To create viable P2P applications, we need to resolve several fundamental issues. These are the significant requirements for general-purpose middleware:

Cross platform. This is a massive requirement with multiple facets: device, hardware, and software. In support of heterogeneity, the P2P infrastructure must provide a consistent set of middleware services on a multitude of devices. These devices range from a handheld wireless device or an appliance, to a laptop and a PC, to a server farm or supercomputer. The same device type, a server, for example, may have a number of architectures. Across any device type there are multiple hardware platforms. And across device types and hardware architectures within device types, there are several operating systems with their own file systems and internal mechanisms, all of which may need to be supported. To this software variety we must add the choice of programming languages for the application, from Java to C/C++ to XML and more.

An implementation that does not comply with the full range of platforms limits the environments where it is applicable. For practical reasons, a middleware implementation must almost always support a subset of all possible platforms. It is wise to include the hooks and capability for adding new platforms in the design.

Interoperability. Interoperability is a central theme in this book, and, clearly, a requirement placed on the infrastructure. At the very basic level, a P2P application must interoperate between, at least, two computers. But this is not enough. Once the P2P middleware runs on multiple hardware and software platforms, these different peers (and servers) must cooperate in running the same application. In fact, when the reservoir of resources for the application is out there all over the net, it is inconceivable that any popular application not support interoperation between peers. Flexibility in choosing APIs contributes to the need for another aspect of interoperability. The same application, a messaging application for example, may use different APIs on different systems. The different set of APIs may be the result of the native operating system or language-implementation choice. At yet another level, the common middleware may facilitate two or more different applications to communicate with each other. The use of this middleware, then, is the mechanism for integrated applications. Interoperability may also provide the desirable feature of migrating a P2P application from one peer to another. This migration may be necessary, for example, when one peer becomes unavailable, and a new peer is found.

Security. Assuming there is a set of middleware services for a peer networked application, satisfying the cross-platform and interoperability requirements makes it possible to create P2P applications. To make it possible and safe for users to join such an application, a layer of security needs to envelop the exchanges. The security requirement covers several functions – authentication for validating visitors to your system, authorization for allowing access to your computer, and measures for assuring data integrity, confidentiality, and privacy. Security is fundamental to establishing trust between peers. Security affects any communication and access the application performs, and security must be designed into the services from the start. Also, security mechanisms and policies must not overwrite and compromise those policies that exist on each peer computer. Security is discussed in more detail in Chapter 9.

Local autonomy. Any service offered by the P2P middleware has to respect the autonomy of the peer. The user determines how, when, and to what extent resources are available to P2P applications. The user also determines who can access the peer computer. There are times when the conditions that are set render the peer not suitable for the P2P application. The services need a way to check and handle this finding. One approach towards non-interference with local autonomy and security is to create a trustful mechanism for defining a "sandbox" within the peer system to which the guest application is confined.

Persistence. One serious difficulty with P2P computing is the intermittent presence of peers. The services must assume that peers may not be available until a task or a session is done. Yet, the application is expected to continue and complete reliably. To deal with intermittent peer presence we need a transparent migration or replication of resources. When a peer disconnects from the application another one may or may not join. It is essential that data that was on the disconnecting peer be available. The capability to move or recreate that data makes it persistent as far as the application is concerned. To make this possible, the peer environment must have a single namespace. A file that started on one peer may end up on another, so there can be no name conflict across the whole system from which peers may be drawn. Again, the naming of files and other objects must not interfere with local settings.

Scalability. The scope of P2P applications is spread across the Internet. The number of possible peers continues to grow. The design of the architecture must allow for scaling up. All the services must be designed so the load on any one node does not increase indefinitely with the number of participating peers. The services must be distributed. This caution is directed to application designers and developers, since the middleware cannot always compensate for centralization brought about by the application.

Extensibility. High-volume P2P is still at its infancy. New devices will be introduced, and new features will be added in existing devices. Opportunities for collaborative applications for the home and for businesses are only beginning to evolve. We can't tell what new services will be needed in the future, nor what features will prove missing in near-term services. A few years from now we may refer to the middleware described here as merely "first generation P2P." It is for these reasons that the architecture and the middleware implementation must be modular and extensible.

Other attributes can make P2P more readily accepted and adopted:

- **Fault-tolerance:** In some ways the P2P concept increases fault tolerance. Access to vast amounts of distributed resources allows for redundancy and replication that, with the right tools for handling exceptions, help overcome local failures. The notion of decentralization that is common to many P2P applications, means that in many cases there is no single point of failure. On the other hand, the reliance on unknown systems, whose presence may be intermittent in a heterogeneous environment, increases the odds of failure. Event and exception handling services will mitigate the risk, as will the resilience that should be built into the applications themselves.
- **Transparency:** With the appropriate abstractions built into the architecture, and an implementation of a unified namespace, the user need not be concerned with the physical location of resources. Switching to a replicated file, or moving a processing task to another peer during the session, should be transparent. Recovery from a failed event should enable smooth continuation of the process without the need for human intervention. Well thought out middleware and a well-designed application should exhibit this transparency. More on this in the discussion on complexity below.
- **Reliability:** Reliability is not addressed through fault tolerance alone. There are two special issues specific to P2P – availability of resources when they are needed, and trust that results delivered by other peers are correct. The guarantee of resources, or acceptable level of service, can be helped by the middleware design. The more versatile and robust the infrastructure, the wider the peer participation, and the more likely requested resources can be found. The other side of providing a reliable service is a function of the business model, marketing, and incentives; these topics are not discussed in this book.
- **Small footprint:** Some of the devices that are potential peers have, at least in the near future, limited storage capacity compared to PCs and servers. Such handheld and other wireless devices may need a minimal set of services that fit their smaller memory and storage. This should be possible with a modular design, since it is likely the storage-challenged devices will not be expected to be full-function peers.

- **Performance:** Performance of P2P applications requires a thorough study. We know that design and run-time decisions have a great impact on the resulting performance. Placing data at the right place relative to the peers that need it, choice of peer types and locations, communication routing services, or process scheduling, all impact the performance observed by the users. Performance considerations must be part of the middleware and application design decision.
- **Development tools:** P2P presents a complex computing environment. Its emergence is characterized by new applications that involve dynamic configurations and intermittent presence of resources. The fluctuations, uncertainty, variety of resource locations, and availability of resources add to the existing list of challenges faced by developers of networked applications. The more development tools the infrastructure providers can supply to the application programmers, the faster applications will appear. And peer computing users will not be far behind. A positive example in this area is the approach taken by Groove Networks. Their approach provides basic collaborative tools while shielding the basic services, such as those listed in the next section.

One other factor looms large over the design of the P2P infrastructure: **Complexity**. The list of challenges and requirements for the P2P architecture is daunting. Heterogeneity is extreme and spans hardware, software, and network components. The architecture and its infrastructure have to support a set of very different application types, from distributed computing to instant messaging to gaming. These applications may be written in a number of languages with different access methods to resources. The configuration on which the application runs can vary from two nodes to millions, and the number may not be fixed even during a session. Local policies, security, and trust levels may vary from one end of the spectrum to the other. And the list goes on.

What can be done to manage this inevitable complexity? The architecture and the associated services can be abstracted and defined with conceptual simplicity. Application developers will find their task much easier if the details of complicated interactions and multitude of parameters are hidden from them. The menu of services and their implementation may help accomplish this goal. Design decisions and clever implementations that are helpful to application developers and to users are described later in this book.

Some items are still left over for the application developer to worry about and take into account when designing the application. For example, network bandwidth limitations and bandwidth variations between peers and locations cannot always be hidden by the middleware services. The services are expected to find the optimum routing for a file transfer, and a suitable location for moving data to the edge. The application developer, however, has to treat communications differently depending on whether the application targets an enterprise network or a collection of home PCs.

Middleware Services

The P2P middleware interfaces to the physical layer underneath it, and to the applications above it. Its purpose is to provide a set of services that are required by P2P applications. Figure 4.77 depicts one way to stack the elements that the middleware services need to address. This is not a diagram of a proposed set of services, only a convenient way to list areas the middleware needs to handle. Once an architecture is defined it may be appropriate to have more than one service for some of the layers. For example, the "Naming, Discovery, Directory" layer may be implemented as three or more separate services. Similarly, the architectural solution may dictate that a layer may not have a single service associated with it at all. Security and Monitoring, for instance, may have functions associated with them integrated into other services as needed.

Each of the topics listed as layers in Figure 4.7 receives fuller treatment in Chapters 6 through 10. The "Identity, Presence, Community" and "Naming, Discovery, Directory" layers are discussed in Chapter 7. Comments on administration and monitoring are found with descriptions of the other services. Here is a preview of these components of the middleware.

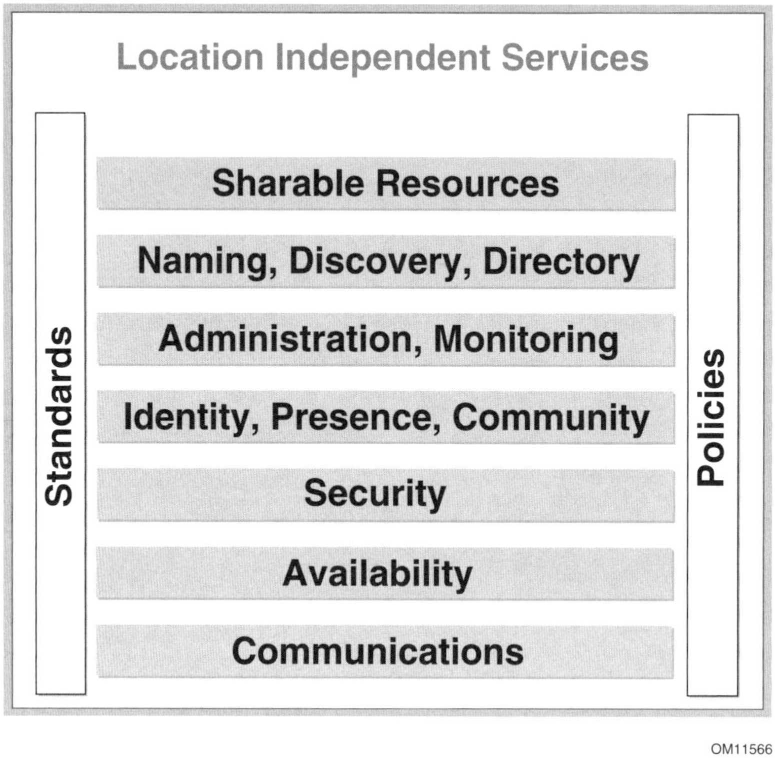

Figure 4.7 Components of middleware layer

Starting at the bottom of the illustration, the first capability needed for P2P computing is **Communications**. Common protocols, such as HTTP or SOAP, or the simple mechanism of sockets, effect exchanges between systems. Service, or services, supporting communications deal with crossing firewalls, and network address translation (NAT) between a local node identifier and an assigned Internet Protocol (IP) address. Network bandwidth is a resource, and network traffic may be audited and accounted for by a suitable accounting service.

Availability, in the P2P context, takes on a new dimension. Peers are expected to exercise intermittent presence on the network. The principle of local autonomy makes it difficult to enforce restrictive policies. The middleware must enable the application to deal with a number of related issues. An attempt to reach a peer may fail, and the application has to deal with it. The solution may involve queuing a message, or a notification, or a search for another peer, and so on. The service supporting such a solution will, likely, monitor events and deal with exceptions.

Another aspect of availability is content. An application may expect some content to be persistent, ever-present. This may require replicating files in a way that assures the required presence. Striving for an adequate quality of service may require services such as striping in order to overcome bandwidth limitations and congestion.

Security and trust are the biggest concerns people have regarding P2P computing. Security-related issues show up in the background of almost all other services. The **Security** layer, therefore, represents a number of topics that must be addressed. The user and the application must manage access control between peer computers. Access control involves authenticating the identity of, and authorizing appropriate access and permissions to, the other party. The security capabilities also have to guarantee both confidentiality and privacy at levels acceptable to users. In addition, peers must trust the integrity and authenticity of data and content they receive and use. To implement security measures, people use tools such as keys, digital signatures, and encryption, among others. These security measures are described in Chapter 9. Because security is one of the fundamental elements of an effective P2P computing environment, it manifests itself in almost all other P2P services.

The **Identity, Presence, Community** layer deals with establishing and managing both individual and group identities. The identity is related to the naming scheme, mentioned below, and to the authentication aspect of the security layer. P2P computing engages multiple users, who form groups or communities. These assemblies require an identity. The group identity may have policies and common permissions associated with it. Membership in a group implies acceptance of responsibilities and privileges that are assigned to the group. There is another, sometimes very important, aspect of the identity that is also related to security. Communication with unknown entities can be unsettling. It is useful to include capabilities for *attestation*, making statements that say something about you, and *reputation*, a measure of what others think of you.

In addition to identities and their authentication, the Identity, Presence, Community layer deals with matters of presence and persistence. Presence involves peers being able to indicate their status to other peers, whether the status is offline, connected but not engaged, or active in the P2P exchange. Some applications may need to allow for persistence of presence in the face of gaps or disruptions between sessions. Other applications may require the user to carry over the identity and presence from one device, for example, a PC, to another. These concepts are discussed further in Chapter 7.

Administration and Monitoring, the next layer of technical challenges, takes on a new dimension in the P2P environment. Here we have a vast, decentralized organization of resources and actors. Some P2P applications seek the opposite of monitoring. They seek anonymity and privacy. But there are often good reasons to audit access and actions. Peers may want information about how their resources are being used. Service providers may require usage and identity information. Performance tuning of network traffic and resource allocation requires observing and measuring how the overall system behaves. This layer of administrative system management is not addressed in this book, as it is highly application-dependent. Its services will most likely be embedded within other services, such as those that manage resources.

Naming, Discovery, and Directory are related but are separate services. The Naming portion deals with managing a namespace that encompasses the P2P universe for the application or the environment. Names need to be unique beyond the user's local environment. Names are also associated with groups of peers, where the membership and participation is not constant. But not only users need to be named. P2P, with its shared resources characteristic, requires that all resources be named. Resources include computers, other devices such as handheld devices, peripherals such as printers or CD burners, files of all types, and, possibly, network resources. Some implementations treat the users and all the resources as named objects. The identity and authentication services use the names provided by a naming service. Note that careful thought must be given to the naming scheme so it is scalable to the millions of possible peers and resource elements.

A discovery service provides the applications the means to find out about resources, their capabilities, and their current availability. For example, think of a message broadcast operation where the application wants to check who is connected within a given group. Or, a distributed computing application that needs to discover which computers, with the right resources, are available for its computations at a given time. This service is likely to use metadata for the basic components and objects, such as details of the network, users and their systems, available services, and other devices. The discovery service may include query support; publication, subscription, and catalog services; and metadata schema.

It is useful, at times, to keep some results from the discovery process in a directory. A directory, in this instance, is a repository of information about objects involved in a P2P application. The best known example of a directory is the indexed list of MP3 files that Napster creates for its users. A Napster peer queries this directory for a specific file, instead of having to discover its location by searching throughout the net. Notice how the use of naming, discovery, and directory follow each other in a logical progression.

Sharable Resources are fundamental to P2P computing, and a resource management service is likely to be a collection of services for the different types of resources, and for the various aspects of managing them. Thus you may encounter a service that manages access to storage. This shared storage can be an allocation given on some peer computer or an aggregate of vast amounts of distributed storage. A file service may include a file directory, I/O services, file abstraction for a storage service, and file system semantics. Similarly, a CPU, or cycle-sharing, service can do as little as enabling a guest executable on a peer computer, or as much as scheduling and dispatching a computational task that spans many computers of different capabilities and operating systems. A part of the overall resource management is the enforcement of policies, either on behalf of the networked community or on behalf of the local user. System management services, when needed, aggregate and administer resources from multiple peers, and may also be located with the resource management service.

Notice how a solution for one technical issue relies on solutions from others. For example, resource management, ID, and discovery services use information gathered and provided by the naming and security capabilities.

To complete the conceptual view of the middleware layers, supporting the structure are the standards chosen for the components of the middleware, such as protocols, and the policies that need to be consistent, or at least interoperable, and enforceable across the various services.

Most applications do not need all the services that can be created for the middleware layers shown in Figure 4.7. In many cases, the environment in which the application runs determines what P2P middleware services must be invoked. For example, if you send an instant message to a colleague on your company's intranet, you can be less concerned about authentication than if you send the same message from an airport lounge on your wireless handheld device. The notion that the application type and the computing environment determine the requirements placed upon the middleware should encourage software architects to examine the opportunities for creating a subset middleware for special important cases. For example, one such class might be the handheld and wireless devices whose available footprint, or storage size, is limited.

The top of Figure 4.7 declares that the middleware contains **Location Independent Services**. Location independence manifests itself in a couple of ways. First, the service looks the same regardless of the platform where it is used. The same is true when accessing the service from a different device. The services look the same on various devices, though their functionality may be limited on, for example, handheld devices. Second, the user interacts with the object in the same manner whether it is local or not. When you view a file via a P2P service, it should not make any difference where this file is stored.

In Chapter 1, we saw a layer of application interfaces that resides between the middleware and the P2P application. The concept of an interface layer between the middleware services and the applications is a powerful one. It preserves the benefits of a common infrastructure while allowing developers to employ their favorite language and development environment. The presence, underneath, of the common services enables the universality of communications and integration between peers.

Allowing the APIs to be defined outside and on top of the middleware also enables a common middleware to coexist side by side with a native infrastructure. For example, a Java P2P application may use its own APIs to call Java services, thus bypassing the common middleware. Alternatively, the application may target its calls to the common set of services presented above. The application makes this choice while using the same APIs.

The following chapters in this book describe implementations of P2P middleware or infrastructure and how they tackle the technical issues discussed above.

Design Approaches

This section presents short descriptions of some of the current P2P framework approaches, and shows the variety of implementation philosophies in P2P infrastructure. The architectural approaches listed below are from Endeavors Technologies, Inc.; Applied Meta, Inc., now AVAKI Corporation; Proksim Software; and Foundation for Intelligent Physical Agents (FIPA). These approaches have been formally submitted as proposals to the peer-to-peer working group.

This section also includes segments about Groove and Grid Computing, and the work these companies are doing on P2P infrastructure.

Endeavors Technologies, Inc.

Out of research at the University of California at Irvine comes a set of P2P products that include wireless P2P capabilities.

Endeavors Technology's product is called Magi. Four design decisions dictate their approach to P2P architecture and infrastructure.

The first design principle is to build on top of the Web's infrastructure. This implies use of HTTP, Web Distributed Authoring and Versioning (WebDAV), URIs and URLs, and MIME. HTTP was chosen because it is an open protocol, has standard semantics, and is widely adopted. WebDAV provides a means for using the Web as a writable medium, and helps with sharing content. URIs and URLs are used for all the resources from Web pages to files and devices. Magi uses MIME to encapsulate the representation of a variety of file formats, such as HTML, XML, WAP Markup Language (WML), and others.

The second design principle is to build an architecture based on components and events. Components are useful objects for reasons of customization, reuse, and extension. The architecture needs to cope with events as much of P2P occurs through independent entities interacting with each other. The flexibility offered by the modular approach of components enables a version of Magi that has a small footprint and can be used in wireless handheld devices and embedded devices.

The third principle of Magi's design is that it should be a platform that allows other applications to integrate into the infrastructure. This integration is made possible through the absence of user interface constraints, use of open standards, use of open source components, and support for multiple implementations.

The fourth design principle is the independence and autonomy of the peer. It achieves this by letting the application make the determinations about how to handle resources when creating local copies or global replicas.

Applied Meta, Inc., now AVAKI Corporation

The high-performance distributed computing community contributed some of the early examples of resource sharing between remote users across the net. The following is a P2P solution based on ideas whose origins were in high-performance scientific computing.

AVAKI has a middleware product (it used to be called "Legion" when the proposal was written) that, as stated in the proposal to the working group, is an "integrated infrastructure for distributed resource sharing in a mutually distrustful setting. The middleware is best compared to an operating system, since it provides core services analogous to what an operating system provides, such as process management (creation, control, scheduling), interprocess communication, persistence via a file system, resource management, security for both users and for resource owners, transparency via naming and binding, accounting and resource management, and an application development environment. The middleware provides these capabilities in a platform-independent manner, running on top of existing host operating systems such as Linux, Solaris, and Windows." In line with the middleware structure proposed above, "Legion allows users and programmers as much flexibility as possible in their applications' semantics, resisting the temptation to dictate solutions." The implementation of the middleware is object-based. All the entities involved are objects that communicate via method invocation. The object-based nature of the middleware does not exclude procedural languages. Users can write objects in C, Fortran, C++, and Java. The unified naming scheme allows for transparencies of location and access, migration, and replication. Failure is transparent when recovery is possible.

Proksim Software

The sharing of information represents the motivation behind the approach taken by Proksim Software.

The main issues that the Proksim architecture addresses are coherency of shared data, limited network bandwidth, latency, reliability, and performance. The underlying means Proksim employs is a technology called Duplicated Objects (Proksim, 2001). The technology Proksim developed is an amalgam of distributed objects and message-oriented middleware. The object-oriented approach of Duplicated Objects resembles that used for distributed objects, but with a full local copy of the object and access to all its data locally. All the copies stay coherent through an automatic update mechanism. The Proksim technology addresses the fundamental issue of how to deal with entities required for P2P. It enables other capabilities to be built upon it. These capabilities include simple namespace management, load balancing, fault tolerance, extensibility, scalability, local site autonomy, aspects of security, multi-language support, monitoring and accountability, and more.

Foundation for Intelligent Physical Agents (FIPA)

A different approach for constructing P2P architecture and services is based on the use of intelligent agents, a technology described separately in the context of some possible P2P application usages in Chapter 7.

FIPA's goal is to promote interoperable intelligent agent applications and agent systems. To this end, the organization created standards for agent communications. An agent communication language (ACL) helps manage the complexity inherent in network-based applications. FIPA uses a holistic approach for architecture that can accommodate a wide range of commonly used mechanisms, such as those used for transports, messaging, directory services, and others. In the abstract architecture described by FIPA, an agent is a computational process that implements the autonomous, communicating functionality of the application. The architecture allows the specific implementation to choose the message transport service to be used for messages between agents. The P2P middleware elements that are addressed by the FIPA architecture include site autonomy, security, namespace, extensibility, scalability, discovery, fault tolerance, and exception management. The FIPA proposal does not address intermittency, persistence, I/O, or accountability.

Groove Networks, Inc.

Design approaches for collaborative computing are being developed. One of the products being talked about is called Groove†, from Groove Networks, Inc.

Groove provides a secure environment for collaborative computing. In Groove's terminology, this environment is called "shared space." It is a virtual space for small group interaction. A user can be a member of many shared spaces. Users, sharing a space, can chat, share a drawing, communicate by voice, send instant messages, update a calendar and plan events, share a file, and more. All these actions are done using a basic set of tools that can be added to the space. People join by invitation, and security is provided by Groove. Security is transparent as far the users are concerned. Groove is implemented with XML, and treats the content as objects to store and to route around. Authentication is built in, authorization is handled through the invitation process, and a sizable number of tools support the shared space. The space itself resides, visually through the GUI, in a window-tool called a transceiver. A relay service provides a solution to intermittent connectivity by peers.

Groove is a platform developers can use to create new collaborative tools to build more complex or more specialized business applications and solutions.

Grid Computing

Originating from the public sector, in academia and national research laboratories and institutions, grid computing techniques are being developed to support distributed computing, high-end collaboration, and distributed data analysis applications. Grid computing researchers, through their Global Grid Forum, continue to develop services that are relevant to P2P infrastructure. Membership in the Forum now includes commercial groups. More information on their activities appears in Chapter 13, where P2P distributed computing is described.

Grid computing differentiates itself from conventional distributed computing by its focus on large-scale resource sharing (Catlett, Foster, 2000 and Foster et al., 2001). To this end, grid computing practitioners define an architecture for "flexible, secure, coordinated resource sharing among dynamic collections of individuals, institutions, and resources." The approach is guided by the principle that interoperability is a key to the architecture, and, therefore, protocols are the basic building blocks for defining mechanisms by which users negotiate access and resources, and exercise sharing and collaboration. There are a number of projects, involving computations and data sharing, associated with the grid computing community. One of these projects, the Globus Project, adopted the approach of creating a tool kit as a programming abstraction, and its Globus Toolkit provides the infrastructure for numerous large-scale grid deployment and application projects in the U.S. and Europe. A key differentiator of the Globus approach is adherence to "open architecture, open standards, and open source." There are other interesting projects such as Condor (http://www.cs.wisc.edu/condor/) from the University of Wisconsin at Madison, for high throughput by harnessing idle cycles on networked computers, the Legion project at the University of Virginia (http://legion.Virginia,edu) that is being commercialized by AVAKI coprporation, and Globe (http://www.cs.vu.nl/~steen/globe/), in Holland, for wide-area distributed systems using distributed shared objects. For more information on grid computing projects, including those mentioned above, see (Foster, Kesselman, 1999).

There are other variants on the approaches to P2P infrastructure. Descriptions of other offerings are included in greater detail in the following chapters.

Some larger corporations also have noteworthy initiatives, in various stages of progress, which involve network computing and services. These companies include Microsoft, Sun Microsystems, IBM, and Hewlett-Packard. This book is not about these initiatives, but about the work done by the smaller new companies whose main focus is P2P.

Chapter 5
An Overview of Reference Architectures

In Chapter 4 we saw the benefits common middleware can bring to developers and users. Unfortunately, there is no such common infrastructure at present. There is no single implementation of an architecture that developers of P2P applications rally behind. Some application developers created the P2P services needed for their application. Others, however, set out to create an infrastructure, or a platform, on which P2P can be developed. So far, all of these platform developers address a specific type of P2P application. Essentially, they offer a partial solution to the general problem of a general-purpose P2P middleware. We examined a few of these platforms at the end of the previous chapter.

This chapter presents infrastructure designs that target specific areas of applications. Each of the classes of application has more than one solution. There is no single "right" architecture, not even for any one segment of the P2P computing space. It is also true that no one solution is a complete and finished product. The new era of P2P computing is too young for definitive products. The platforms described here are still evolving.

The multiplicity of offerings and their still-evolving state present the P2P community with both a challenge and an opportunity. The application developer must choose among several possible platforms to build upon. Each platform may or may not evolve in a direction favorable to that particular application. To understand the opportunity presented by P2P platform solutions, let us turn again to interoperability. Study and usage of available middleware products or infrastructure solutions helps P2P users and developers select the best practices, and make them common, even standard. Developers and users must learn how to interoperate between infrastructures and across platforms without a common and complete P2P infrastructure platform. In the early stages of the widespread adoption of P2P computing, commonly used solutions are good, or best, at certain functions. Interoperability can still be achieved through a relatively small number of interfaces.

This architectural discussion categorizes the platform solutions by the main computing environment they support. This is not the only way to classify the solutions, but it is one that makes the most sense from the viewpoint of an application developer. The P2P platforms described here are grouped as follows:

- **Distributed computing.** This category focuses on applications where peers cooperate in solving computational problems. The cooperation is also referred to as *cycle-sharing*. Grid computing is closely related to P2P cycle-sharing, but its origins are different. Though cooperative computation is the impetus for solutions in this space, you will see examples of ideas and services that have far wider applicability.
- **Content sharing.** This category includes P2P platforms that offer tools and services for applications that enable sharing and delivering of content, and sharing and distributing storage.
- **Collaboration.** This category includes platforms that support applications where peer collaborate online. What differentiates collaboration from the two other classes is the need for synchronous presence of the peers. The peers work together on some shared resource, such as a document. Or, they engage in a real-time exchange.

Technical implementations of solutions for content sharing and for collaborative frameworks are different in an important way. Content sharing applications must maximize services to reach a wide community. The primary effort of collaborative applications is to minimize response time for communications between peers. Keep these separate goals in mind as you read this chapter.

Each of the three categories listed above is illustrated by several solutions. A variety of approaches address different slants of what is, essentially, a similar issue.

Before delving into the details of these reference architectures, let us add some context to help us appreciate the design choices made by the platform designers. Chapter 2 listed 18 scenarios that our fictitious Peer acts on in a typical day in the near future. Each of these scenarios can be placed into one of the three platform categories:

Table 5.1. Platform categories for everyday scenarios

Platform Category	Scenario
Distributed computing	Contribute to a large computation.
Content sharing	What's going on in the world?
	Start thinking about work.
	Notify the team,
	IT needs your attention.
	A quick search.
	Take a class.
	En route.
Collaboration	The family.
	An instant message.
	Meeting with the boss.
	Collaborating with the project team.
	A virus alert.
	Collaborate across the firewall.
	The family web.
	A group play.
	Meeting the neighbors.
	Local trade.

The fact that more situations fall into the collaboration and content sharing categories indicates the rich possibilities in those types of activities.

This chapter focuses on the problem the developer is addressing, the architectural design assumptions, the underlying technologies, and some special features and attributes. Chapters 6 through 10 describe the major technical areas for which P2P computing must provide solutions.

Infrastructure for Distributed Computing

By *distributed computing* we mean, most commonly, distributed computations, or cycle-sharing. In its broader meaning, distributed computing includes using other distributed resources, notably storage. In a P2P infrastructure, the distributed computing category includes the tools and services needed to manage resources shared across peers. The examples in this chapter come from companies that are examining how peers participate in large-scale computations. The activities needed for cooperative computation include resource discovery, requesting and granting access to peer systems, naming of objects and entities, assuring data integrity, and dealing with intermittent presence of resources. When these tools are available, data can be distributed for storage or delivery. We can expect commonality in services between those provided for distributed computing and those that are content-focused. Indeed, there are applications that incorporate elements from both cycle-sharing and content-sharing. Examples of applications that perform a P2P-style distributed search are provided in Part III. For now, note that a P2P search involves gaining access to peer computers, performing processing to look for items specified by the search criteria, and sending results back. The results in this case are synthesized content.

Again, note that the basic services needed for different types of P2P applications do have a lot in common. This section describes two P2P infrastructure solutions that support distributed computations as the initial or primary application.

Distributed computing comes in a number of flavors, depending on the application and the context in which it is run. The most difficult problem for distributed computing is when a single application, with a single dataset, has to be run one time to produce one result. To use thousands of peers for this application, developers must "parallelize" the application (see Chapter 3). There is also a complicated trade-off between the size of the computational tasks and the latency and bandwidth of the network. This is not the place to delve deeper into these issues, and if interested, you are encouraged to look up a reference on parallel, distributed computing.

The more common, and practical, network-based computations are those where the whole application runs on each peer, and there is no need for any communication between the peers. For example, if there are many sets of data that are to be processed independent of each other, each peer can get one set, process it, then get another one, and so on. SETI@home is such an application. Another type of computation, called a *parametric study* computation, occurs when the same computation is performed for each of a pre-defined set of values. Think of a fluid dynamics simulation of an aircraft that has to be checked against every possible angle of attack. Each peer receives the whole application and a value of the angle to which it applies the computation.

Entropia: Internet-based Distributing Computing

Entropia came into being in 1997, before P2P became a household term. Entropia focuses on performing large-scale computations by distributing them across many thousands of processors located on Internet nodes. The goal is to take scientific-engineering distributed processing beyond the realm of supercomputers and data centers, and extend the network-based clustering of several computational facilities. The result is a large-scale Internet grid, made up of many thousands of PCs. Chapter 11 describes the interesting computational problems that are being tackled by the Entropia computational grid.

What are the design principles for this computing platform?

- **Security.** Security for distributed computations is a two-way street. The guest application must be protected from intentional or accidental intrusion by the user who owns the host machine. And the host must be safe from any possible side effects caused by the guest application.

  The Entropia platform protects the applications running on the host machine from malicious or accidental intrusion by the user of the machine, and protects the user from the application through the use of strong encryption technologies.

- **Flexibility and Fault-tolerance.** The network and scheduling infrastructure must tolerate and quickly adjust to peer nodes joining and leaving the network. Entropia provides a centralized management console to manage peer nodes joining and leaving, pooling resources, defining scheduling policies, and tracking job submission and completion.

- **Scalability.** The network must function smoothly when the number of nodes increase to very large numbers. After all, the ability to create a huge network is a cornerstone of network-based distributed computing.
- **Language Neutrality.** The platform infrastructure must handle an application written in any of the common programming languages. Entropia uses binary integration of the applications and as such, any program or executable that runs on the Windows platform can be integrated into the Entropia system without any source code modifications.
- **Ease of Integration.** The platform must allow existing executables to be plugged into the system without any changes made to the application. There is no need to use source code.
- **Non-intrusive.** The guest application and the Entropia middleware must not interfere with the host computer's installed software and applications. This includes protecting the user's computing experience, and the host's software and network environments.

The idea behind P2P distributed computing is to harness under-utilized network-based computer resources to deliver a high-performance computing platform. And, as with any high-performance computing platform, the keys to success are the ability to achieve this high performance combined with the ability to write applications for the platform.

The first Entropia network proved that, for certain kinds of applications, using the spare cycles of personal computers distributed around the world could provide high performance. The Great Internet Mersenne Prime Search (GIMPS), for example, is now a network of 175,000 computers, all over the world, that has already discovered the two largest known Mersenne prime numbers, the largest of which has 909,526 digits. The combined power of the GIMPS network was close to 1 teraflops (at the end of 2000), as compared to 2.1 teraflops for the most powerful supercomputer at that time.

Achieving the second goal, the ability to write applications for the new platform, requires a host of new technologies that shield the developer from the difficulties of the harsh wide-area Internet environment. These difficulties include the use of firewalls that restrict communication, machines that are connected by low bandwidth modems, users who are concurrently using their machines for other purposes, users who turn off their machines, failures attributed to any of the above difficulties, and security considerations that require both the user's machine as well as the application to be protected from each other. These difficulties are dealt with at the system level thus making application development on such a dynamic platform simpler and less forbidding.

The Entropia platform does not dictate how the user application is implemented. The application must run on a Windows operating system, but can be a binary file or code to be interpreted at run time, from any language that is accommodated by the Windows environment. The motivation for this approach is the belief that trusted code that has evolved to solve a particular problem does not need to be rewritten in order to take advantage of distributed computing. Security is maintained through the use of proprietary sandbox techniques. This sandbox ensures that the application is well behaved and non-intrusive. The concept of a sandbox is described in Chapter 9.

Figure 5.1 shows how the Entropia system works.

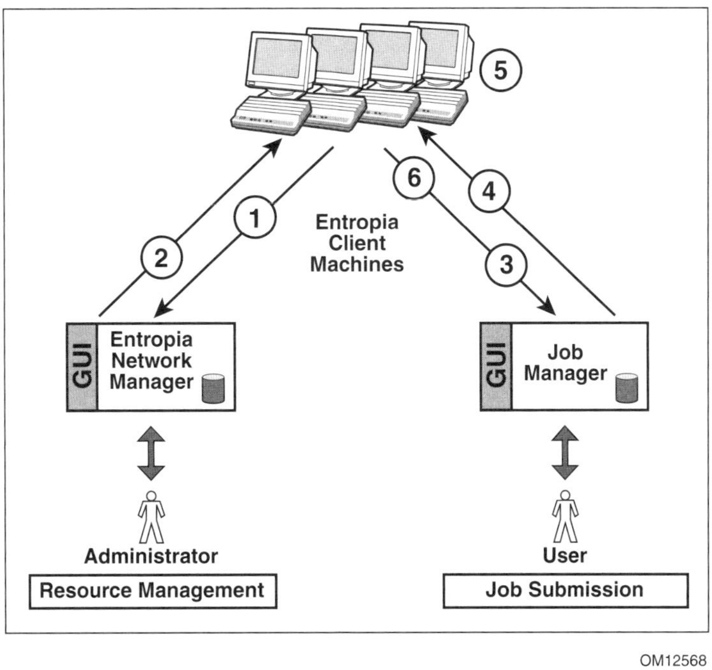

Figure 5.1 The Entropia system

First, in step 1, an idle host contacts the Entropia Network Manager and requests an application package. The Network Manager sends an appropriate application package to the host for execution in step 2. The package is unbundled and the application manager is started on the host machine. The application manager coordinates the execution of the application on the host with a Job Manager that determines the parameters for the execution of the job and prepares the application for execution by staging the necessary data files. These parameters and input files are specified by a user of the system who inputs jobs for decomposition and execution. The Job Manager accepts the job and generates sub-jobs that require execution at available hosts. The sub-job specification is communicated to the application manager in steps 3 and 4 of the figure. In step 5, the sub-job is computed through the execution of the application with the specified inputs. The results are subsequently transferred back to the Job Manager in step 6 and eventually to the user who submitted the job.

United Devices: Creating the MetaProcessor[†] Platform for Tapping into Unused Resources

United Devices began in philanthropic, or public service, projects as early as 1997. The people who founded United Devices came from projects such as SETI@home and distributed.net (commonly known also as d.net), and they put together computational communities to tackle a number of cryptographic challenges.

United Devices provides both software and services for creating and deploying distributed computing applications over intranets and the Internet. The basic premise behind this quest is that only a few machines fully use their network, storage, and computing resources. The MetaProcessor platform developed by United Devices allows a quiet, non-intrusive tapping into this unused power and resources. The platform manages delivery of computational tasks to thousands of networked computers. Typically, these tasks represent the same computation done on different data for one large project. A number of some large computational projects can, and do, exist on the Internet at any given time. As each computer on the network completes its task, the results are sent back to a central database for analysis and placed into the context of the larger project. The distributed computing platform allows very large computing projects to be completed faster and cheaper.

What are the design principles for this computing platform?

- **Simplicity.** Installing the peer software, receiving the computational task, sending the results back, querying the system, and so on, is effortless. Much of the interaction is automated.
- **Portability.** The platform runs on, and tasks move between, multiple processor types and under a number of operating systems. Current Windows operating systems are supported now, and support for Linux is planned for the future.
- **Manageability.** The platform provides easy ways to discover resource capabilities, and easily determines the status of computations scattered around the net.
- **Scalability.** The platform and its associated tools need to handle projects that last for weeks and months and execute on millions of devices.

The choice of technologies gives rise to some useful features:

- Communication is established through HTTP over TCP/IP. An agent, called the UD Agent (see Figure 5.2), is placed on every peer. This mechanism and the nature of the application make firewalls and NATs (see Chapter 6) less of an issue.
- APIs are written in C/C++, with wrappers that offer interfaces to other languages.
- Security is implemented with industry standards. The MetaProcessor platform uses authentication, encryption, and signing throughout the architecture. Triple DES (Data Encryption Standard) encryption protects all communication and storage of data. The UD Agent and customer applications are protected by mechanisms that prevent users from tampering with files or data or from returning false results. User devices are protected by authenticated, encrypted transfer of code and data, and a constrained application execution environment.
- Peers and system administrators can set up a *preference profile* that specifies which applications can run on the host, and when.

Figure 5.2 describes the MetaProcessor architecture. The platform consists of a specialized scheduling and distribution server; a database storing and tracking all work performed by devices on the network; and the UD Agent, which resides on each desktop and workstation on the network. The UD Agent is a small software program that runs on the peer. The UD Agent enables the MetaProcessor platform to work with the participating device for downloading applications, processing work units, and returning results and device information. The web console, also on the peer system, is the user interface for managing the platform, testing, scheduling, receiving new data, and sending results. The other components of the architecture are a central MetaProcessor (MP) server, and the database attached to it. The server manages intelligent scheduling, secure communications, workload distribution, collection of statistics, and other infrastructure management functions. The database contains information about both the application and its work units, and about the users and their UD Agents (see also United Devices, 2001).

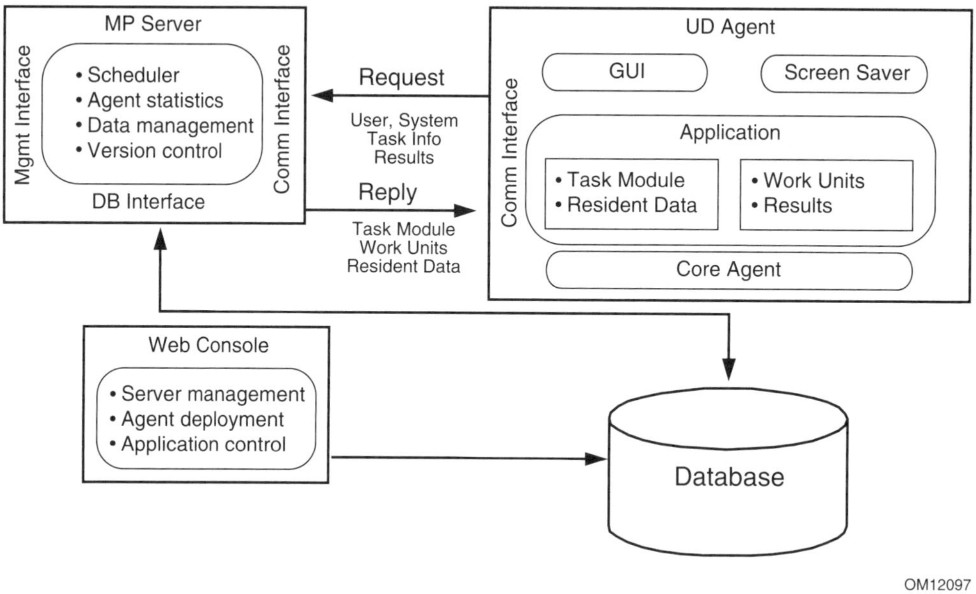

Figure 5.2 The MetaProcessor and UD Agent architecture

Here is an interesting byproduct of Internet-based distributed computing: Building a network of connected computers provides an infrastructure for measuring performance on the network. United Devices is developing technologies and tools for measuring actual bandwidth and latency for various loads on the net, the storage components, and the processing power. This approach has the potential to deliver reliable measurements of real-life workloads. Such benchmarks can be used to remove bottlenecks and improve delivery of content and messages across the network.

Environments for Content Sharing

In the previous section you read about several design approaches that enable distributed computation. In some sense, this is the least complex type of P2P application, since management and monitoring of the process can be handled from a single control point. This controlling function is handled by the peer that is issuing the computational tasks.

Now we can move on to the next level of complexity, to the class of infrastructure solutions that addresses *content sharing*. The term *content* encapsulates messages and files of all types—text, music, graphics, video, source and binary software, and any other content that can be digitized.

Content sharing encompasses several types of activities:

- **Messaging.** This activity sends text, with or without attachments, to someone's attention.
- **File delivery, also known as file sharing.** This occurs when a peer pulls a copy of a file from another system.
- **Distributed storage and distributed, shared file systems.** This is a community activity, requiring some kind of an agreement among the participants.
- **Caching and edge services.** This activity moves content closer to where it is needed. The action is typically initiated by the party that provides the content.
- **Content distribution.** This is a one-way transfer of content from a single source, or a coordinated set of senders, to many recipients.
- **Knowledge management.** This activity uses P2P services to help customize, organize, filter, coordinate, and discover content.
- **Content management.** This activity supports knowledge management by handling content versioning, production, checkout, etc.

What does this mean in terms of the requirements placed on the infrastructure for content sharing? For distributed computing the application must discover available systems, manage requests and grant access to computation cycles, and monitor the presence of the participating peers. The need to establish trust is mostly one-sided. The computing peer must trust the source of the executable program being loaded into the peer computer. Content sharing applications require all of the services that are needed for distributed computing, with the exception of managing CPU cycles. The services also become more complex. Every peer must establish, with confidence, the identity of everyone else. Unified names are needed not just for the computer systems and the users, but for all files. Presence of peers, in the content sharing context, involves not just availability of computational results, but availability of files and storage locations as well. Finding and managing content involves more complex and ever-present discovery and monitoring capabilities. And, whereas in distributed computing all the participating peers make up a single group, content sharing environments need to manage multiple groups, or communities.

In what follows you will learn how developments from OpenCola, Mangosoft, NextPage, and the Escher Group approach these challenges.

OpenCola: Delivery of Relevant Content

The "COLA" in OpenCola stands for Collaborative Object Lookup Architecture. OpenCola agents collaborate among themselves to look for documents and files. The "Open" part of the name implies openness both in the "open source" sense, and in the network sense of being distributed and collaborative.

What is OpenCola about?

OpenCola is developing a product, called Folders, to address the problem of how to conduct effective searches on the Internet. Their premise is that traditional search tools do not cope well with the explosive growth and the dynamic nature of the information on the net. Traditional tools do not discover new pages as quickly as they are created; the search engines re-visit all previously visited sites to check for changes; and the results returned from a search tend to be too narrow or too broad, as they cater to the "average" user.

The OpenCola software uses agents that are programmed to look for content that is likely to be of interest to the individual peer. Folders searches constantly without requiring supervision or input. It performs its tasks in collaboration with other OpenCola agents on the network. Where standard search engines consist of a single central database that uses spiders to search for new resources, and a data mining engine to make the data searchable, Folders send spiders to the Net themselves.

OpenCola products discover resources, or find "things," on the Internet, then evaluate the content for relevance, and deliver only the files that contain relevant content for that user.

A guiding principle for OpenCola is "Computers aren't as good at determining document relevance as human beings are." Much of P2P is about aggregating resources. OpenCola aggregates decisions. Human decisions are instrumental in routing documents to other humans.

The OpenCola tools create virtual neighborhoods of relevance, or communities of shared interest. Whereas Google ranks relevance by the popularity of the reference, OpenCola measures "similarity." Looking at it from the user's viewpoint, this means that if the user finds a document from John helpful, chances are other files from John on the same topic may also be of interest. And if John has references pointing to Cindy's system, it is likely the user will find Cindy's documents and files also relevant. More information about using search techniques to establish relevance is in Chapters 7 and 11.

OpenCola is a system, rather than a single application. It consists of both software and incentive methods to encourage people to establish peer networks. These networks can be viewed as interlocked web rings, where each ring consists of a set of people whose similar interests have led them to band together to hunt for resources. Key to the design philosophy of OpenCola is the idea of a distributed and collaborative system.

Being truly decentralized allows the OpenCola network to be scalable. The search methodology favors the creation of focused peer communities with shared interests. Scalable, therefore, means the ability to support any number of communities of interest. These communities may overlap, thus providing a means for hopping from one group to another. So, scaling in the OpenCola context does not mean that the whole net is one gigantic community.

The OpenCola network also self-organizes. When you participate, your nearest neighbors are best qualified to respond to your queries. As the number of peers increases, the correlations between neighbors in each network neighborhood are refined. The agents fine-tune their searches and "compare notes" with other agents. A peer can always look for better buddies in this pool. It can discard old, less relevant buddies in favor of the new ones. The total number of buddies for a peer's Folder, i.e., the size of its "neighborhood," need not change; it is simply that a more suitable buddy moves in. Because peers operate within relatively small neighborhoods, messages have a finite and predictable scope and life span. The only activity that takes a peer outside the neighborhood is the ongoing search for new buddies, and the peer controls the duration and resources applied to such investigations.

The kernel in OpenCola Folders is called the *clerver* (from "client-server"), and it provides basic messaging services between components. The clerver allows plug-in components, written in C, to be linked to it dynamically. One such component is Folders, mentioned above.

The term "clerver" implies that each node, a peer, acts both as a server and as a client. The clerver can host software, such as plug-ins. It can communicate with objects, via XML. And it can integrate software through a plug-in that enables bringing in new plug-ins or modifying existing ones.

Each clerver plays host to a number of collaborative software programs. The clerver takes care of basic administration tasks, including shunting incoming messages to the correct module. The OpenCola clerver is a small (about 500K) C++ program that takes plug-ins written in C.

The clerver architecture uses several technologies. Software agents and spiders perform searches. A proprietary communication system is built on XML and HTTP with interfaces to other protocols. The communications protocol XRoad resembles SOAP (Simple Object Access Protocol), but it relies on XPath and does not specify what the XML looks like. The clerver need only understand XPath.

The clerver is analogous to an HTTP server in many respects. It can communicate with the outside world using HTTP, and it can serve up web pages from a local directory. Its main task, however, is to host collaborative software, and facilitate communication between the software objects inside it and other clervers. Picture a clerver as a web server that allows you to read and write to specific documents inside it using a very simple protocol. From outside, everything in the clerver looks like a document, and can be addressed using simple URLs. The clerver handles external client requests such as serving a local file in response to an HTTP GET request; passing HTTP POST requests to modules like the Folders manager and relaying the XML responses; and, serving HTML presentations by transforming them from XML. The clerver is the only OpenCola component that handles network and local requests. The clerver allows plug-in components written in C to be linked to it dynamically.

The Folders component we looked at earlier is a plug-in into the clerver. One user's Folders is visible to other peers, which allows for faster discovery. Folders contains, in its simplest form, a relevance engine, a list of similar Folders (buddies), and a list of scored documents. Relevance engines employ various algorithms to determine if a document or a file is similar to the content the user is looking for. There is much work to do in identifying algorithms for evaluating similarity and relevance. The OpenCola philosophy is that human involvement and interaction is essential for "training" the relevance engines. The Folders plug-in is discussed in detail in Chapter 7.

In addition to Folders, another important component of the OpenCola system is the *document fetcher*. The fetcher is the tool that retrieves documents for other components, such as spiders. The fetcher uses the spider's configuration file to locate and download files. An OpenCola system may have any number of spiders working from a given clerver. For example, a spider may be a "crawler," going from peer to peer looking for "buddies." Or, a spider may go on a search when directed by the user. Spiders also decide where to go next, based on the relevance level of documents it sees.

It is no longer true that spiders that understand HTTP and NNTP can find most of the documents people are looking for. They will not fetch files that are encapsulated by SOAP, or by protocols from Napster, gPULP, Freenet, or Gnutella, for example. The OpenCola architecture creates fetchers that can communicate with these other protocols.

OpenCola is a system of peer networks. These networks are interlocked web rings, where each ring consists of a set of people whose similar interests band them together to hunt for resources. Such rings can overlap where people's interests overlap, or they may be autonomous with respect to the rest of the OpenCola network. As mentioned above, each node is both a client and a server, by virtue of running the OpenCola clerver. This is exactly what is referred to as a peer in this book.

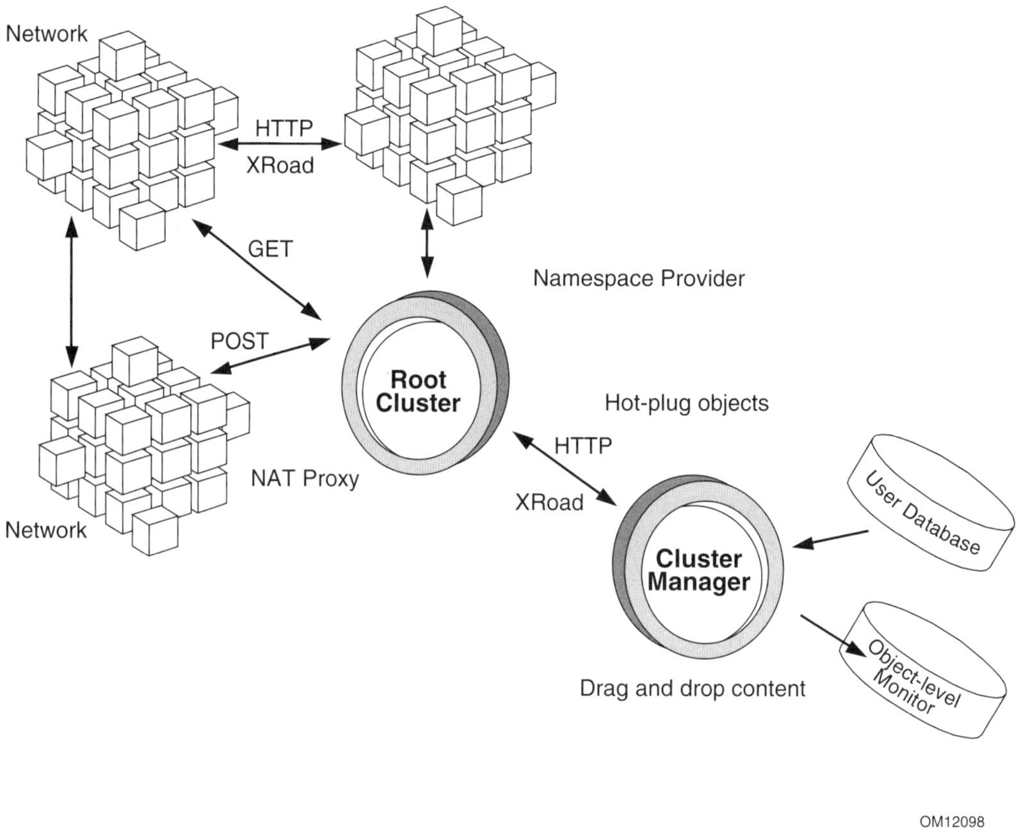

Figure 5.3 The OpenCola network architecture

The OpenCola network consists of three elements:

- The Cluster Manager that controls, administers, and manages a cluster of up to 1024 root nodes. Think of the cluster manager as a super-peer.
- Root nodes that manage OpenCola namespace indices. Root nodes use all of the basic OpenCola technologies to provide public addresses to OpenCola leaf nodes, including desktop machines behind firewalls and dynamic IP addresses which previously were not part of the DNS namespace.
- Leaf nodes that are the peers. Each leaf node is assigned to, and interacts with, a root node. Leaf nodes also belong to a cluster, managed by a cluster manager.

Mangosoft: Clustering and Technologies for Distributed File Systems

Mangosoft arrived on the P2P scene through its patented technology known as "pooling." Pooling is a peer-to-peer clustered caching technology. It utilizes system and network resources for efficient delivery of web content and file services over the Internet.

Mangosoft products provide web caching and secure Internet file service that does not require VPN (virtual private network). Its computing environment encompasses LANs with the enterprise, bridging multiple intranet locations, and storage servers on the Internet. Strategies include P2P clustering, distributed caching, intelligent distributed directories, and dynamic data migration.

Mangosoft currently offers two products of interest to the P2P community. Cachelink† is a web caching software that increases the delivery speed of Internet and intranet content to end-users. Mangomind† is a virtual file service on the Internet.

This chapter focuses on the pooling technology, with a brief overview of Mangomind and Cachelink. You will find more about Mangosoft's storage technology and products in Chapters 10 and 11.

Pooling is a clustering technology that unifies the memory and disk resources of networked computers, making the network appear and act like a single system. Users no longer need to know network addresses and topology to access files and services. Pooling is constructed using caching and virtual memory techniques. It uses pervasive industry standards, Windows, TCP/IP, and Ethernet. Pooling presents an adaptive, transparent, and automatic network solution, where the attached PCs work as both a client and a server; in other words, our definition of a peer.

Mangosoft pooling is adaptive. Logical resources and services are moved dynamically between systems on the network to optimize performance and throughput. The pooling technology is like a dynamic cache, automatically moving web content and files closest to the users that access them most often. Therefore, access happens locally and network performance increases.

Pooling is modeled after the modern computer system's virtual memory mechanisms. All objects in the system have universal, virtual addresses, a 128-bit string, that all systems in the network use to reference them. These addresses are mapped to the physical incarnation of the object on one or more systems. With this universal address space, objects can migrate dynamically between systems, based on the load and where they are needed.

Borrowing from virtual memory techniques, Pooling applies similar concepts of dynamic binding and on-demand resource acquisition to client-server systems. The result is simpler and less expensive scaling for distributed applications. This mode of computing is serverless distributed processing. Mangosoft has devised a pure P2P directory technology built upon hierarchies of recursive caches.

The universal address space makes the physical distribution of resources transparent and universal. Pooling provides a single, location-independent address space to applications for dynamically locating resources throughout the network. Pooling keeps track of the migration of these resources and, in fact, dynamically migrates and maintains coherency of resources based on application requirements. Information is organized based on the logical, intuitive structure of the data, not the physical network topology. Thus the benefits to the user are higher performance and higher availability.

Virtual storage is the unification of memory and storage resources of all the systems on the network into a single, dynamic pool. The technology that makes this possible is the Distributed Storage Engine. The Distributed Storage Engine manages both memory and disk resources across the systems as a unified shared virtual memory. The engine recognizes two broad types of pages, *volatile* and *persistent*. Frequently accessed files are cached on the local disk, thus improving data access performance. The data is kept consistent by using the same techniques applied to local memory. The storage engine uses file system techniques such as logging, replication, and quorum management to ensure that undeleted regions of the global virtual memory remain available when a machine crashes. Fault-tolerance is improved. Data does not have a fixed home under the storage engine's management. It migrates according to access patterns and availability requirements. This provides another performance boost. The distributed storage engine is described in more detail in Chapter 10.

The Mangomind service is an adaptation of the pooling technology that delivers an Internet-based virtual file system. The service looks and works just like a user's local drive and is completely integrated into Windows. Windows-based applications operate exactly as they do on a local drive. Mangomind provides file access even when the user is disconnected from the Internet. Users work on cached files while offline and Mangomind automatically synchronizes the files once they reconnect.

Mangomind is a secure, multi-user, Windows file system, that offers flexible permission settings by user or by group. Mangomind uses client-side encryption before sending data out for storage.

Mangomind extends the reach of LAN-like file sharing to the Internet, facilitating the secure operation of inter-company workgroups as shown in Figure 5.4.

Some of the useful features of Mangomind are:

- The file system allows multiple authorized users at any location to simultaneously access and share files. Each authorized user has access to the latest copy of the file stored at a secure location.
- Windows applications work natively over the Internet with Mangomind, the same way they work over a LAN.
- Mangomind properly arbitrates between readers and writers of files, ensuring that your files are up to date, and that changes are never lost.
- Unlike e-mail and internet storage services, applications operate directly on the files, without any additional copies being made.
- Users can create an identity profile for a drive, giving them access to a single Mangomind drive from multiple computers.

Mangomind is described in more detail in Chapter 11.

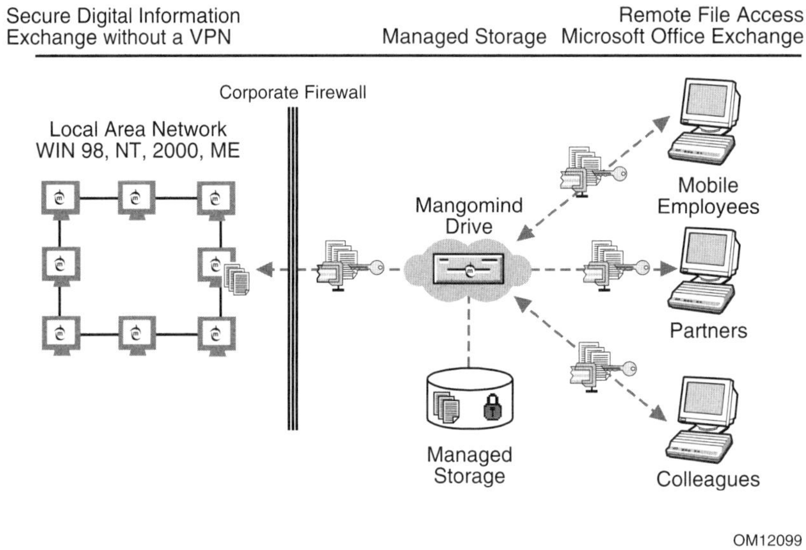

Figure 5.4 Extending a file system service from the local net to the Internet using Mangomind

Mangosoft's Cachelink brings pooling concepts to the Internet by creating a virtual LAN-wide web cache appliance, entirely in software. Cachelink technology augments and pools browser caches in individual LAN-connected PCs into a single cache image for all users, creating a virtual web cache appliance. Thus, access from any one system causes a cache copy to be available to all other systems. Cachelink allows web page fragments to be resolved from the local LAN instead of from the Internet or intranet, with the help of a distributed directory. In doing so, Cachelink reduces the need to access the web, and thus decreases the load on the network. The users are likely to view page fragments faster, and duplication of cached data decreases.

Figure 5.5 shows two machines that are configured to share their HTTP caches. Although only two machines are shown, the design is scalable to any number of cooperating machines on the local area network.

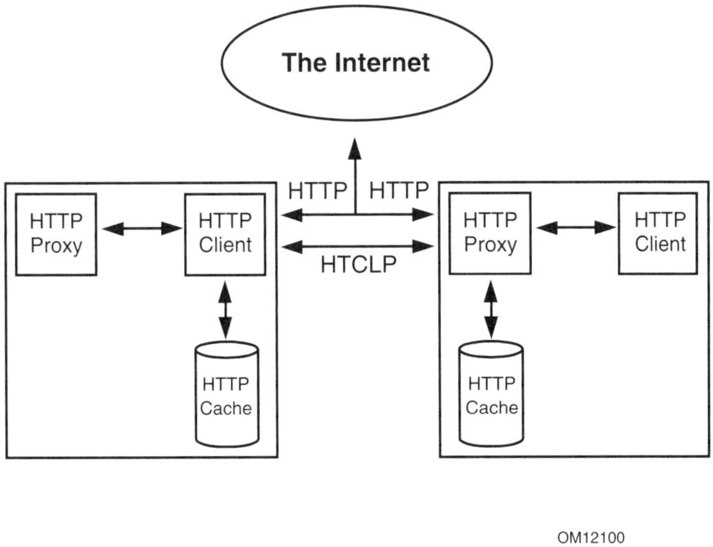

Figure 5.5 Cachelink architecture

Each machine is outfitted with a local HTTP proxy and each HTTP client application, a browser, on the machine is configured to access the Internet via its proxy agent.

The proxy agent, operating out of the HTTP Proxy in the figure, is the heart of the Cachelink product. It makes use of a proprietary hypertext Cachelink protocol (HTCLP) to query cooperating proxies for specific cached data, and then retrieve it. The proxy agent maintains a local store and index of its cached fragments of pages using a persistent hash table mechanism. This augments the browser's local cache during the installation and configuration of Cachelink.

NextPage: Unifying Content without Centralizing

Businesses are struggling to sort through vast amounts of data to deliver the knowledge that's critical and relevant to their stakeholders. The NextPage† platform addresses the problem of lack of productive access and delivery of business critical information to the people who need it.

NextPage's Content Networking platform simplifies access, management, and exchange of pertinent information. Its purpose is to provide information with a purpose. It is a vendor-neutral platform for networking and assimilating content from multiple locations, in a variety of data formats.

The product is both a platform and an environment. Users can install and start using its functionality, or they can build applications on top of the platform. The services and the architecture provide distributed navigation and search capabilities. The platform's features support applications that deal with content collaboration and proactive notification. They can also tie together disjointed content islands across the enterprise and in separated locations. In essence, NextPage provides a secure environment for information exchanges that does not require installing a VPN (Virtual Private Network).

Figure 5.6 shows the degrees of centralization we encounter in P2P computing. As we move out from the center ring, we experience a greater level of decentralization. The inner two rings represent large-grain P2P, within groups and organizations with administered at the group level. Here we include the possibility of server-to-server connections. The outer ring represents the edges of the net, the leaf nodes, where the systems are controlled by individuals. NextPage emphasizes the important role that can be played by the more centralized configurations. Their current products focus on content collaboration that uses the inner rings.

This view provides a framework for bridging the space between the client-server and the P2P models. The computing tasks move from the center outwards. The work done by peers in a given ring replaces the work done by a server in an inner ring. When we reach the edges, the P2P network as a whole becomes the server.

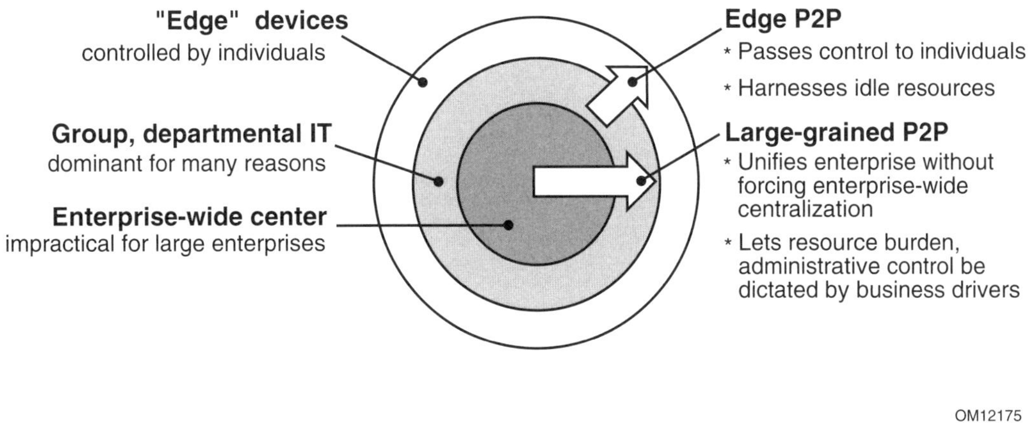

Figure 5.6 Rings of decentralization

The environment that interests NextPage is the multi-location enterprise that conducts business online with suppliers and customers. Even the inner two rings in Figure 5.6 may involve policy and confidentiality issues that occur among business entities.

NextPage uses XML over secure HTTP for communication. This provides a mechanism for crossing firewalls (see Chapter 6) with the help of a SOAP-like protocol. Developed for Windows, the NextPage software now also runs on Solaris.

The heart of the NextPage framework is the NXT e-Content Platform. This consists of several modules that provide the different features and services of the platform, as illustrated in Figure 5.7. We look here at the NXT 3 version.

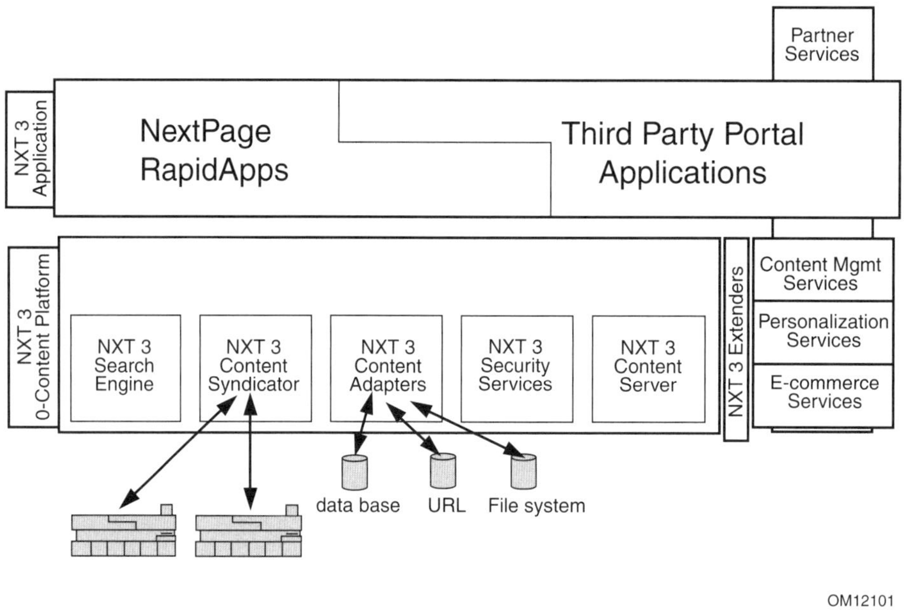

Figure 5.7 NextPage architecture

Let's look at the main modules of NXT 3.

- The NXT 3 Content Server is the piece that aggregates and maintains content from various data sources on the Internet, intranet, or extranet. The NextPage solution is threaded to allow scalability of the number of users and the number of large collections of content.
- The next piece is the Content Syndicator. NextPage uses a non-traditional model for syndication, different from replication. This syndication model enables real-time access to distributed information through a protocol that allows users to search all available information in the network. The content is maintained in its native format, by the owner of the content, and then delivered to the user in a simple consolidated framework.

- The Content Syndicator works with the Content Adapters, which provide real-time access to disparate types of data. Numerous data types are supported, and additional adapters can be created without disturbing the existing infrastructure.
- Finding the content in the first place is the responsibility of the search engine. It provides distributed search functionality that spans the NextPage network of peers (see also Chapter 11). Search results are ranked and presented in their native form or in a browser. The user can provide feedback on relevance of the results for further refinement. NXT 3 allows supplementing the content with metadata that is useful to future viewers.
- The final component of the Content Platform provides Security Services. NXT Security Services has three parts: authentication, authorization, and metering. Metering is the process whereby the user is further authorized based on some usage-based criteria such as number of page views, users concurrency, or resource usage.

The Application Framework resides above the content platform. The framework provides a means for incorporating existing or new applications into the services and capabilities embedded in the NXT content platform.

The Escher Group: Data Management and Distributed Messaging

The Escher Group's product, called WebRiposte[†], has been evolving since 1994. WebRiposte is a distributed messaging and data management platform that supports highly reliable distributed transaction processing and content distribution. WebRiposte is deployed within large (1000 – 100,000 nodes), highly distributed (100 – 20,000 geographic locations) enterprise networks, and is also used to provide connectivity between enterprises.

Three fundamental design principles motivated the WebRiposte architecture:

- **High Reliability.** WebRiposte supports mission critical applications that must operate in a distributed environment and be highly resilient to failure. Several techniques are used to achieve high reliability. Replication provides data availability and automatic recovery of lost data in the event of failure. A loosely coupled message based model provides a basis for distributed processing which is resilient to temporary losses of connectivity and the failure of individual application components.

The need for high reliability drove the decision to use a P2P model. The P2P model maximizes availability in a distributed environment, since the nodes maintain local autonomy and continue doing useful work in the presence of failure. In addition, peers also act as a backup for other peers in the network.

- **Adaptability.** WebRiposte operates as a platform for a diverse set of heterogeneous applications that may consist of multiple distributed components. These components may be developed by different development organizations using different tools and development methodologies. New applications are introduced on a regular basis, and changes to existing applications emerge as business needs change. Accommodating this level of change in a large distributed network presents particular challenges—at any time there may be different versions of the same application operating simultaneously at different nodes in the network, and it must be possible to propagate changes through the network gradually and gracefully. Also critical is the ability to interpret data correctly and preserved it, so that today's version of an application can still process data created ten years ago by an earlier version.

  The need for adaptability drove the decision to use self-describing messages, represented in XML, as the basis for all application communication and all information storage. In a highly distributed heterogeneous environment, a single global schema that all applications understand and adhere to is not viable. All data must carry its own description with it so it is understood and processed independently.

- **Cost of Ownership.** WebRiposte can be installed and operated in a large number of heterogeneous locations, with little or no local IT support needed. The system manages and administers itself and does not require local administration to perform backup, recovery, audit, security features, data organization, configuration management, or performance tuning.

  Low cost of ownership is reflected throughout the implementation of WebRiposte. It has a small footprint, self-optimization, automated backup/recovery, and built-in audit and security features. Since WebRiposte requires no local administration, overhead is reduced.

Here is how the WebRiposte architecture achieves the three design principles:

WebRiposte provides a web-enabled HTTP interface, with support for Web-based transactions and web-based application development. WebRiposte is XML-based and conforms to XML standards for data interchange. It provides public XML-compliant programming interfaces to build web-enabled, interactive, business applications for accessing and manipulating data in a Riposte Message Store.

The WebRiposte infrastructure provides a secure messaging system solution that includes distribution and message storage as well as a content delivery platform. The Message Store and Message Processor are coded in C, and some of the servers at the top boxes use COM.

WebRiposte ensures secure transmission of data through encryption and authentication. These are implemented via the security standards SSL and TLS. In addition, WebRiposte supports the definition of Access Control Lists (ACLs) on objects. This feature allows specific users and user groups to permit or deny access to content stored in the Message Store.

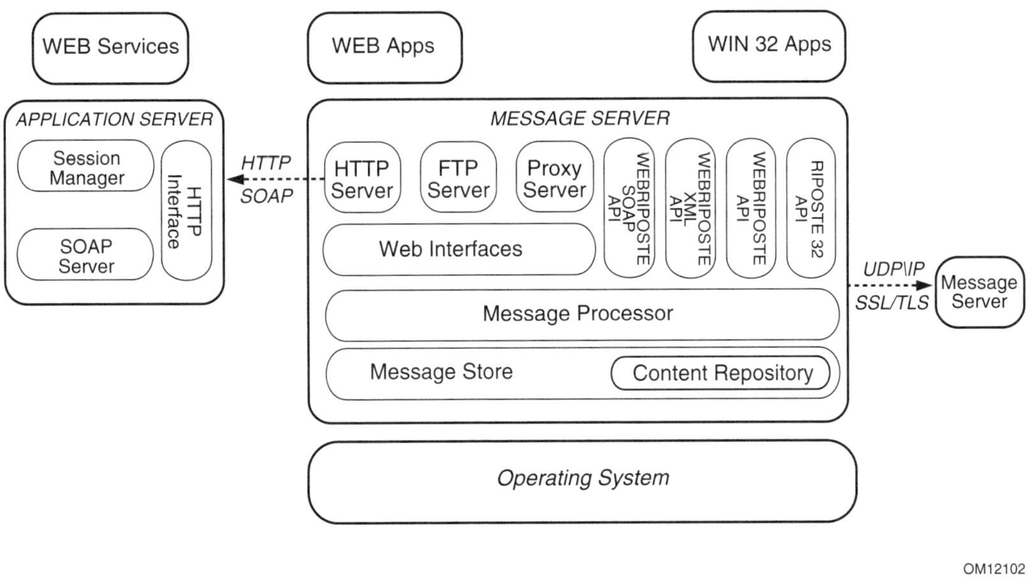

Figure 5.8 WebRiposte system overview

The other main components of the Message Server, which resides on the user's workstation, are the HTTP Server, the FTP Server, and the Proxy Server, and they are described below.

- The HTTP Server provides a standards-compliant web-based interface to the Riposte Message Server, and is compliant with the World Wide Web Consortium HTTP/1.1 specification. It transparently serves content stored in the Message Server to a browser via a standard HTTP interface.

  The HTTP Server also services requests from XML-based client applications that issue API calls via the SOAP programming interface to the Message Server. It supports HTTPS, which provides secure connections using the SSL or TLS protocol; provides a standard web logging facility; and generates performance statistics that can be monitored via the Riposte Performance Monitor utility. The HTTP Server is the single point of contact for applications to access the WebRiposte system. Applications access web services via HTTP using SOAP and XML.
- The FTP Server supports data transfer between the Riposte storage system and a native file storage system. The FTP interface is used by client applications, connected locally or remotely, to store and retrieve data in a Message Store. The server supports transfer of files native to Windows and Unix.
- The Proxy Server provides secure access to third-party web content. It stores content in the Message Store and distributes content via the messaging system, by maintaining a dual-level distributed store of cached web content. The Proxy Server uses the Proxy Agent to service remote client requests for content, either from the cache or from the origin server. The Proxy Agent forwards requests for content that has not been cached to the origin server, and then distributes the response to the client and updates the cache. This agent also automatically re-verifies content freshness, for any content served from the cache. The Proxy Server supports cache management on the WebRiposte workstations, and special support servers, called Correspondence Servers.

As illustrated in Figure 5.8, the Application Server is another part of the WebRiposte system. The Application Server runs as a separate process from the HTTP Server, and in parallel with it. It receives HTTP requests, and invokes the service objects via one of its components, the SOAP Server.

The Application Server manages the execution environment, including threading and session management for multiple users. Through its Session Manager, the Application Server allows web services to persist in memory beyond a single session or SOAP call. This is useful for processing large sets of reference data, and provides performance efficiencies with through data availability and response time.

The Application Server provides a SOAP interface to web services from within a WebRiposte environment. A client application can request services from the web service through the SOAP Server.

The Session Manager component of the Application Server stores and retrieves session state information. The Session Manager offers a number of services that help a WebRiposte client application manage access to, queries from, and requests of web services.

WebRiposte applications use the core Web services supplied with the product. For example, applications use the Session Web Service to manage user sessions with logon and logoff functionality. In parallel, organizations can develop their own custom web services that encapsulate their business logic for shared use by their user applications.

WebRiposte supports the use of Web Service Description Language (WSDL) to implement web services. WSDL provides extensions for SOAP and HTTP, thereby providing a common language across all platforms.

Let's leave our view of the WebRiposte user, and look at the WebRiposte network and caching architecture.

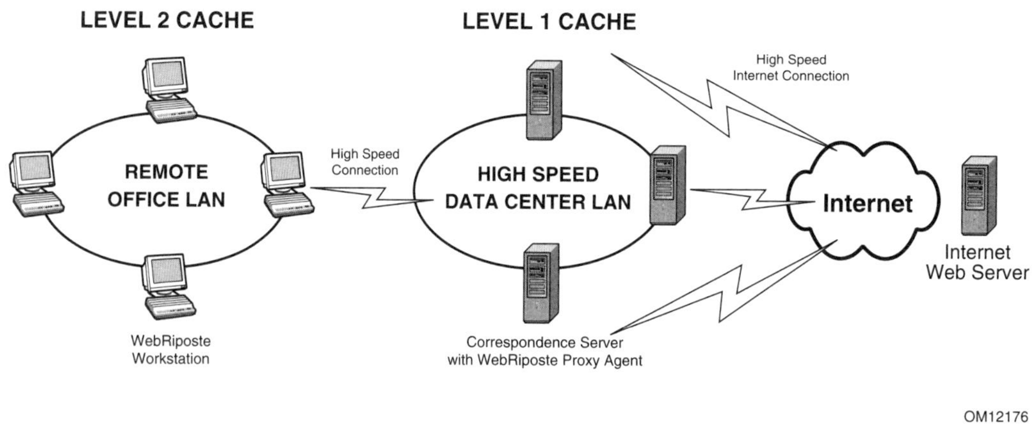

Figure 5.9 WebRiposte network and caching architecture

Figure 5.9 shows that the typical WebRiposte application supports multiple local groups. Each local group maintains a single cache of all web content retrieved by any node in that group. This is called Level 2 cache in the WebRiposte architecture. Level 2 caches are synchronized with a Correspondence Server.

All the Correspondence Servers are configured as a group that maintains a single cache of the content retrieved by all the group's users. This is called the Level 1 cache. This network architecture provides a framework for system-wide caching and consistent shared data among all users.

Frameworks for Collaborations

Content sharing and distributed computing bring to the fore many of the services and capabilities required for reliable, secure, and effective P2P applications. They involve communications and sharing of resources. They accommodate pull and push styles of content exchanges. They rely on negotiated or agreed-upon access with provision for trust and security. But there is more. The collaborative class of P2P applications is characterized by ongoing interactions and exchanges between peers. A collaborative application may involve several users reviewing and modifying a file simultaneously. It assumes an immediate response. The collaborative applications also must respond in real-time. The immediacy of the interactions exposes the environment to possible human error and misjudgment. Thus, assuring security and integrity of content becomes a greater challenge, compared with the two other classes we looked at before.

This area of direct collaboration between peers is where new applications, not yet conceived, may appear. Where distributed computing and content sharing make great use of the resource sharing capability of the P2P computing model, collaborative applications add strong emphasis to taking advantage of the direct exchange feature enabled by the P2P model. Direct exchanges provide the immediacy that cultivates person-to-person interactions, which are the essence of collaboration.

Let us now see how some of the pioneers of collaborative environments for P2P computing overcame the technical hurdles.

Groove Networks: Internet-Based Collaboration

The software and services from Groove Networks address the business demand for online direct and personal communications. The medium is the Internet, and the model is P2P computing. The product, called Groove, enables real-time, small group interaction and collaboration across and between organizations.

Groove's goal is to make the Internet an effective medium for personal communication and interaction. Groove can be applied in two modes:

- As an environment that is immediately useful for all sorts of multimedia communications. It allows the user to create context for business, entertainment, school, and many other social settings.
- As a platform for developing collaborative P2P applications. In this mode, developers use the Groove capabilities to create new and specific applications. They create their own tools, and present users with a custom-made environment. For example, a financial institution may use the Groove platform to present its analysts with a P2P way to implement exchanges based on information pulled from the enterprise database.

Groove is a platform for solutions that intersect P2P interaction and back-end business systems. It does so by providing a shared space where the peers can encapsulate content and function from a server-based system. The security measures in Groove provide the means for managing who has access to what within the shared space.

The architecture for such a collaborative environment has to enable a few important attributes:

- Personal control that comes from storing the shared content on the user's system.
- Shared context through jointly working on the shared content. This is a consequence of the immediacy of the communications.
- Security for sharing content with group members as it travels over the net. P2P lends itself to secure communications by not relying on a third-party intermediary.
- Flexibility for a platform on which other applications can be built. For Groove, flexibility means:
    - — Control of which tools the group shares and uses for its development.
    - — Automatically adapting to network and firewall settings.
    - — Real time interaction.
    - — The ability to work online and offline, and from any location.

Cost effectiveness and speed are by-products derived from collaboration the P2P way. Cost effectiveness comes about when a team sets up their own collaboration space, uses and manages their own resources. Content sharing and immediate interaction speeds up development and decision-making.

The fundamental component of Groove is the notion of *shared space*. The central idea is that each member of a group owns a copy of the shared space. Changes made to the shared space by one of the group members are automatically and immediately synchronized with other members' computers. When a peer works in the space offline, the changes are saved and then synchronized when connected.

More important design principles arise from the overall goals above:

- The product must be peer-to-peer in that users can communicate directly with each other without requiring a server.
- The platform must be secure, automatically and transparently, in several ways:
  - — Users are authenticated with public keys.
  - — Data is strongly encrypted, end-to-end, both on the host machine and on the wire.
  - — Components of Groove, and imported components, are digitally signed.
- Groove is network flexible. It can operate on the Internet, on intranets, and on private networks. Groove supports HTTP and SSTP protocols. It can be used on devices other than PCs, such as mobile phones, tablets, and PDAs.
- Groove is development-environment flexible by being language-independent and based on the COM specification.
- Operations in Groove are Asynchronous to insure immediacy and speed. The user interface is not interrupted by background activity. Groove performs multiple send and receive operations among the users.
- A number of measures are taken to insure data is persistent. These measures include use of XML for interoperability and extensibility.
- Groove enables privacy by allowing the user to control the presence of data. The user also grants and revokes permissions to others for access to data.
- Groove is a multi-threaded platform that provides flexibility for applications design and use of Groove services.

Figure 5.10 shows how the Groove architecture appears to the user and to the application developer.

The portion of Groove that is visible to the end user is called the *transceiver*. It contains the user's variety of shared spaces with differing sets of members, and the collection of tools available within each shared space. The tools can be many and varied. Examples of tools include instant-messaging, chat rooms, drawing tools, or any components users add or create.

The underlying peer services include security, local XML object storage, and XML object routing services.

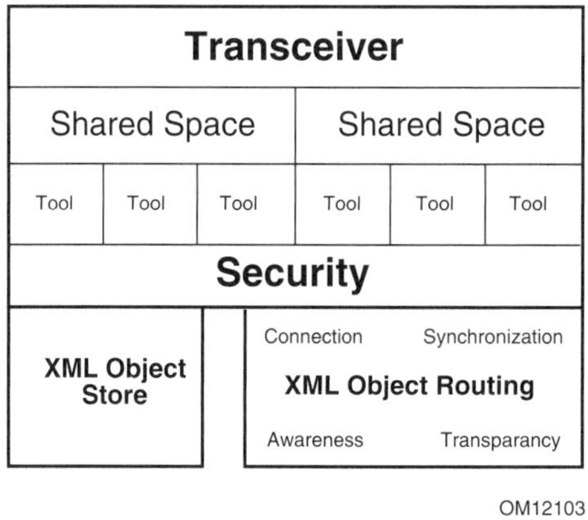

Figure 5.10 Groove architecture

The lower half of Figure 5.10 shows the following components of Groove:

First, security. All shared spaces in Groove are fully private. Only members specifically invited by other members can see or create content. Authentication and end-to-end encryption ensure the confidentiality and integrity of all content and activity, both on the disk and over the network. Groove supports "whispering" between two, or more, members so that private conversations can take place within the context of a larger group.

Second, the XML Object Store. This is the local container for all content and activities. The use of an object store instead of an XML file system improves system performance. Groove also compresses the XML content for efficiency.

Third, the XML Object Routing component. When Groove stores content and activities locally, it also passes all changes to the XML object routing service. Then it passes the encrypted content to the appropriate end points on the peer network. This service supports a number of important communications capabilities:

- **Transparency.** Groove connects peers across corporate or personal firewalls. Groove's routing services automatically and transparently cross firewalls and network address translators, so that users never need to go through special steps to set up a shared space.
- **Awareness.** Groove keeps track of what other devices and/or users are doing online at any given moment, and where other entities are "located" in Groove. That is, users can tell at a glance who else is online at the moment, which shared spaces they are in, and what each person is doing in each space.
- **Adaptability.** Groove checks all members' online status, their position inside or outside a firewall or behind a network address translator, and how to most efficiently move content across the network.
- **Mobility.** Groove allows disconnected members to continue to work in a shared space, propagating all changes made by all members whenever an offline member reconnects. Groove manages this using a relay service. This is typically a server that holds all the changes sent to members who are not connected at the time.

In summary, here are two final observations about Groove:

First, Chapter 2 described the need to let users present different aspects of their lives by membership in specific online communities. To promote online community participation, Groove enables the use of multiple identities, or personas, by the same person. This feature allows Groove to better support users on multiple computers. Groove copies and updates the content relevant to the persona that connected through that device.

Second, in Groove there is no "save" command. Every keystroke is saved in the XML Object Store. This means that even if the computer crashes, all the content is saved.

Endeavors: Inclusive Peer-to-Peer Collaboration with Magi

Another example of collaborative P2P computing is the Magi† framework from Endeavors. Magi focuses on the sharing of information, and acting on it, anywhere and at any time. To achieve this goal Magi provides what amounts to a web server with chat and messaging capabilities on any Internet-enabled device. Magi is, therefore, a vehicle for event-driven, multi-way communications between servers, PCs, PDAs, Internet-ready phones, and embedded chips.

Magi addresses the needs of collaborative business applications, or P2P-based commerce, and emphasizes the incorporation of multiple types of devices among peers with varying capabilities.

Four design principles shape Magi:

- Take advantage of the existing internet infrastructure. Whenever possible, use existing protocols and tools that provide the required feature or capability.
- Make the Magi architecture event-based and component-based. Being component-, or object-, based makes it possible to customize solutions for specific needs. It also allows easy reuse of modules, or removal of unneeded components. Being event-based enables Magi to handle interactions between entities, such as humans or programs, when the timing of such exchanges cannot be predicted or determined in advance. Magi events decouple components and allow them to be more dynamic and distributed. Magi events are asynchronous and can broadcast to other peers over the network.
- Magi must be a platform on which others can develop their own applications. Several decisions support this goal. The user interface is platform-independent. In addition to the open standards mentioned above, the core infrastructure is available in an open source fashion. Since Magi uses open protocols, the architecture itself is platform-independent with multiple implementations that bind the architecture to a particular platform. The platform-independence makes it more convenient for application developers to develop on top of Magi.

- Maintain local autonomy of the user at the edge of the net. The application running on the peer system, and not the infrastructure, dictates what services execute on that node, and what entities will be replicated there. The application determines the resources used by the peer.

As mentioned above, the choice of technologies for Magi is motivated by the desire to use existing standard protocols. The basis for the Magi infrastructure is a Java† version of Apache. Magi employs four standard elements:

- HTTP is the default communications protocol.
- An extension to HTTP, the Web Distributed Authoring and Versioning (WebDAV) provides facilities for remote document manipulation and editing. This tool enhances the web by turning it into a writable medium by clients at the edges.
- URIs and URLs are used to refer to all network resources.
- MIME, which encapsulates the variety of file formats permeating the web.

Magi security uses standard encryption and authentication techniques. SSL (Secure Sockets Layer) is used to create "signed" notification and management of events, thus allowing for secure events over insecure communications channels. We will discuss this further in Chapter 9.

XML is the vehicle for expressing exchanges between the modules of Magi. And Web-XML is used for modifying the Magi configuration on non-PC devices.

The Magi framework from Endeavors is an example of the trend to change existing practices and migrate to a more extensive, even exclusive, use of XML and SOAP for expressing and encapsulating information.

The goal of the Magi architecture is to be a platform for P2P applications. The model is that of a web server on each peer, while being able to accommodate the limited space available on handheld devices.

Figure 5.11 describes the architecture of the node, or what Endeavors calls the "canonical peer." The presence of the web server on the client side, or the edge of the net, creates the client-server combination that, in Magi parlance, is called the "Magi servlet."

The P2P infrastructure is run through the servlet engine. These two layers comprise the "web server foundation." Above the foundation are the core components: the Request Manager that directs all requests to the appropriate service, the Event Service that handles the communications between peers, the Access Controller that manages the access by other peers, and the Module Container that dynamically loads other services and provides access to APIs used by applications built upon the core services.

The vertical columns in Figure 5.11 are examples of services that can be built with the help of the core components. With the inclusion of APIs these tools are a part of applications that the end user can invoke. The services, at that level, offer such capabilities as chat, meta search through WebDAV, presence information, web interfaces, and more. The openness of source code extends, beyond the core components, to these extension modules that are related to open standards, such as HTML, WAP (Wireless Application Protocol), and WebDAV.

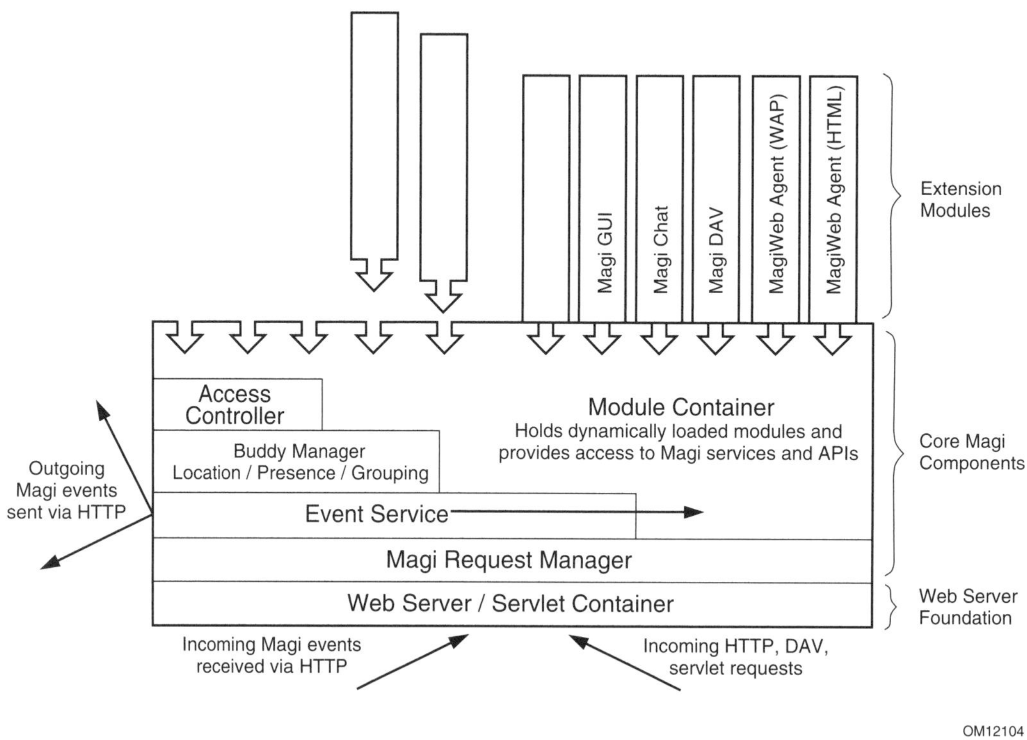

Figure 5.11 Architecture of the Magi client, or "servlet"

The user model that fosters the collaborative aspect of Magi is based on "buddy" lists and groups. Chapter 7 provides more information about this model, and describes how presence and persistence of information is managed via Magi's folders.

The network view of Magi covers the important common configurations from simple peer-to-peer direct communication, to the presence of a firewall between the communicating peers, to the use of NATs (Network Address Translators). These concepts are described Chapter 6.

Engenia: Information Sharing and Interactivity

Engenia's goal is to provide software that enables effective online collaboration for businesses. Underlying the design philosophy of Engenia is the conviction that the paradigm of "storage and filing," commonly used for information handling, does not reflect the true needs of today's enterprise. Instead, Engenia advocates a P2P solution built on information sharing and interactivity. Eugenia's product can be described as a collaboration system with a web portal presentation interface.

The basic requirements for the design of the collaboration platform include elements that are important to emerging business models and practices:

- The system must be adaptive, in the sense of being able to evolve in response to future needs.
- The information and data must be provided in context, and this means carrying knowledge about the content.
- The user must be able to see and operate the whole system, including its lower-level parts.
- The system must have the capability to establish self-forming web-based relationships among individuals and groups with shared goals or interests.
- All the interactions have to be secure.
- The system should look easy to use.

The architecture's fundamental entity is an object that possesses context and that can communicate with other objects. An object has a set of properties and comes with methods that define its behavior, the user interface, and its interaction with other objects. At its basic level, the Engenia platform is a virtual distributed file system that allows its users to share information no matter where it resides within the Engenia environment.

The object model is built on XML and JavaScript†. JavaScript enables the product to be hosted easily on any number of platforms. In addition to Windows, there is also a Linux version. The code includes a JavaScript interpreter. The object model extends JavaScript to support inheritance, polymorphism, and other programmatic constructs. JavaScript functions of an object are directly mapped to URLs, so they are called directly from a browser.

In many ways, the user's view is that of a small, JavaScript-based, XML-based web application server that lives right on the desktop. The XML part of the object model defines the structure of an object such as properties, relationships, and security policy.

Other architectural components are defined as a part of the object model. The important ones are desktops, servers, and connectors.

Desktops are the peers. An Engenia desktop is the user's primary vehicle to view and access objects in the peer computing environment. Objects, files, or applications appear to be local, regardless of where they reside. An Engenia server acts as a super-peer. This means it hosts a large shared collection of objects. A server also provides directory services that help desktops, or "regular" peers, locate objects elsewhere. Servers can form federations, through which they spread their services across multiple locations and extended intranets.

Engenia adopts the hybrid P2P model that allows for the presence of servers. In their terminology, node is the entity that encapsulates both the desktop and the server. The node, be it a desktop or a server, can communicate with other nodes. It may represent a single computer or it can be a cluster of computers using a round-robin DNS (Domain Name Server) technique or similar to connect the browser to one of the nodes on demand. Note that this model allows for P2P-like interaction between servers, and does not involve humans. A node may also represent a more complex configuration of computers, a useful abstraction for a higher-level resource that acts as a single object.

A connector is a special type of object. It is an interface to resources that are external to the P2P Engenia environment and allows access to other systems. For example, a connector can be constructed as a search API that ties to an external search engine. Another connector can be crafted for access to financial and other ERP systems, or to various other databases.

Figure 5.12 shows the Engenia platform architecture.[1] The connectors are the double-headed arrows that connect the external applications to the platform core. The top of the figure depicts some of the collaborative applications that can be created on top of the Engenia platform. The browser provides the HTML-based interface from the objects to the user's view. The other boxes illustrate the main technologies that are employed, for communication and for interface with applications. Adaptive XML is Engenia's mechanism to describe objects and create metadata with the help of JavaScript.

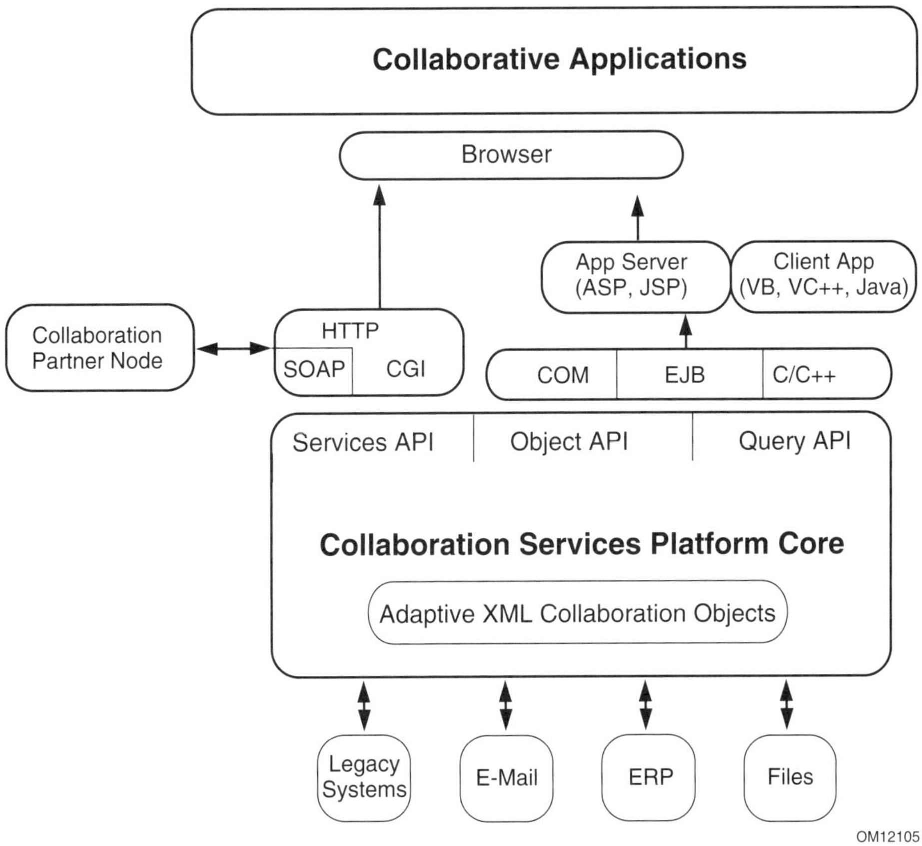

Figure 5.12 Architectural view of the Engenia platform

[1] Engenia has recently acquired technology from Roku, which was integrated to the Engenia platform in the form of Desktop Access Module. Many users prefer to access the full Engenia node through the Desktop Access Module. It connects to Outlook, Notes, and other e-mail services. It also looks at user's file system. The Desktop Access component uses an Engenia node as a rendezvous point. Users mostly open a web browser to the Engenia node, which allows them to redirect into their own desktop.

Note that Engenia is moving towards adopting SOAP on top of XML as a means to describe data and context in the future. Now, every object is structurally represented as an XML file.

In this desktop architecture, the user can use a browser to drag and drop and double-click objects. An object supports multiple HTML views, as defined within the object XML file. There is considerable power vested with the Engenia user, but objects are protected with access control lists and authentication mechanism (see Chapter 9 for more information on Security).

To summarize the technology and the architectural approach, note that the distributed object approach allows objects to evolve independently. Objects can run either on-line or off-line. Objects can communicate with each other without the need for a centralized administrator. Objects can model a variety of enterprise entities, such as tasks. As each new object enters the system, it can interact easily with existing objects. The ultimate flexibility of the system is preserved with this approach, allowing the system to grow organically within an enterprise.

Towards a General-Purpose P2P Infrastructure

There is no comprehensive infrastructure that encompasses all the usage models and application types that we associate with peer computing. That said, there are architectures that attempt to provide a more generic, or general-purpose, P2P platform.

The two architectures described here, the middleware from Avaki, previously known as Applied Meta, and Globus from the Global Grid Forum community, have common historical roots. The approaches taken by their respective developers are different, though. Avaki, the commercial successor to Legion, is built as a complete system with inter-related services and capabilities. It is a bottom-up, integrated solution. The Globus project provides a set of tools, based on common and standard protocols, which work on multiple platforms. Think of this approach as a top-down design. The necessary services are provided, and application developers decide how to couple them and which ones to use.

Describing these two approaches to P2P infrastructure is an appropriate conclusion to the survey of solutions presented in this chapter.

AVAKI: Integrated Architecture for Secure Resource Sharing

The technology developed by Avaki originated from work done in the context of high performance distributed computing. The goal of Avaki, though, is to enable all forms of P2P computing. Their product, called Avaki†, is an integrated platform that runs on all major operating systems. The vision for the product is ambitious – create the illusion and the benefit of a single virtual machine that encompasses devices from supercomputers to handheld devices, crosses organizations and geographical boundaries, and incorporates diverse architectures and operating systems.

Avaki designs its products for the enterprise, and, therefore, develops the class of services that global organizations require when managing complex, mission critical, and distributed systems. Avaki is positioned as middleware that is an infrastructure for distributed resource sharing in a mutually distrustful setting. It provides core services analogous to some that an operating system provides, such as process management (creation, control, scheduling), inter-process communication, persistence via a file system, resource management, security for both users and for resource owners, transparency via naming and binding, accounting and resource management, and an application development environment. The middleware is platform-independent and runs on existing host operating systems such as Linux, Solaris, and Windows 2000.

The Avaki architecture exhibits these attributes:

- Interoperability across multiple and different hardware platforms, operating systems, files systems, and network infrastructures.
- Scalability in size and number of resources, including fault-tolerance.
- Security through policies that are enforced within separated domains.
- Deployment that minimizes impact on existing policies and operations.

Avaki's P2P infrastructure is an object-based system comprised of independent objects that communicate via method invocation, the technique by which objects call each other. The fact that the middleware is object-based does not preclude the use of non-object-oriented languages or non-object-oriented implementations of objects. In fact, the system supports objects written in traditional procedural languages such as C and Fortran, as well as object-oriented languages such as C++ and Java.

The infrastructure must be flexible enough to accommodate all sorts of user constraints, application types, and platforms. The object model specifies the functionality but not the implementation of the system's core objects; the core system therefore consists of extensible, replaceable components. Avaki provides default implementations of the core objects, although users are not obligated to use them. They can construct implementations that answer their specific needs. The middleware is an open system, designed so that a third party can develop new or updated applications, and add run-time library or core components.

Figure 5.13 shows a high level view of the Avaki architecture.

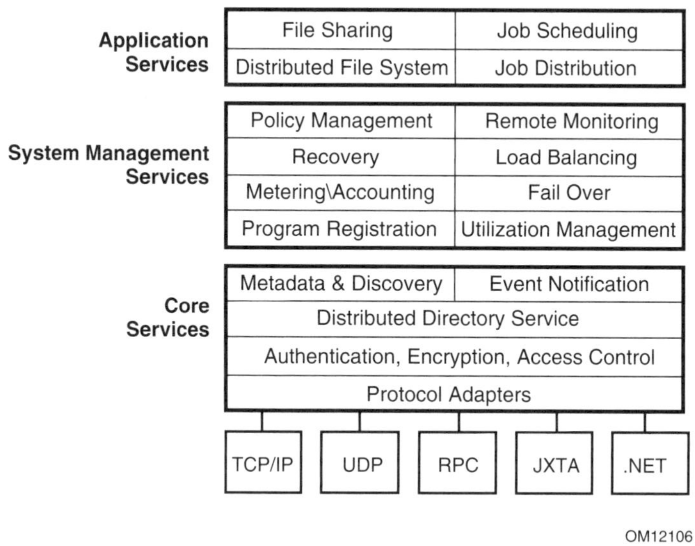

Figure 5.13 Avaki's distributed middleware architecture

The middleware platform is organized as three separate layers: a Core Services layer, a Systems Management Services layer, and an Applications Services layer.

The Core Services layer provides a set of primitives for building P2P and distributed computing applications:

- Protocol adapters enable the middleware to work seamlessly over a wide variety of different networking environments, including TCP/IP, UDP, RPC, and FTP. This service layer also includes the interfaces for interoperability with platforms such as .NET from Microsoft and JXTA from Sun Microsystems.
- The security capabilities offer public key authentication, SSL data encryption, and group-based access control. Together these provide strong security and fine-grained control over resources. Interoperability with Kerberos is also supported.
- The Distributed Directory Services provides a secure three-tier naming system that is used for each resource (a resource might be a device, a file, applications, etc.). The three tiers are: a human-readable name, a location-independent identifier, and a physical address. Each location-independent identifier includes an embedded public key, providing seamless, decentralized authentication for all node-to-node communications.
- Metadata repositories and resource discovery services enable users and applications to find files or other resources.
- Event notification service enables publish and subscribe messaging between networked resources. Files, applications, devices and other resources can initiate an event; and that event can propagate to other resources that have registered an interest in it.

The System Management Services layer includes the services that help organizations implement and manage distributed resources and solutions. The purpose of each of the services is identified in Figure 5.12. Utilization Management refers to starting a program or an action when the load on the host has dropped below a previously specified level. The Program Registration service allows system administrators to control which programs can run where, and which users are authorized to run which programs. The Metering and Accounting service measures usage of resources such as storage and processing time. And the Fail Over service increases fault-tolerance through replication of data and caching of metadata, files, and services, as set by the application. Recovery may use techniques such as checkpoint and restart.

The Application Services layer provides higher-level services to construct P2P applications.

- The Distributed File System enables the virtual collection of storage across a wide variety of platforms and devices. This service includes configurable policies for managing file replication, localized caching, and version control.
- File Sharing provides capabilities for access control to files that includes strong authentication.
- Job Scheduling is priority-based, and is used for distributed computations.
- Job Distribution services automate the process of moving application binaries to different hardware platforms, and propagate them as specified by the application or the policies.

Grid Computing for Large-Scale Resource Sharing

Grid computing is the concept, and the Global Grid Forum is the organization that, for the purpose of this discussion, represents work done with grid computing. The Global Grid Forum is an umbrella organization with members from over 90 institutions in 20 countries. Most of the researchers involved with grid computing hail from national laboratories and federal agencies, and are starting to engage some commercial corporations who have challenging computational problems.

Though grid computing has its origins in high-end scientific and engineering computations, in practice, however, the "Grid problem" is broader. The grid problem is about resource sharing and coordinated problem solving in dynamic multi-organizational virtual communities. The grid problem deals with issues that are also shared by the content-sharing and collaborative application developers for P2P computing. Specifically, all developers have to deal with lack of central control, and establishing trust across geographical and institutional boundaries.

There are quite a few projects under the umbrella of the Global Grid Forum (see Chapter 11). This chapter focuses on the Globus project (http://www.globus.org), as a representative of an architectural approach to grid computing.

The type of problems Globus developers address include:

- Interactive coupling of computers and smart instruments, such as wind tunnels and particle accelerators, with databases and users.
- Distribution of computations among networked desktops, or between a smaller number of supercomputers.
- Collaborative design through virtual spaces that allow interactive manipulation of shared data.

To support these computational problems, Globus developers are engaged in research and development in these main areas:

- Resource management.
- Data management and access.
- Application development environment.
- Information services.
- Security.

Note how the research in the grid computing community overlaps with all the major technical topics of interest for P2P computing.

The factor that has influenced the Globus design the most is the requirement that sharing relationships can be established between any potential participants. This mean interoperability in the sense of communication between different platforms through the same Globus services. The other assumption is that it is not practical to create multiple bilateral interfaces for any possible pairing of platforms. Therefore, in this context, interoperability means the use of common protocols.

Using protocols as the basis for commonality has another important benefit. Since protocols govern interaction between components, and not their implementation—which may be platform dependent—local control is maintained and lightweight exchanges are feasible.

Above the protocols there are services. A service defines a behavior that is superimposed on usage of protocols. A service, for example, facilitates access to data or performs a discovery. The applications access the services through APIs or SDKs. Their presence helps application developers.

It is interesting to note here that without using common protocols, achieving interoperability through the APIs implies a single implementation of the services everywhere. And this is not feasible in many environments of interest.

The design approach advocated here, then, is to use common protocols, build P2P services on the protocols, and, add SDKs or APIs that call the services. The result is not a tight framework, but, rather, a toolkit that allows the application to use components without being forced to a particular programming model or language.

Globus builds on standard protocols. For communications, it uses protocols from the TCP/IP stack. Globus's security infrastructure for authentication, protection of transmissions, and authorization extends upon TLS, the Transport Layer Security, it can be integrated into local security mechanisms, such as Kerberos, and it uses X.509 format for certificates to establish trust between users. Information gathering services use LDAP (Lightweight Directory Access Protocol), and resource access and management services are based on HTTP.

The Globus toolkit provides C and Java APIs.

Figure 5.14 shows grid architecture from the application developer's view.

There are protocols, services, and APIs, and they are layered by function. APIs and tool kits are superimposed on the grid architecture. The services define functionality; the SDKs add interfaces and the usage model. The APIs use grid protocols to interact with network services that provide capabilities to the end user. Higher-level SDKs provide functionality that is not directly mapped to a specific protocol, but may combine protocol operations with calls to additional APIs or implement local functionality.

The following layers are illustrated in Figure 5.14.

- The fabric layer represents the resources that are available to other services and the application. These resources are computational, storage, network, code repositories, and catalogs (query-capable information repositories, such as databases).
- The connectivity layer includes protocols and APIs for communications and authentication. Communications enable exchange of data between resources, while authentication mechanisms provide a secure means to verify the identity of users and resources.
- The resource layer includes two main categories of protocols. One category lists the protocols that gather information about the resource,

and the other category shows the protocols concerned with managing the resource by negotiating access and terms.

- The collective layer deals with aggregating information from multiple resources. This is the layer where global information is collected. Working through the "narrow" resources and connectivity protocols, collective services provide sharing and shared information for a variety of purposes. Examples are: Directory services; co-allocation of multiple types of resources, and scheduling and brokering such resources; monitoring and diagnostics; data replication; software discovery services; enforcement of community policies; and collaboratory services, such as commodity groupware and specialized coordinated exchanges.
- Applications in the applications layer are constructed by calling the services in the layers below, through the protocols or SDKs or APIs. The "languages and frameworks" notation at the top Figure 5.14 refers to the possibility of using high-level systems, such as COM or CORBA, to construct applications. These systems, in turn, can build on the protocols and services provided by the grid architecture.

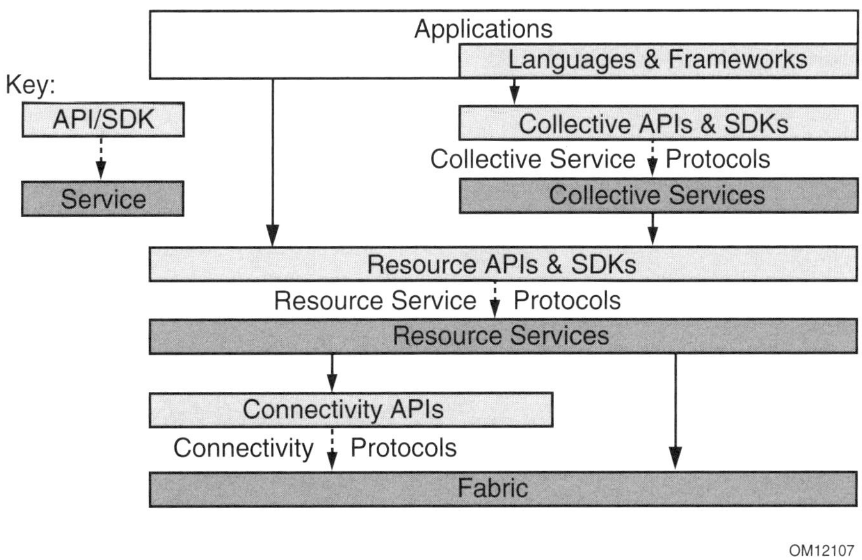

Figure 5.14 An application developer's view of the Globus architecture

Summary of Approaches and Objectives

One of the goals of this book is to examine the benefits and status of interoperability in the P2P world. The P2P platforms and products described in this book are all different. But there are some trends that make us hopeful that interoperability is indeed possible and feasible.

Let us consider the choice of protocols.

Almost all implementations use standard protocols. Using common protocols serves as a basis for interoperability. The communications mechanisms all rely on the Internet Protocol (IP). But, at the transport protocol level, some of the companies use TCP, others use UDP. The choices reflect the needs and priorities of the platforms. At a higher level we notice that SOAP and XML become common tools for P2P services, though the schemas used are not the same.

Security is applied in different ways and to varying degrees in the platforms examined above. Again, this is a function of the needs of the environment the infrastructure addresses. Nonetheless, all of the security solutions employ the same mechanisms. The protocols are SSL, and its successor, TLS. There are some differences in the extent to which security function are used. The differences apply to use of digital signatures and certificates, or the choices made for encryption. But, as you will see in Chapter 9, it is important to gather a basic set of security services from which all the applications can pick and choose.

As for feasibility of future interoperability, you will notice that most of the developers employ a modular structure. There are layers of services, and a set of interfaces that allows communications among them. This modularity increases the chances that modules can be replaced easily so that interoperability may increase. Short of replacing modules, a well-defined set of interfaces can facilitate the creation of one-to-one interoperability between a pair of P2P middleware solutions.

Things are not as clear when we look at the higher level services.

In particular, every platform uses its own technique for creating the namespace and names for its universe. Naming is one area where a mapping from one solution to another seems quite straightforward. It is a one-to-one mapping. Of course, it is not advisable to carry along too many pair-wise conversion tables for names. And, remember, the list of names is very dynamic.

The actual list of services depends on the type of problem the platform addresses.

There are common threads among the design principles that govern the resulting architectures.

The notable similarities include the attention to security, and the means for dealing with intermittent connectivity by peers.

How about the infrastructures themselves?

It is striking that a number of solutions described in this chapter follow a three-tier layering of the components. At the lowest level, the *core* if you will, there is the interface to the operating system. This core contains services such as establishing presence and communications. It sets the infrastructure on which to build a P2P environment.

At the other end of the stack, users interact with the software and perform useful work. This is the application layer on which higher-level applications can be built. During the application development phase the developers discover that other tools are needed. And these tools have value beyond that of a single application. Here are three examples from this chapter:

- OpenCola created the clerver as the core for their applications. Their goal, and application, is Folders†, a file system for sharing content. Along the way they had to solve the problem of moving popular large files without incurring a bandwidth bottleneck. The developers came up with Swarmcast. Though packaged as a stand-alone application, which it can be, Folders uses Swarmcast† internally. Swarmcast is also used to break up a large file, and send pieces of it to different peers. The peers continue to pass the pieces they have and get pieces they are missing from others until all have a complete copy of the file. The file reaches multiple destinations when only one copy left the source.
- Another example is Mangosoft. The core is the Pooling technology. The application, or solution, is Mangomind, a secure system for network-based shared files. Files shared on a network can benefit from caching. And Mangosoft's pooling technology makes it possible to aggregate desktop resources for caching. The result is a product, Cachelink, which serves as an application in its own right, and also supports other applications.

- In Groove, the core is the XML store and XML routing engines, combined with the security mechanisms. The set of tools plays the role of the middle layer. The applications, as the outer layer, need only invoke the tools.

The point here is that between the infrastructure that makes P2P possible, and the uses that developers have in mind, there is a layer of useful tools and services. This middle layer can be an application, or a tool for other applications; but it is not required for the P2P environment to function.

Perhaps not surprisingly, we begin to see common themes at the applications level, too. Here is one example:

One of the difficult problems Internet users face is how find the content they are looking for, but avoid the deluge of information they do not wish to see. We saw that developers who are concerned about content, OpenCola and NextPage for example, use the "relevance factor" in content searches. What emerges as common wisdom is that, for the near term at least, relevancy is only effective when machine and humans interact. The software agents can be "trained" and will improve, but for that to happen the human user has to provide feedback. This feedback is in the form of feedback to the agents, indicating which returned content is useful and which is not. It is reasonable to expect that we will see more easy-to-use user interfaces for providing such feedback.

Finally, it bodes well for the future of peer-to-peer computing to see general-purpose P2P infrastructure designs. These comprehensive designs demonstrate a consistent and holistic view of P2P as a computing platform.

Some of the comments above will become more concrete as you read through the next chapters. Each of these chapters covers a major technical topic that was touched on briefly in this overview chapter. The P2P technologies to be described are grouped as follows:

- Communication.
- Naming and discovery.
- Availability and fault-tolerance.
- Security.
- Management of shared resources.

Chapter 6
First, Peers Need to Communicate

Communication between peers is at the heart of P2P computing. Without communication there is no P2P activity, just as if we had no processors or devices to work with. Every single scenario described in Chapter 2 uses communication in one form or another. This chapter covers some communication issues that affect P2P computing. It contains a few fundamentals of Internet networking, but is not a comprehensive tutorial.

The exponential growth of the Internet introduced challenges in assigning network addresses to each computer. The solutions involve non-fixed (dynamic) and private network addresses. Enterprises had to introduce security measures that entail funneling communications through proxy servers. All of these get in the way of simple and direct exchanges between peers. This chapter explains the problems and suggests directions for solving them.

You will also find the choices that P2P developers made with regard to communication protocols and services. The complexity of P2P communication arises from the variety of networks that need to be accommodated. Communication within the enterprise is different than that on the open Internet. Communications that cross the boundaries between intranets and the Internet (and make exchanges between separate intranets) present their own challenges.

About Addresses, Names, and Protocols

This section is a quick introduction to some of the communication protocols and mechanisms that are fundamental to P2P connectivity, naming, and discovery.

It is customary to use the OSI (Open System Interconnection, an ISO standard) model as the frame of reference for discussing communication protocols. The OSI model has seven layers: Physical, data link, network, transport, session, presentation, and application. These are depicted on the left-hand side of Figure 6.1, where you can see the kind of actions taken and control assumed by each of the layers. The way to view the communication process is to start with one station, or node, on the network. At this station, control is passed from one layer to the next, starting with the application layer and proceeding to the bottom layer. Then the "message" is carried over the channel, or the physical connection, to the next station and back up the hierarchy of layers from the bottom layer to the receiving application layer. OSI itself has not become the universal communication model as was expected, although most of its functionality still exists in all communications systems (though some layers may be combined). This is exactly the case for TCP/IP, which is the protocol that governs communications on the Internet. TCP/IP, and in particular the IP part of it, is a basic component of any P2P infrastructure. The Internet has made TCP/IP the *de facto* standard network protocol.

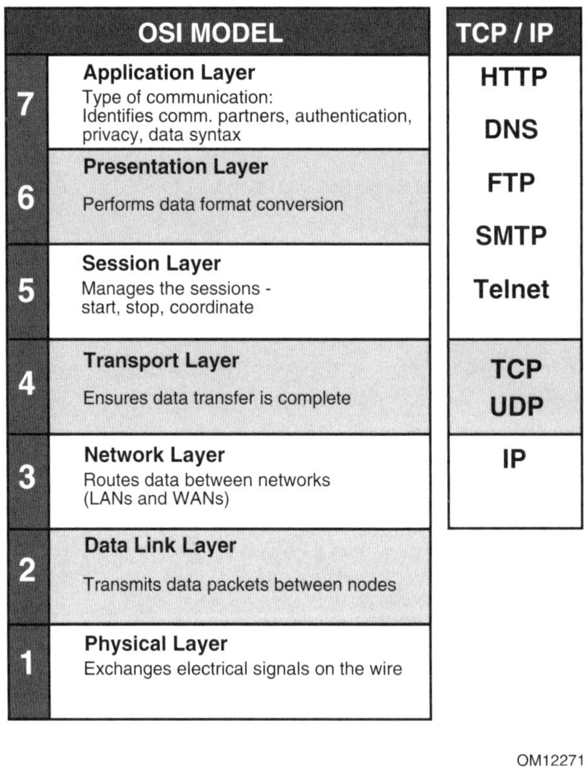

Figure 6.1 Mapping TCP/IP to the OSI Model

What is TCP/IP?

TCP/IP stands for Transmission Control Protocol/Internet Protocol. It is an open protocol that enables all types of computers to transmit data to each other via a common communications language. It was first tested in the early 1980s on ARPAnet, the U.S. military's Advanced Research Projects Agency network, the world's first packet-switched network. The Internet has pushed TCP/IP, its native protocol, to the forefront of communications. In doing so, it is enabling the world to migrate to one global data communications system.

TCP/IP is made up of three layers: The Internet Protocol (IP), the Transmission Control Protocol (TCP) and an application layer. First, in Figure 6.1, observe that TCP/IP covers layers 3 to 7 of the OSI model. We start with the IP, a network layer, which is responsible for routing data based on network addresses. TCP/IP is a routable protocol. In a routable protocol, all messages contain not only the address of the destination station but the address of a destination network as well. This allows TCP/IP messages to be sent to multiple networks or from network to network and around the world, hence its use in the worldwide Internet. IP has become "the" standard protocol for communicating all common forms of electronic data, including voice and video, wired and wireless. It is the foundation for networked computing.

Second, note the transport layer. TCP provides transport functions, and ensures that the total amount of bytes sent is received at the other end. TCP establishes a connection at both ends and guarantees full, reliable delivery of the sent message. TCP tests for errors and requests retransmission, if necessary.

User Datagram Protocol, or UDP, is an alternative to TCP as a transport layer protocol. UDP is also a part of the TCP/IP suite. In contrast to TCP, it does not guarantee that all the data packets have been delivered. UDP, however, is widely used for real-time voice and video transmissions where erroneous packets are not retransmitted. It is often the preferred transport protocol for multi-casting, when the transmission should not be interrupted if some nodes are having difficulties. UDP is also the transport protocol of choice for a number of P2P implementations, as you will see later on. If UDP is used and a reliable delivery *is* required, then the application must check the packet sequencing, notify errors, and take appropriate action.

Third, note the TCP/IP application layer. It corresponds to the top three OSI layers – the session, presentation, and application layers. Here you will recognize such utilities as FTP (File Transfer Protocol), SMTP (Simple Mail Transfer Protocol), and Telnet. But the two entries that are really important for P2P are HyperText Transport Protocol (HTTP) and the Domain Name System (DNS). These are some examples of protocols that provide the communications interface for end-user applications. There are other protocols – for remote access and for specific operating systems, for example.

What defines the protocols in the application layer is that they initiate the communications between nodes on the network. P2P services can call the TCP/IP application protocols in order to initiate communications. Some P2P applications skip the TCP/IP applications layer and make direct calls to TCP or UDP. To the TCP/IP applications, it doesn't matter what programming languages or formats the P2P developers may use. TCP/IP is handed a string of bits that constitute the data, or message, which it must transport. The protocol attaches the appropriate headers and trailers and sends it off.

Addresses on the Net

The functions performed by the protocols layers tell us how the transmission work is allocated. To begin understanding how it all works, we need the concept of an address. Each node in a TCP/IP network has an *IP address*. An IP address[1] is made up of four numbers; each number can range from 0 to 255, with periods separating them. These four numbers are called *octets*, as each is 8-bit long. The string 123.4.98.06 is an example of an IP address.

A central authority allocates IP addresses, otherwise we could not assure that each port has a unique address. Nor could we overcome the difficulties described below.

Every connection to a network requires an IP address.[2] This applies to any device that is connected, not just PCs and servers. Printers and storage devices can also be connected directly to the network. And with wireless IP, all network-capable handheld and mobile devices need IP addresses

[1] The description here applies to IP version 4 (IPv4), the current version of IP. The next IP version, IPv6, will have a different address format.

[2] There are other network protocols, and each defines its own address format. IP addresses are what interest us as this is the protocol used on the Internet.

when connected. Each device connects to the network via a *network port*, or just *port*. Every network adapter has a port, and a device has a separate port for each network it might be connected to. Computers, typically, belong to a local network, and some also have connections to a wide area network and the Internet. In particular, a typical enterprise user connects to the outside world through a server. This server has at least two ports – one port for the local network to which it belongs and a second port connecting it to the external network. The organization of content places more requirements on IP addresses. When a server hosts multiple web sites, for instance, each one of the sites must have its own IP address.

Is it possible to allocate a fixed IP address for every port? A 32-bit container can generate up to four billion different positive integers, but not all the numbers get used. It is similar to why telephone numbers run out well before all possible numbers have been allocated. The first part, or parts, of the IP address acts as a telephone exchange number. It points to a group of numbers, referred to as a *subnet*. There are several classes of addresses and subnets. The size of a subnet can be very large — about four million when only the first octet is used. About half the available addresses have been given out in 'chunks' of this size. The remainder is divided into two smaller-size classes, and there is a range that is held back. The hierarchy of subnet-device helps make routing efficient, and it is good for performance. But it brings about another consequence – we cannot plan on being able to use all possible IP addresses. Some subnets will be used up before others.

The number of bits allocated to create an IP address is simply not large enough to have each desktop own a unique, permanent IP address, even though we don't yet have four billion ports to connect. For most computers, therefore, their IP addresses are not permanent. That is, a new address is assigned every time the computer connects to the net. The application may not, in general, assume that a client system will have the same IP address in a future session. Because the address is not fixed, or static, we refer to these one-time addresses as *dynamic* IP addresses.

A new standard is coming for the IP address (it's called IPv6). Among other changes will be its size – the new address will be 128-bit long. This will allow for more addresses than we can possibly use for decades to come. But do not expect the new version to do away with the need for dynamic IP addresses. First, the new format has not been deployed yet. Second, even when it is, many parts of the network will continue to use the current version (IPv4) for quite a while. The changeover is not trivial, as it requires changes to routers and interfaces between IPv4 and IPv6.

Even with plenty of addresses, there are several operational reasons for continuing to assign temporary addresses. The ISPs, serving the home users, understand that only a small fraction of all their subscribers will be connected at the same time. They install many fewer phone lines than the number of their users. An ISP is given a block of IP addresses to manage. Its size is commensurate with the expected peak number of active connections. They are assigned dynamically as users log in.

Enterprises, for reasons of privacy and security, do not wish for every employee to have a public IP address. Desktop computers, and mobile systems in particular can, and do, get assigned different IP addresses at different times.

The self-management of IP addresses is helpful in dealing with the address shortage. There is a server with an application that recognizes the IP addresses given to the organization's users. They do not need to be known externally, and IT operations prefer it that way. An address that is locally used can be utilized on another local network without conflict. Indeed, the governing body of IP addresses set aside blocks of addresses to be used as "private addresses." Any local network can use addresses from these private ranges, so the same address can be used multiple times. For the scheme to work, there needs to be a service that mediates internal and external addresses.

The common use of dynamic IP addresses presents a challenge for direct peer-to-peer exchanges. It makes it more difficult for one peer's application to find the IP address of the other. Without an IP address for a destination a transmission cannot be completed. Without a known IP address, a computer cannot offer a service, and the ability to function as a server is what makes a client a peer.

TCP and UDP append a header to the message. In addition to the address it contains a *port number*. The port number, a 16-bit integer, is a way to identify a specific process to which a network message is to be forwarded when it arrives at its destination. The port number should not be confused with the network port, or network adapter. It is a logical number that is assigned to each application.[3] The port number allows a simple association of incoming data with the right service. Some

[3] "Application" in the sense of network protocol layers. HTTP or FTP, for example.

applications have conventionally assigned permanent port numbers, which are called "well known port numbers." For example, HTTP, which delivers web traffic, always communicates through (logical) port 80. This will be pertinent when we discuss P2P connections that must pass through firewalls. In other cases, a port number is assigned temporarily until the application finishes its action.

Associating Names with Addresses

As with phone numbers, no one wants to have to remember a numeric IP address. Of course, we have also seen that many computers do not have permanent IP addresses, so each device gets a name that is made up of a string of characters. It is supposed to be easy to remember. A name looks like the string of characters that follow the @ sign in your email address. Indeed, that string is the name of the server through which you send and receive email.

The domain name system (DNS) is the way Internet domain names are located and translated into Internet Protocol addresses. A domain consists of a set of addresses, which are organized by levels. For DNS, a domain is a name under which there will be records of sub-domains or hosts. These records map a name to an IP address. The sub-domains and the host names only need to be unique within that domain. The lists of domain names and IP addresses are distributed throughout the Internet in a hierarchy of authority. There is probably a DNS server near your access point to the Internet. It maps the domain names in your Internet requests or forwards them to other servers in the Internet.

There is a useful protocol that automates the assignment of temporary IP addresses. This is the Dynamic Host Configuration Protocol (DHCP). DNS servers translate people-friendly names to IP addresses. DHCP servers assign users temporary IP addresses. Clearly, it is desirable that the DNS databases are in sync with the DHCP servers. The integration between the DNS domain names and the DHCP pools of available IP addresses is service called Dynamic DNS, or DDNS. Unfortunately, not all DNS servers are a part of a DDNS. As a result, it is not easy to find a host with a temporary address without the help of a mediator system.

This is a difficult challenge to direct peer-to-peer exchanges.

For home users, it is possible for network applications to find their computer. One way is to get a fixed (static) IP address from the ISP (for additional charge). Another way is to use a service transparently. There are quite a few companies[4] that offer a service where the user's system is provided with an Internet name and will automatically map to the user's current IP address. This way, the absence of a fixed IP address doesn't stop a desktop user from offering services from that computer. The potential clients have a way of finding the service provider.

Neither method provides a general solution to the difficulties in providing services without a permanent and fixed IP address.

Figure 6.2 illustrates the relationship between TCP, IP address, port, and name.

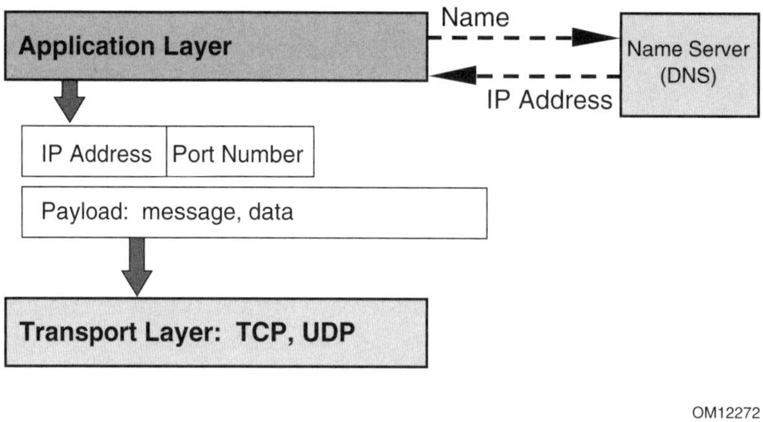

Figure 6.2 TCP, IP address, port, and the application

The application gives the DNS server the name of the destination computer, and is assigned an IP address. This address, along with the port number, defines the destination – location and application. The address, port, and data are packaged and delivered to the TCP or UDP for transmission.

Good sources for learning more about TCP/IP are (Davidson, 1988) and (Comer, 1991). There are also numerous online tutorials. For a clear and concise tutorial, see (PC Network Advisor, 2001).

---

[4] For a comprehensive list of such offerings see, for example, http://directory.google.com/Top/Computers/Software/Internet/Servers/Address_Management/Dynamic_DNS_Services/.

The Tree of Protocols and other Standards

The use of standard protocols simplifies and accelerates development for multiple platforms. The presence of common protocols does not guarantee interoperability, but it moves us closer to it. There are several application layer protocols that are popular with the P2P developers. This is a short reminder of what they are:

HTTP

HTTP (Hypertext Transfer Protocol) is the set of rules for exchanging files on the web. The rules apply to a variety of media, including text, sound, graphics, and video. A basic concept is the idea that a file can contain reference to other files. A selection, or a click on the screen, will produce a request for another transfer.

Some of the P2P implementations described in this book use HTTP as their communications protocol. Using HTTP frees the developer from having to be concerned about HTTP implementation differences across device types.

XML

XML stands for extensible markup language. It provides a way to share format and content on networks. The XML markup symbols, and associated character strings, indicate how the file looks when displayed. This is not surprising as XML extends HTML, the Hypertext Markup Language we have all been using. XML is much more powerful. It can be used to describe the logical structure of the document. In XML, you can use tags that describe the content by specifying what data is being described. The known syntax thus makes it possible to use software agents to gather information and act upon it. XML is *extensible* because, unlike HTML, new markup symbols can be defined and added indefinitely.

For an introduction to XML and a tutorial on how to use it, see http://www.w3schools.com/xml/default.asp at the W3C Schools sites.

SOAP

The Simple Object Access Protocol, or SOAP, builds on XML and HTTP (though it can use other transport protocols). SOAP provides a mechanism for communications between programs running on different computers. These computers may run different operating systems, and the programs can still "talk" to each other via SOAP. With HTTP and XML, programs can communicate across platforms. SOAP specifies exactly how to encode an HTTP header and an XML file so that a program in one computer can call a program in another computer and pass information to it. SOAP also specifies how the called program can return a response.

SOAP is a suitable component for a P2P environment, because it enables the exchange of information in a decentralized and distributed setting. Communicating via HTTP is an advantage. HTTP uses one of these "well known port numbers," and many firewalls allow its exchanges to go through.

To learn more about SOAP, visit the W3C SOAP site at http://www.w3schools.com/soap/default.asp.

WebDAV

The "DAV" in the acronym stands for Distributed Authoring and Versioning. Web is added at the front to emphasize it is web-based. WebDAV is a set of extensions to the HTTP protocol. This standard enables users, separated from each other on the net, to jointly and collaboratively edit shared files, with one editor at a time. These files may be located on remote servers, or on a peer system that supports WebDAV hosting functions. This kind of collaboration is a powerful capability for P2P computing.

The significance of WebDAV is that it adds web-based *write* capability to the *read* access afforded by HTTP. It also allows collaborations on the Internet that were only possible over an intranet.

You can read about many useful features in the WebDAV Resources site: http://www.webdav.org/.

UDDI

The Universal Description, Discovery and Integration (UDDI) is a platform-independent, open framework for describing services, discovering businesses, and integrating business services using the Internet. A UDDI operational registry exists today. The UDDI project takes advantage of standards such as XML, HTTP and DNS protocols. UDDI uses Web Services Description Language (WSDL), an XML-based language used to describe the services a business offers. WSDL is the language used by businesses to list themselves and their services in the UDDI registry. Cross-platform programming features are addressed through the use of SOAP. The UDDI specifications and registry allow business to discover each other and define how commerce should be conducted between them.

You can read more about UDDI at http://www.uddi.org/about.html.

UDDI provides a partial interoperable solution to an important P2P activity – the discovery of resources. This is an example of a tool, developed for use by business-to-business exchanges, which can be extended and become a general-purpose discovery tool.

XPath

XPath is an XML Path language. It is designed to help find parts of a document. As its name indicates, XPath defines a standard XML syntax. This is an example of how XML can be used to create standards for specific operations. In this case, XPath defines a syntax that is based on the path through the document's logical structure. What differentiates XPath from descriptors is that it specifies a route, not just a point.

This approach is a powerful aid when the application deals with relevance and "closeness" of the discovered content. As such, it is useful for P2P applications involved with content sharing.

For more details about XPath, visit http://www.w3.org.

Constructing the Tree of Protocols

There are many protocols, and they are used for different purposes at varying levels. You saw how the communication protocols are layered. The protocols higher-up on the "tree" use those that are below them, closer to the system software or the computer hardware or the network wires. Figure 6.3 is a useful way to remember the roles and relationship of some of the protocols (including the few described above).

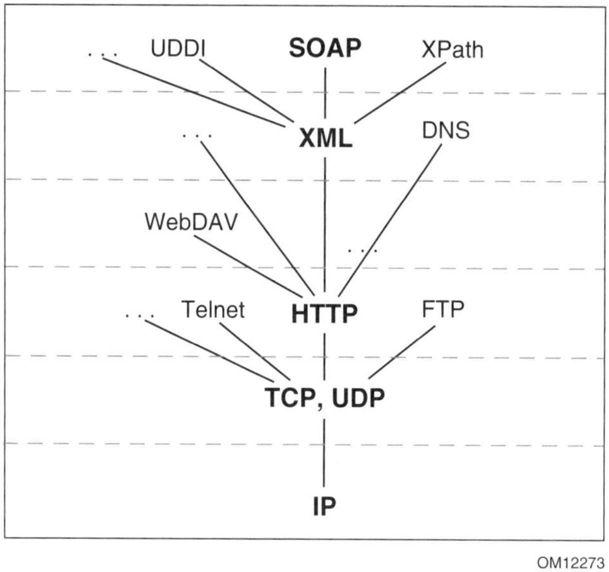

Figure 6.3 The tree of protocols and standards

TCP and UDP are the two most commonly used transport protocols that sit on top of IP, the Internet Protocol. There are several network application protocols, of which we are mostly interested in HTTP, the Hypertext Transfer Protocol.

HTTP is used by higher-level protocols that are employed by network applications. In particular, P2P developers use WebDAV, DNS, and XML. XML, itself built upon HTML, is a building block of a family of diverse protocols that provide standards for a focus area. SOAP is of major interest to P2P, as is UDDI for discovery, as well as XPath for content-related inquiries.

Most of the interoperable technologies on the Internet are being developed in the World Wide Web Consortium (W3C, http://www.w3c.org) and the Internet Engineering Task Force (IETF, http://www.ietf.org). Much of the information above was derived from these bodies.

Dealing with Firewalls and NATs

NAT is short for Network Address Translation, or Translator.[5] We need devices that map names to network addresses because most of the computers and devices that can be peers in a P2P environment do not have a permanent network address, or their IP address is not visible to the originator of the communication. The reasons for dynamic or private IP addresses are:

- The address range of IPv4 is insufficient for everyone to have a permanent IP address.
- Enterprises, organizations, and individuals, do not wish to expose internal systems and resources to direct external communication.

Security is a major motivation for the separation between internal networks and the outside world. A firewall is a service that offers greater security, and is located at a gateway to a network. The purpose of a firewall is to prevent outsiders from accessing resources on the networks it protects, and it may control what outside resources its own users have access to as well.

NATs and firewalls serve different purposes, but they do have things in common: NATs and firewalls are located at an entry point to the organization's internal network, and they both inspect incoming and outgoing messages. For that reason, they are often implemented on the same server and function as an integrated pair of services.

The presence of firewalls and NATs impedes direct P2P communications. Two factors determine the extent of the obstacle and what can be done about it:

- The types of NATs and firewalls involved.
- The topology of the network connecting the peers.

[5] At least some of the IETF documents use "translator", including RFC 2663. It is more convenient to talk about the translator, as a device or a service, instead of the translation, being the action.

We will consider these aspects next. But first, what is the nature of the "NAT/Firewall problem"? NATs and proxy service firewalls, for instance, act as protocol end points and interfere with true end-to-end peer interactions. Moreover, NATs and firewalls hide peers and other resources, making peer and resource discovery and direct communication more difficult.

NATs and firewalls can also limit communication so only responses to requests that originated behind the devices are allowed back in. This blocks communications from hosts outside of the protected domain to those inside the domain. Often, certain ports/services are closed down completely and access is denied. Address translation and other packet modifications by NATs and firewalls can break end-to-end security operations by requiring (or not detecting) modification of encrypted data payloads.

Most firewall solutions only allow outbound communication that is initiated internally. And most NATs coexist with firewalls as the gatekeepers of exchanges between the internal and external networks. A common assumption is that one cannot trust communication created from the outside.

Much of the end-to-end transparency of the Internet has been lost because of NATs and firewalls. This means that essential P2P functions such as addressing, discovery, and communication are impeded.

NATs and How they Work

This section refers to the NAT as a translator (rather than the translation). In other words, it refers to what a NAT *does*. A NAT straddles two networks and relates to two separate sets of addresses. It translates an IP address used within one network to a different IP address; one that is known within another network.

Here is a typical scenario:

An organization uses an internal network[6] with private IP addresses. These addresses are not valid on the public network. The internal network includes a NAT, which has two addresses, each belonging to a different network port (an adapter, not a port number). One port connects

[6] A private, or local, network, as used here, has the property that within its domain every IP address is unique. This property defines a network domain that is sometimes referred to as a realm.

to the internal network, and the other is a public IP address for connectivity to the external network.

The NAT does nothing and will not interfere with exchanges between nodes on the internal network. How does a computer on the internal network communicate with an external computer? The IP packet sent out contains the source's address and port number, and the destination's address and port number. The port numbers are attached so that different sessions between the same two computers can be kept separate. The source's address is not valid outside the organization's network. The NAT is the gateway between the two networks. It replaces the source address with one of its own public (external) addresses. It may also replace the port number of the source so it is unique among all communicating internal computers. The transformations are kept in a table that the NAT manages. The destination computer replies to the NAT's public address. The NAT knows where the source is, from the unique port number listed in the translation table. And so the exchanges go on.

In this scenario, it is not possible for an external computer to initiate an exchange with an internal node. You see that this NAT solution fits nicely within the client-server model. The client is a desktop and a node on the internal network. The external computer is a server. The client initiates the communication by making a request, and the server replies. The mechanism is not adequate for the symmetrical exchanges that are fundamental to P2P.

A NAT service may use more than one global IP address, and it has access to a pool of such addresses that the organization owns. The NAT, then, also acts as a multiplexor between many local nodes and a few global IP addresses.

NATs come in a number of flavors. Some of them are:

- *Traditional*, or *outbound*, NAT (the example above describes this type). We saw that a traditional NAT works when external addresses are unique in both external and internal networks. But internal addresses are unique only within the internal network. This means external addresses can be advertised everywhere, but internal addresses can only be advertised internally.
- *Bi-directional*, or *two-way*. This NAT is used when sessions can be initiated by any node, whether on the internal or on the external network. This is possible when an internal node is bound to a unique global address. An external computer initiates communication with

an internal computer by sending a message to the internal computer's global address. The NAT still needs to map this unique external address to the internal computer's private address.

- *Twice* NAT is a NAT where both destination and source addresses are translated. Such a NAT is necessary when the same address may exist both in the local (private) network and as an external (public) address. This situation should not happen, but it does, occasionally. The address collision occurs when addresses from the public IP address range are assigned locally. It can also occur when a site changes its Internet provider, but continues to use the addresses from the ex-provider internally.

There are more types of NATs, but this selection is sufficient for highlighting the challenges that face P2P communications. A general solution to the NAT traversal problem must cater to all the NAT flavors that are expected.

There is another level of complexity. Altering the packet headers is sufficient for correct routing, as handled by the transport protocol. But many applications also exchange network address information within the message payload. This information pertains to the network application protocol, and it needs to be modified when the NAT processes the header of the packet. For that reason, most NATs are accompanied by Application Level Gateways (ALGs) that perform address translation within the payload. ALGs are application-specific. A P2P application that exchanges network address information must access an ALG (or equivalent) that will track the address mappings as they occur. This ALG is provided with the assistance of the NAT vendor. Even with the ALG, the address translation may still not be possible if the message is encrypted.

The topology involving the network and the NATs (and firewalls) affects the solutions for traversing the gateway. The important configurations are:

- The *single NAT* (as described above). One NAT separates a private network from an external one. One of the communicating peers is behind the NAT within the private net. The other is on the outside, with a public IP static address.
- *Double NATs* topology is when both communicating peers behind a NAT on a private net, with the Internet "cloud" in between.

- *Nested NATs* occur when one of the peers must communicate through two (or more) NATs before reaching a peer on a public network. This situation can arise in a large organization, or when users behind a NAT connect to the Internet via an ISP who runs its own NAT.
- Composite topologies also exist. For example, we can encounter a *nested-double* combination.

Figure 6.4 illustrates the three main variants of NAT network topologies.

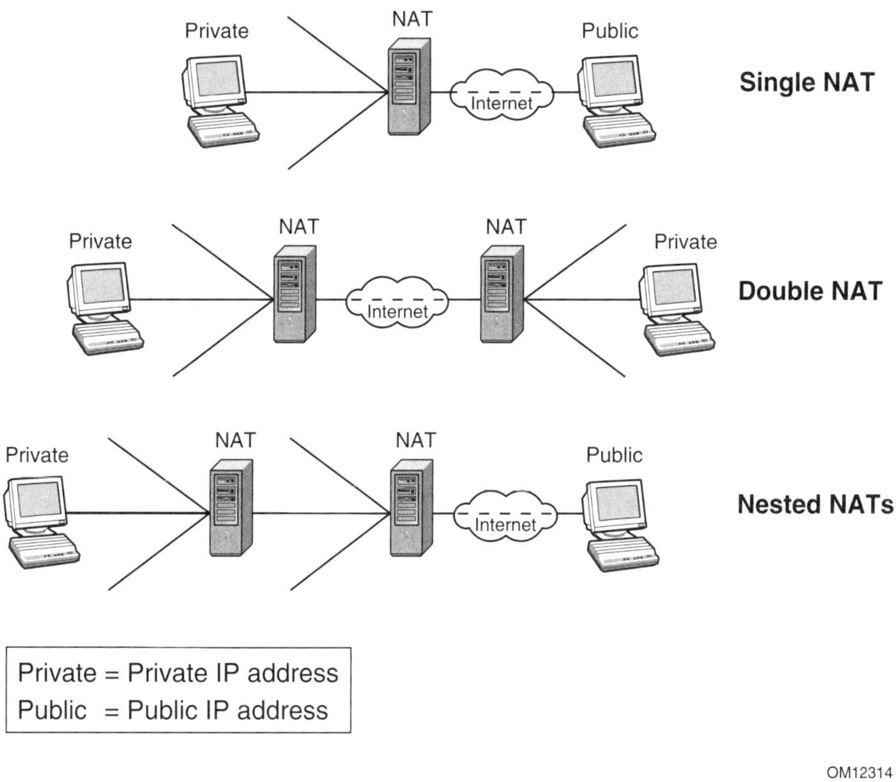

Figure 6.4 NAT network topologies

The subject is more complex than the description here implies. There are variations and caveats that are not included. For more information about NATs, see (IETF RFC2663, 1999 and IETF RFC1631, 1994).

Firewalls

A firewall is a security tool that protects assets of a private network by limiting access from outside the network. To accomplish this task, the firewall is located at the network gateway to external networks. Remember, firewalls and NATs often exist on the same server. Firewalls at enterprises may also screen and act on outgoing traffic, thus controlling what outside resources its own users have access to. In either direction, firewalls impact direct P2P exchanges.

There is no such thing as a "standard" firewall. Firewalls vary greatly depending on the security policies chosen by the organization or at home. All is not lost, however, as firewalls employ three basic techniques:

- A Packet-filtering firewall examines network traffic passing through it and selectively passes or drops the packets. It will look for incoming messages that are not from expected sources, for example. The filtering rules are set to reflect local security policies.
- Proxy service firewalls examine and filter packets, but also act as a relay between hosts behind the firewall and the external network domain. Therefore, a proxy service firewall must perform address translation functions similar to that of a NAT. The external domain sees only the proxy server address; that is, the proxy server and NAT act as protocol end points. There are different levels of proxy services characterized by the level of protocol they examine. The more context the proxy examines, the more stringent filtering it can exercise.
- Stateful inspection methods monitor communication protocol and application-level state and develop a detailed context. The detailed context is then used to more carefully inspect the communication protocol stack, enforce security policies, and anticipate protocol communication actions and requirements. One such action can be to "open" a port associated with an application that just sent an outbound packet. A reply to that communication will go through. This feature can be applied in establishing peer-to-peer direct exchanges. Stateful inspection methods are application specific.

This subject is more complex than the description here implies. There are variations and caveats are not included. To learn more about NATs, see (IETF RFC2663, 1999 and IETF RFC1631, 1994).

Addressing NAT and Firewall Traversal

The lesson from the preceding sections is that NATs and firewalls come in various shapes and functionality. There are also multiple paths between the communicating peers that arise from the networks' topology. As a developer of a particular application, you no doubt understand which types of gateways and networks you prefer. You can also build in a traversal solution if you know the makeup of the communication path. However, we rarely get to choose the gateway and we cannot assume one type and one network topology.

A general P2P solution for transparent traversal of NATs and firewalls does not yet exist. There are, however, partial solutions and promising directions for further investigation.

The ideal solution allows any peer to establish a connection with another peer known by name, as if there was no NAT or firewall in the way. Here are some work-around proposals and directions that are being employed.

- **HTTP port 80**. Many organizations restrict inbound communications, however, they do allow access to the web. The browsing application uses HTTP, which always uses port number 80. Firewalls enable HTTP traffic by keeping port 80 open to communications. Thus, a P2P application that uses HTTP as the communications protocol can get through the firewall.

  This solution addresses a common barrier placed by the presence of a firewall, and it works when the destination's address is otherwise known.

  While the use of HTTP is an ad hoc solution for now, there is a proposal in the making that will standardize this approach. An IETF Network Working Group has a proposal (RFC3093) for a Fire Enhancement Protocol. If approved, it will allow any application to traverse a firewall by layering HTTP over the TCP or UDP transport protocols. Again, this will work in instances where HTTP traffic is allowed to go through, and when the address is known.

- **Relay and Rendezvous servers**. This is a class of solutions that relies on a third party to help in traversing NATs and firewalls. As with the "HTTP port 80" technique, the third-party solutions do not require any changes to the NAT software. Known uses of third-party assistance fall into one of three approaches:
  - Arrange for a node behind the NAT or the firewall to initiate communication. Alice wants to contact Bob, who is behind a NAT or firewall. A third-party, a server used by the application or another user, can contact Bob and others who are behind the firewall. The application allows Alice to tell the third-party to ask Bob to send Alice a message. This message may be a simple packet that will open a port for return communication.
  - Advertise, or register, your presence at a Rendezvous server. Users who wish to participate in a specific P2P application register with a server that maintains current addresses of connected users. The information may include the NAT's global address, the information needed for the NAT to map the message to Bob, and the port number that is open for communication (if not fixed by the application). Alice can now get from this rendezvous server all that is needed to establish a connection with Bob.
  - Use a relay server to place communications that cannot go through directly. This method uses a third-party as a conduit that transmits the message. The relay service may be a central server, one that all users have established communication with. Or, it can be a distributed service. Alice wants to send a message to Bob, but cannot communicate with Bob directly. The application passes the message on to the relay server, where it is forwarded to Bob. Bob replies to Alice directly, or uses the relay server in the same way Alice did. When the relay mechanism is distributed, the application will route Alice's message to Bob via one or more peers.

  HTTP and its port 80, or third-party assisted communications, are the most common means for traversing NATs and firewalls.
- **Configuring NATs**. This is a scheme that works with bi-directional NATs. The external node is aware of the NAT address and appends a port number that identifies the destination node. The port number received at the gateway is redirected to a port on the internal network that belongs to the destination node. The mapping between the internal port numbers and an internal node address can be static (a

fixed port number), or it can be dynamic, when addresses are allocated from a pool of available addresses.[7]

This is an example of a scheme that relies on controlling the NAT server, since it requires modification of the translation table. Similarly, in the case of nested NATs, the method will work only if the appropriate changes are made in both NATs. Single control, or even coordination, between two nested NATs can be problematic. For example, one NAT may belong to an ISP and the other may be at home or at a small business.

- **SOCKS**. The SOCKS protocol, version 5 (SOCKS5, see also IETF RFC1928, 1996) supports authenticated firewall traversal. It is an open Internet standard for network proxies at the transport protocol layer. SOCKS5 requires a SOCKS server, as well as SOCKS support in the client application.

  A SOCKS5 server can be configured to offer external clients access to the internal network using an internal naming scheme. Unlike bi-directional NATs, the SOCKS solution does not require control over the DNS naming service for the proxy on the public network. Alternatively, the SOCKS5 protocol also presents a method through which an application can set up an inbound connection and receive the necessary external addressing information. SOCKS5 proxies may be chained to support multiple levels of nesting.

- **Realm Specific IP**. Realm Specific IP (RSIP) is a solution currently under consideration by the ITEF. Like NAT, RSIP addresses the shortage of available addresses by multiplexing IP addresses in one domain with multiple machines in another (see Borella and Montenegro, 2000 for an introduction to RSIP). As with NAT, multiplexing may be done at the IP address level or at the port level. Unlike NAT, RSIP requires that the clients be aware of the RSIP server and perform explicit negotiation with the server to establish communication channels. RSIP support can be provided to most applications by modifications below the application level of the network stack. In exchange for the required client side changes, RSIP is able to provide additional functionality. RSIP gateway communicates public addressing parameters to the client. Inbound and outbound bindings may be explicitly requested. Lease

[7] In practice, the process is more complicated than indicated here. In some cases, an internal DNS server is required.

information, such as grant and revocation can be provided by the client or the gateway.

RSIP is scalable. It supports arbitrary levels of cascading. Regardless of the number of levels of nesting, only valid public addresses are assigned.

The greatest issues with RSIP are that it requires modifications to all client devices as well as to the gateway. Also, no RSIP products are currently available.

- **Universal Plug and Play, or UPnP**. Universal Plug and Play, also known as UPnP, extends the notion of Plug and Play on the PC platform, primarily targeting the domain of consumer networks. The UPnP strives to make networking invisible and automatic. UPnP is compatible with manual and auto-configuration methods for IP address assignment. Installation of new elements such as computers, printers, consumer electronics, appliances, and residential gateways to the network is simple as UPnP supports automatic resource and service discovery and control by peers. UPnP relies on open, accepted Internet Web standards and protocols such as IP, TCP, UDP, HTTP, SOAP, and XML, but remains agnostic with respect to the network media, OS, and languages (see also http://www.upnp.org).

  While work is still in progress within the UPnP forum, there are some known NAT-related features in a UPnP Internet gateway device that are of interest to us. Among them are:

  — The ability to detect presence of a NAT or an RSIP server, including its external IP address.

  — The ability to add port mappings to enable forwarding of inbound connections to a particular client on the residential LAN. Mappings can be assigned a lease time to support the notion of static (permanent) and dynamic (temporary) mappings. Hosts in the mapping entry can be identified by IP addresses or DNS names. Mappings can also be assigned a description string for reference. Thus, UPnP solves NAT-traversal by a modification of the client software stack as well as through modification of the NAT device.

The current NAT-related services defined for UPnP Internet Gateway Devices do enable some outbound and inbound capabilities for existing applications. These include the ability to transparently map, open, and close ports on the Internet gateway device or the NAT. In some ways, stateful-inspection firewalls can implicitly achieve a subset of this functionality by understanding the communication-level and algorithm-level state, protocols, and context, while operating in a legacy environment. Explicit support as found in UPnP, however, eliminates some guesswork and enables new UPnP-aware applications to be deployed immediately without having to craft or wait for custom firewall rules and action triggers.

Nested NATs within the residential network can be supported via UPnP, where each lower level NAT performs the dual role of a controlled device and a control point or a relay to an upstream NAT device. However, for NATs beyond the edge of the residential LAN, such as those employed by an ISP, discovery or configuration may not be possible.

Much of the work done by the UPnP forum is highly relevant to P2P communications.

- **Middlebox Communication**. A new IETF activity, under the auspices of the Middlebox Communication Working Group, focuses on communication with and through middle boxes such as NATs and firewalls. The focus of the working group will be the architectural framework and the requirements for the protocol between the requesting device and the middle box. The group is also concerned with the architectural framework for the interface between the middle box and the policy entity.

  The Middlebox communication project is an example of an ongoing activity that the P2P developer community should continue to monitor and support.

NATs and Firewalls – where do we go from here?

There are numerous ways to approach the NAT and firewall traversal problem, but most offer only a partial solution, or a solution to a subset of the problem. The majority of the solutions discussed here deal with ways to enable support for inbound connection for those nodes that are beyond a NAT gateway. This is a difficult technical problem, and one for which general technical solutions are badly needed for an easier adoption of P2P computing.

For large portions of the consumer space, addressing appears to be the chief obstacle to connectivity. In the enterprise, and where the integrity of the systems is paramount, the greatest obstacle does not stem from difficulties in address translation, but rather due to security concerns. The solutions for allowing incoming communications directly to the desktop does not need to compromise security. But, even when such guarantee cannot be absolute, there are many opportunities to utilize P2P within the confines of an organization or a local network.

Peer-to-peer computing offers new opportunities for sharing and collaboration of computation resources at the edge of the network. Transparent, bi-directional communication is an essential ingredient for enabling peer-to-peer applications and services across the Internet. Unfortunately, NATs and firewalls (devices that impede transparent communication) have become widely deployed in recent years in response to other security, privacy, management, resource availability, and cost reasons.

Many P2P developers, inside and outside the P2P Working group, are searching for general solutions to the NAT and firewall traversal problem.[8] What we don't have is a general and secure solution. Among the important questions the P2P developers need to answer is the extent to which a universal scheme for traversing NATs and firewalls is desired and feasible. The issues are: how do we incorporate the different types of gateways and different network topologies? And how do we fit the solution, or solutions, to the application and its operational environment?

The P2P Working Group is working on proposals for solving the NAT and Firewall problems for P2P (Peer-to-Peer Working Group, 2001). The final answer will likely involve external standards bodies, such as the IETF and other industry forums. Along the way, the P2P community will develop software and protocol stacks to demonstrate what can be done. And these examples will help shift policies and enable peer-to-peer deployments.

[8] One such example can be found in papers posted at the Clipcode site (http://www.clipcode.com/peer/index.htm).

Current Practices

The infrastructures and services that were introduced in Chapter 5 present a variety of solutions for P2P communications. The target applications and computing environments dictate the choices that were made. We look, mostly, at two aspects of communication:

- Communication protocols used
- Means for establishing communications

The second item is closely related to the topics of the following chapters – naming and discovery, availability, and security, where these topics will be covered in detail.

The Interplay of Protocol Use

Almost all the implementations examined here use HTTP directly or via XML. The advantages of choosing HTTP as the entry point to the communication protocols are:

- It runs on all major platforms and devices.
- HTTP was designed for 2-way communications in the first place. It's PUT command, for uploading data, and it has always been there (even if it hasn't been used much).
- HTTP uses port 80, which is often open to incoming communications through firewalls.

In addition, XML, which is fast becoming the tool of choice for many developers, uses HTTP. Use of HTTP at present allows a smooth transition to XML.

Let's look at some examples.

Endeavors use HTTP as a communication protocol for their Magi environment. The implementation offers an example of the flexibility afforded by using HTTP. Magi runs on desktops and on handheld devices. Magi's HTTP uses TCP for desktops, since it checks for completion of the delivery. But it calls UDP when Magi operates on a handheld device. UDP does not check for complete receipt of the message, and has less overhead than TCP. Indeed, handheld devices are not expected to be constantly connected, and reducing the overhead for these devices is desirable.

The Event Service of Magi manages the communications and the structure of the messages with XML over HTTP. The current model is quite SOAP-like, and Endeavors have plans to migrate to SOAP as the tool for invoking methods on other nodes. Apart from increased interoperability and standardization, the use of SOAP also enhances the connection independence. For example, SOAP allows messages and data to be sent via email. Files can be exchanged with XML over HTTP, too.

Escher's WebRiposte bases its inter-application communication on HTTP or HTTPS (Secure HTTP). Applications also communicate via SOAP, which runs on top of HTTP.[9] The peer-to-peer communication is primarily based on UDP, for reasons related to handling communication failures, better performance, and scalability. However, WebRiposte also uses TCP/IP, primarily when the application requires a security layer. All communication is message-based, and messages are represented in XML. There is an optional support for data-compression that reduces the increased size of messages due to XML.

Similarly, **NextPage**'s NXT communicates with XML over HTTPS. The protocol is quite SOAP-like, and soon will be fully SOAP-compliant It should not come as a surprise if we see other implementations becoming SOAP-proper in the future.

Some implementations define communications through protocols lower than HTTP in the TCP/IP stack. Globus, from the **Grid Forum**, does so. The Globus Toolkit defines a suite of protocols for notification, resource discovery, resource access, and resource management. These protocols are based on a common set of standards-based authentication protocols, the Grid Security Infrastructure (discussed in Chapter 9), and layer variously on HTTP, LDAP, and FTP. A movement to a common SOAP substrate may occur in the future. The Grid Resource Access and Management (GRAM) protocol supports secure access to, and management of, remote resources (such as computers). The Meta Directory Service (MDS) protocols support the discovery and monitoring of Grid resources, and GridFTP supports secure, reliable, access to (and transfer of) data. The flexibility of these different protocols has been demonstrated via the creation of a number of higher-level services, tools, and applications that use these protocols.

---

[9] WebRiposte also supports Win32 RPC interface.

Employing Higher-Level Protocols

Some of the infrastructure and architectures use higher-level protocols for specific types of operations. The use of discovery protocols (UDDI) is discussed in Chapter 7. Here is an example of the use of WebDAV by Endeavors:

WebDAV, above HTTP in the protocols tree, is used for publishing and keeping track of modified files. It is only an IETF (Internet Engineering Task Force) extension to HTTP, and they fit well together. WebDAV does use the PUT in HTTP. With the help of its metadata capability, WebDAV serves as a tool for managing resources. One could utilize it for creating "collections" (a query can produce a list of some specified resource, for example). One could get a list of files without having to parse web pages, as well. WebDAV also provides a facility for locking resources, a useful function for managing coherency of content. Magi will also use WebDAV for versioning and access control.[10]

Proprietary Protocols

In some cases, the developers use standard communication protocols as a stepping stone to their unique communication mechanism. Here are three examples from the architectures examined in this book:

The **Engenia** Collaboration Services Platform employs high-level protocol for communications between objects. The protocol is called Adaptive XML, and it is a proprietary XML schema. The resulting XML utilizes HTTP and its underlying transport protocol.

Engenia defines a special type of an object, called a *connector*, which provides an API for accessing another system. For example, a search API in one of the objects that ties (using COM underneath) to another search engine will do so through a connector. It's an object that is used as a service, and the term connector merely defines its functionality as being able to access other systems.

The **Avaki** Middleware Platform is also object-based. It defines the message format and high-level protocol for object interaction, but not the programming language or the communications protocol.

---

[10] At this time, access control is handled by Magi in a non-WebDAV complaint way.

Avaki uses standard network protocols and communication facilities of host operating systems to support inter-object communication. To perform such communication, Avaki converts location-independent object identifiers into location-dependent addresses through the Avaki binding process. An object address element contains two parts, an address type and the address itself, whose size and format depend on the type. The address semantic field is intended to express various forms of multicast and replicated communication. There are two address types, one uses UDP and the other uses TCP. In addition to the address and port number, the Avaki message header carries another field that allows differentiation between multiple sessions that use the same pair of IP address and port number. The binding between the object identifier and the address also contains a field that specifies the time at which the binding becomes invalid (including never).

The last example of an architecture that establishes communication through a high level proprietary protocol is **OpenCola**.

As a collaborative computing environment, OpenCola relies on the ability of peers (OpenCola calls them *Clervers*, from client-server rolled in one) to communicate with one another. After evaluating many possible communications systems, OpenCola decided to create their own protocol. They call it XRoad.

The design aim of the communications protocol for OpenCola was maximum flexibility. To this end they selected XML as the most generic message-carrying format, and HTTP as the transport layer of convenience. The XRoad protocol resembles SOAP in many respects – it is based on a combination of HTTP 1.1 and XML. In both XRoad and SOAP, a field in the HTTP header is given over to an address, which tells the protocol which method inside the program should receive the XML part of the message. HTTP is used because it provides a basis for a functional RPC protocol. HTTP is widely understood and easily implemented.

One of the key advantages to HTTP is its concept of the URL. The designers chose not to constrain the receiving software to an object-oriented programming model. They also decided not to use any technology that contained any platform-specific (and not easily portable code). For these reasons, in designing a dynamic protocol framework for collaborative computing it was decided to devise a way of extending URLs into "program space." The World Wide Web Consortium's XPath standard is used to targeting a message to an object inside "Clerver space." XPath is a way of targeting a specific node in a document tree according to (possibly) highly complicated and precise criteria. XPath can be added to a valid URL in a way that is compatible with current HTTP, and therefore Web browsers and servers.

The XRoad protocol, therefore, applies a document-based rather than an object-based model to communications. Each program using the protocol may represent itself to the peer as a leaf on a document tree in the Clerver. Messages coming into the Clerver are routed to that leaf according to its XPath, as though the Clerver and its contents were itself an XML document. In addition, programs within the Clerver may represent themselves as XML documents as well, allowing the XPath address to extend inside programs to their methods, as in SOAP.

The XRoad protocol differs from SOAP in the following ways:

- XRoad, by extending URLs to be robust references inside the program space, uses a World Wide Web Consortium standard and does not mandate object-orientation.
- XRoad does not define what the XML must look like. This design choice was intended to make it possible for extremely simple message types to be invented.

Managing on the Net

Not everyone has to worry about the obstacles placed on direct communications by the presence of NATs and firewalls. There are many opportunities for P2P applications within an enterprise, or within a local network. Escher, for example, designed WebRiposte to take place among known and trusting entities. Communicating with nodes behind a gateway is also simplified, since all the nodes receive the same updated data. The synchronization of transaction records is broadcasted to all the peers on the subnet.

Those who address the traversal of NATs and firewalls use variants that fall into one or more of these approaches:

- Arrange for the node behind a NAT or Firewall to initiate communication with a node that is publicly addressable.
- Use a rendezvous server to provide a known location for all to register and to advertise presence and address.
- Use a publicly visible node as a relay, or router, for blocked nodes.

Here are some specific examples.

Let's look at Magi from **Endeavors**:

Magi assumes all the uncertainties and barriers that are common to the net. These include wireless and wired devices that cannot be counted on to be connected all the time. The network itself may contain peers that can connect to each directly — that is, the communication protocol will find the destination's IP address. But Magi also assumes that there may be peers behind a firewall, or whose network address is handled through a NAT server. The NAT difficulty is handled through the use of a proxy. At the start of a session the peer registers (or checks-in) at the proxy, thus making the (temporary) address known to others via that proxy. And HTTP tunneling through port 80 enables getting through firewalls.

The Magi Proxy is a service that provides a mechanism for allowing an application to reach peers with changing addresses using Magi authentication. It also allows other applications to find and interact with mobile Magi servers. The proxy service described here can be thought of as a persistent directory service for allowing peers to find each other.

Firewalls and NATs often coexist, especially within the enterprise, but let's review them individually. Firewalls, for this discussion, can be thought of as a mechanism for allowing only outgoing communication. This means that a peer located behind a firewall cannot be reached by a peer on the other side of that wall. The peer outside the firewall caches (locally) events destined to a peer behind a firewall. And the peer behind the firewall contacts his "buddies," the other peers, at regular intervals to fetch messages. When two peers are behind separate firewalls, a third party is needed. Magi requires an Event Relay, a node in a publicly accessible part of the net. Both peers store the messages to each other on this relay. The relay is set to forward the stored messages when the peers request them. It is not possible to browse peers behind a firewall, nor is it possible to send them files directly.

The action Magi takes to in order to deal with the presence of a NAT depends on the NAT's capabilities. If the particular address translator can map a unique identifier to the peer, a specific port, or an URL, then Magi can establish direct communications with that peer. Otherwise, the peers will communicate via an event relay as done in the case of firewall presence.

Note that the Event Relay is, in effect, a mechanism for supporting asynchronous communications, similar to our regular email. Another by-product of the relay server is that a single cached message can be directed to multiple peers. Sending the multiple copies from a server, rather than a desktop-peer, makes better use of network bandwidth.

WebRiposte from **Escher** operates in a somewhat different environment. All application communication between peers is performed via replication, so that each peer has a complete, fault-tolerant record of both sides of the conversation.

WebRiposte uses the concept of replication groups to restrict the domain of communication, and this also provides an effective way to securely manage communications between enterprises and across firewalls (for more on security aspects, see Chapter 9). A Correspondence Server, outside the firewall, is used to mediate for nodes behind the firewall.

The WebRiposte application does not rely on a pre-defined port number. Instead, this is a parameter that is set by the customer when installing and building their custom application.

Next, let's look at how **Groove** deals with NATs and firewalls:

By default, members of a Groove shared space send messages (deltas) directly to each other. In some cases, Groove members may be separated by a corporate firewall. When Groove detects firewalls, it redirects the content and activity of the shared space to the Groove relay service. The Groove relay service wraps the groove deltas in HTTP and passes them through the firewall.

Groove utilizes, wherever possible, a pre-defined port number (2492). The knowledge of this port number is used to enable direct communication when otherwise it would not be possible. For example, when the source is behind a firewall and inbound traffic is allowed on port 2492. When the target is behind a firewall that allows outbound messages on port 2492, a slightly more complex scheme is possible. The source of the exchange starts via a relay server. The target, after receiving the initial communication, can reply and create a new connection. Now the two parties can communicate directly.

The last example is from the distributed computing camp: how **Entropia** manages communications with its peers.

The Entropia Grid collects spare CPU cycles on member's machines and recycles them for running applications. The members may be corporate employees whose machines have been preloaded with the Entropia software by their IT departments or they may be users on the Internet. In either environment, Entropia must deal with firewalls and Network Address Translators (NATs). Entropia's solution has two components. First, because NATs effectively hide the IP address of the machines that sit behind it, Entropia cannot use the IP address of the host in the naming of the host. Another reason is that for many users, the IP address is dynamic (DHCP for example) and can change on a daily basis. When the Entropia client is installed, a unique Entropia Client ID is generated which uniquely names the client. All communication from the client is tagged with the client ID so that the Entropia servers know the source of the message, despite changes in hardware and network location.

Furthermore, the Entropia client and servers can detect the use of firewalls, and in these cases it uses HTTP tunneling and polling. The polling is used because the Entropia server, sitting outside of the firewall, cannot initiate a connection to the client. Therefore, any server-initiated message is queued. The client, sitting behind the firewall, may initiate communication with the server and periodically polls the server for any new messages. HTTP tunneling is used to get through the firewall itself: the message is packed into an HTTP envelope and sent using port 80.

Concluding Observations

What can we learn from the communication challenges and the early implementation examples?

- A general case solution to traversing NATs and firewalls is eluding us, so far. The problem has multiple faces and the application has multitude of requirements.
- A transparent and general solution for P2P connectivity requires agreement on gateway conventions (NATs, firewalls) that may become standards.
- IPv6 by itself will not be the solution.
- The common means for traversing the gateways involve a third party. The solutions work well, but scaling them to many thousands or millions of users may be difficult.

- There is a noticeable convergent to a set of protocols. The common denominator is HTTP. It provides the interface to calls to TCP and UDP. The trend is to use XML, with more and more SOAP included, running on top of HTTP.

Communication is at the heart of P2P computing, and it is the foundation of other services that are the subject of the next few chapters.

Chapter 7
Next, Name and Find Everyone and Everything

The Internet is not a static entity. Communication messages are going from place to place as content migrates through distribution and downloading. Content can be reproduced through replication and caching. Computers, or nodes on the net, are connected one moment and gone in next. Users move around between a desktop system, a mobile laptop, or a wireless device. And with all this activity, the P2P services need to keep track of where everything is, how to find it, and what to call it. In this chapter, I will introduce the basic technologies and techniques employed by P2P applications to name things, to find out about resources and objects, and to help organize the collection of these details.

Even though new P2P solutions need to be invented, developers still return to existing protocols whenever they exist.

The Name Space Issue

In Chapter 6 we saw that the domain name system (DNS) is responsible for translating names to IP addresses on the Internet. When there were a small number of users on the Internet, one list mapped the names of the computers to their IP addresses. With the incredible growth of the Internet, it has become impractical to maintain one central list. The DNS servers that have copies of the name-to-address translation tables are now scattered all over. Thousands of DNS servers are organized in a hierarchical manner.

The DNS works fine as long as the computers have fixed, permanent IP addresses. But we know most of our computers – the desktops, laptops, and PDAs – do not have permanent addresses. In many cases they don't have routable addresses, since they belong to the private range of IP addresses. Even under these circumstances, the DNS scheme works fine in the client-server model (when the servers have a permanent address). Only the clients make requests, and their requests go directly to servers – not to other clients.

In general, the DNS system breaks down when it comes to P2P computing (Shirky, 2000). If you get assigned an IP address dynamically, it might take days before your name-address mapping is known across the vast array of DNS servers. It simply does not work when a peer is looking for another peer.

The fundamental weaknesses of DNS, as far as P2P is concerned, is that is was designed for static addresses and it cannot deal with intermittent connectivity, even when the address is known.

You read in Chapter 6 about solutions the P2P developers found for dealing with dynamic addresses and with private addresses, even traversing firewalls and NATs. Each solution fits a set of circumstances that its application addresses. We do not have a general solution.

Now we also see that the traditional tool for naming and namespaces on the Internet is not adequate for P2P applications. Even when we have a way of finding a peer's current address, and a method to start the communication between the two peers, the DNS is still not the right tool for mapping names to addresses. DNS is not responsive enough to the dynamic and intermittent presence of peers engaged in P2P computing. But no standard exists (other than DNS), and so developers came up with their own.

Perhaps the most recognized situation where the application takes the users outside of DNS is Instant Messaging (IM). People exchanging instant messages are registered with the application with a name unique to that environment. When a user connects, his or her name is mapped to the current IP address. Direct exchanges between the connected peers can now proceed.

There is another significant difference between DNS names and those created for IM applications: DNS names machines. The name it gives points to a computer. Yes, there is a user name, but it is attached to a host (computer) name. Many of the new naming schemes separate the user's identity from the physical location of a host device. This separation offers powerful capabilities for P2P:

- Users have an identity that is mobile as they are. The context that defines the user is carried over to whichever device is the vehicle for connecting to the net. This mobility gets our network presence a step closer to real life. The analogy here is our use of the telephone; it does not matter which one we happen to dial from.

- P2P naming schemes need to extend to resources other than computers and people. The independence of names from a physical location allows the application to follow a resource as it moved around. A reference to a file may switch to another location if the current host disconnects. A computation may proceed on another platform when the current one becomes unavailable. References and discovery can focus on content, not on a path and a location.

Replacing DNS with new naming mechanisms enables us to name all kinds of objects, and facilitates the flexibility of mobility – both for users and the resources on the net. This is very important.

The freedom from the reliance on DNS is a central component of the decentralization of computing on the net. Moving computing from the center to the edges is what P2P advances. The non-DNS naming allows greater independence from the network of servers that comprise the DNS.

P2P naming is based on rules, or protocol. It is not a mapping to a physical location, such as a host computer. This mapping takes place when an IP address is associated with the name of the object or the user. And, in the P2P world, this association is transient.

There are different solutions to P2P naming schemes, which is not necessarily a good thing. Every P2P environment or application defines its own name space.

Some of the schemes may not scale well because they do not lend themselves to a hierarchical structure. This is not a problem for applications designed for small groups or modest-size online communities.

The multitude of name spaces created by P2P environments may never converge into one. If it does, it may suffer from some of the weaknesses that afflict the DNS today. Fragmentation on the edges on the net is consistent with the type of P2P application we can envision. But it is reasonable to hope that the P2P developer community will agree on a set of conventions – even a protocol – for naming. This will be most helpful for integration of applications and for users who participate in several P2P applications.

There might be a basis for such a protocol that describes how names can be formed, yet offer enough flexibility for developers to specify the name the way they choose. XML has the "xmlns" (XML Namespace) key word that allows it to assign an Internet-wide unique namespace identifier. The identifier is unique since it is an URL, and it points to some (possibly fictitious) document. For example, we can create a tag called "name," whose content is a user name. In its simplest form it might look like this:

```
<x xmlns:sp="http://www.p2pwg.org/namespace"
...
      <sp:name> alice </sp:name>
      <sp:name> bob </sp:name>
      <sp:name> carol </sp:name>
...
```

The prefix "sp" means nothing; it is just shorthand to the full name which is the URL. And the URL does not need to point to an existing document. It only serves as a unique identifier, or a unique name for the namespace. Of course, the content may be much richer than just the first names given in the example, or it may be accompanied by other attributes.

A P2P application or community may have their XML namespace. The name of this identifier offers a structure of "namespace—name" that allows a user to participate in more than one application or environment.

We may not have a universal naming convention with this approach, but at least it will be possible to tell integrated environments how to process names that come from the other list.

Group Identities

P2P computing technologies enables both strong, local autonomy by the user, and permits the easy formation of groups and communities. These two seemingly contrasting attributes coexist in the P2P world because, unlike the image we have of a "traditional" online group, P2P groups tend to be self-governed, self-organized, and decentralized.

The P2P group has an identity. It encapsulates a set of access permissions, policies, and memberships – all of which can change in time. Membership in a group implies specific relationships with other members. These relationships may involve resource sharing, access, and a level of trust.

It is convenient to name a group.[1] It is an entity, or an object, that offers an efficient way of managing properties, permissions, authentication, and authorization for a group of users. In practice, the member's name should not include the group's name. Users may belong to multiple groups, and membership in a group should not be assumed to be permanent. The group, as an entity, manages the list of its members.

In some aspects it is advantageous to think of the "group" as a user. For example, Groove allocates encryption and authentication keys to the group. Of course, it means these keys can be used by all the group's members. The use of the group-wide keys allows easy broadcast of encrypted messages, and it allows for a simple recovery of undelivered messages.

When a group has a name and some user properties, it becomes easy to manage policies, permissions, access control, authentication, and trust.

Examples of P2P Naming Schemes

Let us examine some of the companies featured in this book addressed the naming issue for their environment and applications.

Endeavors:

Magi uses what it calls "buddy" names to represent identities of peers. The Buddy Manager is equivalent to a Magi dynamic DNS. The identity is really a pair of character strings separated by an apostrophe. The first string is the user name, and the second represents a location. For example, Alice'Office, Bob'Laptop, and Carol'Palm, are all legitimate magi names. A buddy list contains all the other peers with whom you, as a Magi user, can connect.

Within this buddy list you can belong to a number of different groups. The association with a specific group defines what resources are being shared among the members and how the access permissions are set. This is an example of the group identity described above.

The buddy manager tracks the users' locations and the presence of other peers. Knowing when peers are on- or off-line permits communications and transfers to be triggered at appropriate times. When a peer starts a session, it connects to a dynamic DNS: a server that is always online. This Buddy Manager is really a specialized peer that uses a SQL database to

[1] I use "group" and "community" interchangeably here.

manage the buddy list. In addition to providing directory services, it is also used for authentication of peers and support of store-and-forward.

Escher:

In the user environment of WebRiposte, an Escher application, the peer is really the workstation that sits in a fixed location. The application synchronizes data in multiple branches of the organization.

Thus a name (and really an identifier) is constructed as a string, which, conceptually, looks like:

[site-ID/group-ID/node-ID]

This name is bound to an IP address. The address is known (local, private) or is found via DNS. This is how it is done for user names.

A WebRiposte object (stored content) also has a name. The object's name consists of a string name and a unique ID. It also carries the node ID, a date/time field, and a version number. An object name conflict can occur when a new name is created while some of the nodes are disconnected. The message server is responsible for version control resolution. This is how:

- If all agree, one of the objects with the same name is selected.
- Sometimes, objects with same name can continue to exist. This occurs when it is known that the nodes where these objects reside are never connected at the same time. The advantage of this circumstance is that other nodes can access the object even when a host that stores this object is disconnected.
- If the name conflict cannot be resolved, then the object gets assigned a new version number.

When the application looks for an object that has multiple instantiations, each with its version number, it accesses (by default) the one with the lower version number. The application can still be directed to look at other versions. Another means of locating the desired version is through indexing. It is possible to index the objects by any attribute, including the body of the message or file.

Avaki:

Note how security is built into the construction of names.

Avaki implements a three-level naming system. At the highest level, users refer to objects using human-readable strings, called *context names*. Context objects map context names to Avaki object identifiers, which are location-independent identifiers that include an RSA public key.[2] Since they are location independent, the identifiers by themselves are insufficient for communication. Therefore, an identifier is mapped to an *object address* for communication. An object address is a physical address (or set of addresses in the case of a replicated object) that contains sufficient information to allow other objects to communicate with it. The address is likely to be an <IP address, port number> pair.

The context names are organized into a classic directory structure called a context space. Context spaces support operations that lookup a single string, return all mappings, add a mapping, and delete a mapping. A typical context space has a well-known root context, which "points" to other contexts, forming a directed graph.

Every Avaki object is assigned a unique and immutable identifier upon creation. The basic identifier data structure consists of a sequence of variable length binary string fields. Four of these fields are reserved by the system. The first three play a key role in the identifier-to-object address binding mechanism:

- The first field, labeled the *domain identifie*r, is used in the dynamic connection of separate Avaki systems.
- The second field is the *class identifie*r, a bit string uniquely identifying the object's class within its domain.
- The third field is an *instance number* that distinguishes the object from other instances of its class.
- The fourth field is reserved for security purposes. Specifically, it contains a public key for encrypted communication with the named object.

Associations between identifiers and object addresses are called *binding*s, and are implemented as three-tuples. A binding consists of an identifier, an object address, and a field that specifies the time at which the binding

[2] RSA public key is a specific implementation of the public key method for encryption and authentication. The concept is explained in Chapter 9.

becomes invalid (including never). Bindings are entities that can be passed around the system and cached within objects.

Groove:

This is another example where security features are an integral part of how a name and an identity are constructed. The Groove scheme also reflects the multiple facets of our lives, and it facilitates the mobility of users.

With Groove, a user may assume multiple identities. Many people will use Groove with different business and social groups. Groove promotes the use of different "personas." A user can have a "work" identity, an "online game" identity and a "family" identity all in one place. Technically, a single account in Groove supports multiple user names.

Many people will use Groove with a desktop, a laptop, a home machine, a work machine, and more. Users do not need to manually keep each of them synchronized. Groove automatically keeps the content of all spaces on all machines in synch. In addition, if someone has spaces shared among several computers and one is lost, damaged or stolen, they will not have lost the content and history of their spaces.

In Groove, a name of an object does not have to be unique. In fact, the idea is to have objects replicated on the members' shared spaces on their own computers. Though the name is not unique, since it is a COM object it has a Global Unique Identifier, or GUID.

Mangosoft:

Mangosoft, with its focus on secure Internet file service and web caching for enterprises, makes use of the established infrastructure. The initial representation of a user is created from their Internet email address. This is then used to transmit a unique join link in an invitation message containing a secret key that belongs only to that user. Once this join-key is used to join a drive, it cannot be used again, so other people cannot impersonate the user later.

Each Mangomind Drive maintains its own unique user list. Each entry in the user list has a unique human-readable username, the user's public key, and a unique ID, which is used for all user-related file system operations (setting file ownership, determining access permissions, and so on).

This is separate from how the other objects of interest, memories and disk space are addressed. One unique aspect of Mangosoft's technology is its P2P directory scheme. Objects comprising the memory or disk storage across the systems are managed as a unified shared virtual memory, and treated as a large, coherent cache with dynamic data movement between systems. This coherent cache actually includes the object directory itself, resulting in a fine-grained, truly P2P distributed directory structure. Over time, both the directory pages and the objects they represent are naturally distributed across the systems based on usage patterns.

Engenia:

Engenia's Collaboration Services Platform treats all entities, resources, and users as objects that must be uniquely accessible. Engenia uses a GUID convention for creating unique object identifiers and ensuring uniqueness. These identifiers are used to discover entities and to communicate with them. Everything in the system must have a uniquely discoverable and addressable name. The objects may move around the system, and therefore require identifiers that are not mapped into the IP address where they were first found or defined. For that reason, Engenia does not use conventional URLs to name its entities.

Users, too, are represented by objects that are named by GUIDs. The user-object may also point to other GUIDs – users or resources of interest to the user. Currently, there is no binding between character-based names to the GUIDs.

NextPage:

The NXT system supports two types of names.

- "Relative pathname" is a location-dependent URL-like string. It points to the nearest node running NXT, as in:
  http://nearestnode.Company.com/resource1/resources1.1/...
  The rest of the pathname points to the location of resources within that node. A special type of such a resource is a link to another machine. This mechanism allows a peer to reach resources beyond those of the nearest neighbor. This method specifies a location of a resource.
- "Absolute identifier" is constructed according to the Digital Object Identifier, or DOI convention (see http://www.doi.org). The identifier is persistent, even when the location associated with it may change. An identifier may look like this string:
  10.1000/123456...
  The string up to the first slash is the prefix. It defines a domain, within which the domain owner is free to choose unique names by any convention.

Useful Technologies

As with existing protocols, there are a couple of software technologies that are particularly useful for P2P computing. They play a special role in the P2P services described in this chapter. The two technologies are:

- Metadata
- Intelligent agents

What follows is a short discussion of the technologies' relevance to P2P.

Metadata for P2P Services

Metadata is data about data. More precisely, it is structured data about data. Naming through XML namespace, as described above, is an application of metadata. You can include metadata with HTML, but with XML the tool is much more powerful. The namespace feature fits very well with the notion of independent communities defining their own vocabulary. The application can allow a collective of collaborators to decide what objects or elements to define and what attributes to assign to them.

The strength of XML, as far as metadata goes, is also its weakness. With the freedom for developers to define their own schema– the set of rules that tell the reader program how to process the content associated with the tags – applications may document different sets of items and attributes. The XML Schema, the XML language for describing and constraining the content of XML documents, allows machines to carry out the rules set up by the creator of the document. But the metadata may not be what another application or another user is looking for. For example, if there was an agreement of what attributes a user name carries with it, then it wouldn't matter if the metadata layout was different. XML allows us to figure it out. There is useful work being done in defining a standard set of elements, which is useful for describing resources on the web. Most notable is the Dublin Core Metadata Initiative, or DCMI.[3]

The obvious usages of metadata in P2P computing involve discovery and search. In particular, the use of metadata can be a powerful tool in identifying relevance of content. With the appropriate metatags it is possible to reduce language-related ambiguity that results from scanning

[3] For more information about DCMI go to http://dublincore.org/ and http://www.ietf.org/rfc/rfc2413.txt

text. A "category" (or "field" or "discipline") tag can tell us if the word "pipe," for instance, relates to software, plumbing, or an oil-drill.

Metadata can be used to aid in describing locations and resources on the network, as well as aiding in locating and filtering information.

Here is an example of taking XML and its metadata one step further:

Engenia's platform is designed around what they call *Adaptive XML*. Adaptive XML is an object definition that ties the logic associated with the business to the data it is expected to manipulate. Adaptive XML is a living entity, not a static data construct. It has the ability to convey data just as traditional XML can. But it also allows an entity, via a script, to perform operations on itself and other entities. Adaptive XML is useful in developing collaborative systems because its elements can have the opportunity to adapt to their environment. The Adaptive XML elements can change their own properties or evolve complex behaviors in conjunction with other objects. In a sense, the Adaptive XML structure is the metadata that is conveyed throughout the system.

Metadata is a powerful tool for naming, discovery, and search. XML is the right tool for delivery of metadata on behalf of P2P infrastructures and applications. The effectiveness of the use of metadata is reduced by the lack of agreement on what items to describe, and how to describe them. As metadata schemas become more common among communities and disciplines, our use of resources on the Internet will be much more effective.

For more on metadata and P2P, see (Brickley & Dornfest, 2001).

Intelligent Agents in P2P Computing

The second useful software technology, which fits so nicely into the dynamic and ever-changing landscape of P2P computing, is the technology of intelligent software agents (referred to as "agents" from here on).

An overview[4] on software agents states: "We have as much chance of agreeing on a consensus definition for the word 'agent' as AI researchers have of arriving at one for 'artificial intelligence' itself – nil!"

[4] "Software agents: an overview", by Hyacinth S. Nwana from BT Labs, see - http://www.labs.bt.com/projects/agents/publish/papers/review1.htm .

My definition of a software agent is this: it is a software component, local or remote, static or mobile, active or reactive, that accomplishes tasks on behalf of its user.

There are important attributes that apply to agents; some of them are whether agents collaborate with each other or whether they modify their behavior through "learning." There are many more, but here I only want to scratch the surface and invite you to explore more opportunities for use of intelligent agents in P2P applications.

Agents are synergetic with distributed computing models. We have multiple systems, often connected by a changing and not-so-reliable network, which must continue to operate and make decisions. Agents can help deliver the level of autonomy that is required.

What kind of operations will benefit from the presence of agents? Here are some examples:

- A distributed function that relies on information and/or action of individual nodes. For example, each node is to report the level and frequency of communication it receives. In this case, the agent is local, static, and reactive.
- Tracking and reporting of changing data that the node is exposed to. For example, some monitoring function aggregates available shared resources on the network (the agent is active). Or, the node responds to a query about what resources it has available for use by the application. The agent is local and static (the agent is reactive).
- Aggregate information across the network. For example, an agent may create a list of all nodes that have a copy of specific version of a document so that it can be updated by newer versions. A mobile agent going from one node to the next can accomplish this function. In this case, the agent is also static and active.
- Event-driven notification. For example, a user needs four other nodes to be available at the same time. An agent, placed on each of the other nodes, tells an agent on my computer when the remote host is available, and sends another message when it is not. The local agent figures out how many other nodes are available simultaneously. This agent is remote, static, and reactive.

These types of operations by agents can be applied in several services that are relevant to P2P networks. Some of them are:

- **Discovery.** Agents can assist in discovery of presence of peers, resources on active nodes, content, etc.
- **Search.** "Search assistant" agents may reside on the network's nodes and respond to queries from authorized nodes.
- **Security.** A specific implementation of an agent may monitor communication patterns in order to alert the network in case of an attempt to hack the system or to start a denial-of-service attack.
- **Update directories.** Other search agents may roam the network looking for specific information or updating directories when related files have been modified, replaced, or deleted.
- **Monitor.** Agents can monitor traffic, bandwidth, performance, usage, and more. They can act on behalf of administration and accounting functions, or for the purpose of benchmarking and optimization of resource utilization.

The degree to which agents are used in current P2P implementations varies greatly. In Chapter 4, FIPA proposed that the whole architecture be based on agent technology. Sometimes it is difficult to tell if the interaction between objects can be seen as typical behavior for agents. It comes down to terminology and definitions. It is likely you will come across software components that perform these and similar "agent" operations, yet their creators do not refer to them as agents.

There are many other possibilities and opportunities for employing software agents. It is true that agent technology is not the only approach that works. It is certainly a technology that promises to be very helpful to P2P applications.

Finding out about things: Search, Discovery, and Directories

In P2P networks, nodes, users, and resources come and go. The transient and dynamic landscape makes it necessary to have an efficient way to find out about resources at any given time. Discovery services currently used tend to be pre-configured. This is the solution implemented for name servers (DNS, DHCP protocols) and other directories, such as LDAP (see below) in enterprise networks.

A fixed configuration file or a database with search results is inadequate. The infrastructure has to support frequent queries for discovery, and it must provide the answers fast, or else they won't be valid.

Discovery, in the P2P context, includes the protocols and the mechanisms by which peers and P2P applications become aware of the resources and services they need. Directories are where the findings of the discovery are placed.

What are the things that need to be discovered in a P2P environment?

- **Resources.** What is out there that my application needs?
- **Presence.** Who is connected? Who is a member (even if not connected)?
- **Content.** What are the topics discussed by this group?

These are just examples of the kind of entities a peer may wish to discover.

In particular, resource discovery is fundamental to P2P. The resources peers are looking for vary by the application, the group, or the community to which they belong.

Why do we need search capabilities that are specific to P2P?

The current search method we all use employs a massive collection of servers that store all the information they have indexed from all over the Internet. These static engines that send crawlers do not revise data fast enough, and, more importantly, don't even reach the peer systems. The well-known search engines search web servers. They are not likely to poke around our desktops (nor are they permitted to).

So, one reason for P2P search techniques is that peers need to search within the P2P network. Peer network and P2P search can also assist the traditional search engines. The peers are able to find information the large search engines' crawlers cannot reach. Endeavors takes advantage of this idea (see below).

There are two aspects of searching where P2P can be useful. First, peers may conduct the search itself. There are circumstances when this method is more accurate and practical. Second, the servers containing the search engine database can communicate as peers. The database is distributed and replicated in a way that will eliminate the single-point-of-failure risk.

Discovery and search capabilities are not new to Internet users or to network applications. But we see that both need to be tailored to the special needs of P2P.

The P2P developers are still improving the techniques for both discovery and search. We know that some mechanisms work well for small groups but will not scale to very large networks of peers (Gnutella is one example). Most solutions for large networks rely on querying and searching via hops from one peer to the next. This approach is susceptible to interference by third parties. Much of this area is still a work in progress. However, we do know that the use of known protocols and metadata can improve quality and speed of search and discovery.

It may be interesting to note the difference between a *discovery* and a *search*. The answer may be somewhat arbitrary. But here is a way to find out.

Whether something is a Discovery or a Search depends on how we ask the question:

When we want to know *what* is out there, that's discovery. For example, "Who's currently connected in my P2P network?" or "What music categories does Joe have on his system?"

When we want to know where *something* is, we conduct a search. For instance, "Tell me who has the group photo from last week's picnic?" or "Show me the weather in the San Francisco Bay area."

Of course, we are not likely to make these queries in plain English.

The lines between discovery and search can be blurred indeed when searches become more sophisticated. For example, OpenCola adds "similarity" and scores "relevance" of our search. Is this when Search becomes Discovery?

Directories are repositories for information. In P2P networks, we need to consider distributed directories, as well as those that reside on servers. Some P2P infrastructures include directory services. These services provide the means and the interface for fetching information from the directories, or updating the user's data. The functionality of the directories improves when they interface through a standard protocol (see LDAP below), because different applications can then access the same data.

Protocols

We referred to existing protocols aiding in performing P2P services whenever possible. For discovery, there was UDDI (introduced in Chapter 6). There is more to say about UDDI, Web services, and P2P. A popular protocol for directory services is Lightweight Directory Access Protocol, or LDAP. It is introduced below.

More about UDDI

Universal Description, Discovery and Integration, or UDDI, defines specifications for the discovery of information and for publishing one's own information. It was designed to support Web services between businesses. The goal of UDDI is to provide means for building a registry where businesses can find out about other businesses. In particular, the registered company publishes information about its product offerings and Web services it offers. The result is a directory that is similar to the white and yellow pages of a phone book, supplemented by "green" pages that contain information about the company's Web services. UDDI is based on XML and uses SOAP to allow one application to interact with others.

The three basic functions that UDDI users can perform are:

- **Publish.** The user or company register the Web services they offer.
- **Find.** A user, or an application, can find Web services offered by others.
- **Bind.** An application can connect to, and interact with, a Web service it has found.

You can learn more about UDDI from http://uddi.org. The target audience for UDDI is businesses seeking services from other businesses while offering their own. But the functionality of UDDI can be imported to a P2P network, where a peer replaces the business as the user of the service. The same UDDI specification allows peers to register and publish. What the peers publish need not be a Web service. It may be content, or a list of files, or any other resource and service. The scope of the UDDI service can be the P2P network, and not the whole Internet. The binding capability specified by UDDI can be used in connecting P2P applications that are published through the UDDI-generated directory.

LDAP

LDAP is a Lightweight Directory Access Protocol. It is a lightweight (less code, less complexity) version of an access protocol that was previously defined as a part of the X.500 standard for network-based directory services. The LDAP protocol enables anyone to locate organizations, individuals, and other resources such as files and devices in a network, whether on the Internet or on a corporate intranet. LDAP only specifies the interface protocol to the directory and does not specify how the actual directory is implemented. It is an open standard and platform-neutral. An application that uses one implementation of LDAP can interact with any other LDAP interface. For these reasons, LDAP is fast becoming the *de facto* directory protocol for corporate intranets as well as the Internet. Most middleware products for networks support LDAP.

There are additional features that make LDAP appealing to P2P environments:

- The LDAP design allows for the directory to be distributed. The directory is replicated on multiple servers, or peers, in the P2P case. LDAP has a mechanism for periodically synchronizing the replicated versions.
- LDAP includes security measures within the directory. Two security elements are employed: Authentication and access control. The authentication established the user's identity and the credentials associated with it. These credentials specify the level and type of access the user can have with the directory.

The popularity of LDAP on network platforms and its features make it a strong candidate for use in P2P as a tool-defining interface to directories.

Discovery and Search Practices

This section contains a sample of usages and implementations of discovery, directories, and searches that are typical for P2P.

First, let's look at discovery and directories:

For **Endeavors,** discovery involved finding out the presence and location of other peers, or buddies. The peer will first look for a Magi directory service. If the directory is not available, the peer will rely on cached information from previous sessions. If all fails, the peer will broadcast to the local network in an attempt to find other buddies. Once buddies are located they can provide information about their system's capabilities, so that it will not be asked to perform functions for which it is not suitable. The discovery process uses standard protocols, and the UDDI infrastructure, in particular.

WebDAV, introduced in Chapter 6, is another protocol that allows publishing and searching. Magi uses WebDAV for discovery of resources.

The architecture proposed by the **Global Grid Forum** advocates the use of LDAP to define a standard resource information protocol and associated information model. The Globus Toolkit's Meta Directory Service (MDS) defines and implements a secure, scalable architecture for discovering and monitoring resources in a distributed environment. A large, distributed collection of generic information providers allows access to information about individual entities, via local operations or gateways to other information sources. Information is structured in terms of a standard data model, taken from LDAP: an entity is described by a set of "objects" comprised of typed attribute-value pairs.

Higher-level services collect, manage, index, or respond to information provided by one or more information providers. Aggregate directory services facilitate resource discovery and monitoring for communities, by implementing both generic and specialized views and search methods for a collection of resources. Other higher-level services can use this information or obtain information directly from providers for the purposes of brokering, monitoring, and troubleshooting.

Interactions between higher-level services (or users) and providers are defined in terms of two basic protocols: a soft-state registration protocol for identifying entities participating in the information service, and an enquiry protocol for retrieval of information about those entities, whether via query or subscription. A provider uses the registration protocol to notify higher-level services of its existence; a higher-level service uses the enquiry protocol to obtain information about the entities known to a provider, which it merges into its aggregate view. Integration with the Grid Security Infrastructure (GSI) provides for authentication and access control to information.

This architecture has a number of desirable features. The separation between information retrieval, on the one hand, and discovery and monitoring, on the other, means that a wide variety of discovery and monitoring strategies can be supported. This is done by implementing different tradeoffs between query language expressiveness, information timeliness, and cost, and without modifying the various resources and services that comprise the Grid. The distributed architecture and use of soft-state registration makes the system highly fault-tolerant: a component failure or network partition affects only those components that fail or are separated from the observer.

Read more about MDS in (Czajkowski et al, 2001).

Distributed P2P searching presents technical challenges that affect the user experience. **NextPage** addresses the issue of delivering search results corresponding to what the user has actually asked for.

All of us have had the experience of typing in a query and receiving thousands of links – of which only a few are relevant. P2P searching makes this problem worse unless it is done correctly. The idea behind a more targeted search is to focus on the concept that is being searched.

For example, suppose you are a university research librarian with access to multiple departmental libraries in astronomy, biology, chemistry, and a dozen others. If someone were to ask you for references about the appearance of stars in classical mythology (and you behaved like most distributed search engines), you might request the top twenty hits from each of the departmental libraries. You might receive a few relevant references, but they are usually buried amid hundreds of irrelevant hits from libraries that have little to offer on this topic (such as chemistry, music, and zoology).

The issue described above arises because the information comes from multiple sources. A correctly designed search would take the steps necessary to treat the collection of libraries as a single information source, prioritizing across the entire collection and therefore taking the most results from the source that has the most to offer. In this case, it would be the library for classical literature. To do this correctly requires a multiple-pass P2P search protocol, which is how the NXT Search module works.

Endeavors has taken another interesting approach with Magi in order to help peers improve search operations. Traditional search engines use crawlers to collect and refresh information. The approximate time elapsed between visits to a particular page or site may be any period between 24 hours and 60 days. Magi can index the sharable information on a peer and push it to the repository of major search engines. This is an interesting way of combining P2P services with a server-based application. The peer files are partitioned to private, public, or shared directories. This designation is respected when performing indexing for search engines.

Much of the focus of **OpenCola** is to seek relevance in searching the Internet. It is a more detailed description of the theory and practice, as implemented in OpenCola Folders (see also the OpenCola section in Chapter 5).

With OpenCola Folders ("Folders" from here on), individual users can create Internet-searching strategies suited to their particular needs.

The search results can remain "fresh." Folders can update the search returns with a single mouse-click, and it is trained to sharpen or broaden the search's focus as the user's needs change. Relevant resources are brought to the user's attention; irrelevant resources are ignored.

Here is how it works:

Folders can be described as a host for a series of single-purpose search engines. Each document (text file, movie, piece of audio) in your Folders library can search the OpenCola network for similar documents. These searches are performed in collaboration with other OpenCola agents on the network. Because each document searches for a limited set of similar documents, searching and discovery are faster and more efficient, and searches never have to be reconfigured. Whenever you want to initiate a search, the search criteria are already in place.

Folders can cooperate in conducting their searches and aggregate their efforts. The application builds many small, nimble networks that cooperatively search for relevant resources. At the same time, each document you place in your OpenCola Folders library is published to the OpenCola network. As such, it is available to other OpenCola Folders users who are looking for documents.

Also, the search engine can be trained. Initially, this training is automatic and proceeds without input from the user. In the final product the user will be able to "reward" Folders when it retrieves subjectively good documents, reinforcing its propensity for locating similar documents.

To aid in locating the right kind of document, Folders can use a variety of` "similarity engines" in their searches. To actually retrieve documents from the network, Folders uses a fetcher that is built into the system. This basic architecture allows for much variation and for many additional programs (for instance, chat programs that search chat "histories" online to find the kind of conversations you'd like to join).

Folders is a plug-in program designed to work with the OpenCola kernel, or Clerver, that was described in Chapter 5.

Folders itself contains components that perform specific functions related to OpenCola Folders operation:

- A relevance queue that stores found material and searches for new documents that match the user's criteria.
- A parser of web pages that retrieves new links for the relevance queue.
- A similarity engine that compares metadata of found documents with that of the document which launched the search and scores for similarity.

Folders supports two methods of searching:

- Document search "spiders" the OpenCola network looking for documents whose metadata is similar to that of the document that launched the search.
- Keyword search allows you to type a keyword or phrase commanding OpenCola Folders to search the Web for documents containing the string.

Folders follows links present in a document that was found. But, more importantly, the metadata in the document is assessed as to its similarity to the searching document (keyword search checks against the string searched itself). The application then calculates a relevance score that is placed as a "suggestion" in the Suggestion pane. The user can accept the find by moving the reference to the "My Library" pane. A document that is added to the library can initiate further searches for similar documents (documents that stay in the suggestions pane are deleted). This is the process by which the search is fine–tuned, and it is how the search engine is being trained.

Folders, as an OpenCola plugin, can locate peers. It can find documents the peers have and it even adds to the other peer's own OpenCola Folders. This way, peers can also be rated for relevance.

For Folders, a document can be any one of numerous file types – text, images, music, multimedia, and so on.

One of the appealing by-products is that the relevance score can be applied towards the creation of communities of peers with shared interests.

In Closing

There is tedious work to be done before we can get to the more satisfying job of creating and running applications that use the resources available at the edges of the web. These are the details without which we cannot do the more exciting stuff.

All entities and objects need to have names, and the names must be unique within some environment. We have to have a reliable way to map the names to addresses or locations, and we simply need to know how to establish communications with them.

We learned that existing network protocols might be borrowed by and employed by P2P practitioners. But applying these protocols must be tailored to the needs and the characteristics of a P2P network.

The few examples presented here demonstrate the wide variety of naming schemes in use by P2P developers. This is a challenge for the users or developers who try to communicate across communities that employ different naming mechanisms. It is a challenge for integration of applications where names are constructed according to different rules.

And, most significantly, peer computing opens up new opportunities in which to enhance the scope of discovery and meaningful searches on the web.

Chapter 8
Then, Peers Wish to Stay Connected

One of the least glamorous aspects of software projects is maintenance: what needs to be in place and the tasks that need to be done to keep things going. This is particularly important for P2P computing, given the premise of the concept.

P2P networks harness resources at the edges of the net, relying on components over which the application has little or no control. The participants exercise local autonomy over their own systems, and in many circumstances the peers join and leave the network at will. Communications are carried over external networks, which are sometimes unreliable. Often, the systems on which computations are run are unknown. Content that is found may disappear or move the next time it is sought. And the list goes on.

In this chapter, you will find how the companies we are following have addressed the issues of intermittent connectivity, availability of resources, and fault-tolerance in the face of a very dynamic setting. The various topics are presented by way of solutions offered by one or more of the companies. These topics are:

- Managing intermittent presence
- Fault-tolerance
- Maintaining content coherency
- Availability of resources
- Availability of content
- Fault-tolerant use of servers
- System Management

Intermittent Presence

In this chapter, all the topics will deal with intermittent presence of peers on the network.

The Endeavors approach introduces the presence issue in a fairly generic manner.

The Magi Event Service handles most of the communication tasks for the Magi peers. It uses simple XML constructs to identify the purpose of the event. Each event contains information about its origin, time of creation, and order in a queue relative to other events from the same peer. If it is a response to another event, it will also have information regarding the request to which it is responding.

Intermittent connectivity is accepted, and Magi makes no strong guarantee for delivering all messages. As described in Chapter 6, Magi uses a store-and-forward mechanism, when available, for delayed delivery to peers who are not connected when the communication is initiated. An event, though, has a "time to live" attribute, which prevents the relay from holding onto undelivered events indefinitely (when peers have left the peer group, for example). In some cases, a short "time to live" attribute is assigned because the information will have no value if not delivered immediately (think of stock quotes, for example)

Handling intermittent connectivity is done by a combination of the event and the cache services. Three methods are available:

- Keep undelivered messages in the outbox folder. They may be sent when the intended recipient is connected.
- Route the message through another peer using the store-and-forward technique.
- Make use of a central store-and-forward capability (a server, for example).

The choice of mechanism depends on how the Magi environment is configured, and whether the event is delivered also depends on the event's "time to live" stamp. When a peer joins a Magi environment it registers, an act that triggers delivery of outstanding events addressed to the peer. Magi uses three types of folders (and files, by extension): Public, which can be accessed by all; Private, which are just that; and Shared, where specific peers are given access permissions. The joining peer will receive the messages and content according to the access permissions granted to him or her.

Fault-tolerance

Avaki implements a general approach for fault-tolerance in P2P networks. Avaki defines all the environment's entities in terms of objects.

In large distributed systems, resource failures will be the norm, not the exception. At any given time, at least some resources will be in a "failed" state. Fault-tolerance involves redundancy in time or space and thus entails higher costs with respect to resource consumption. The Avaki architecture allows users to balance their desired level of fault-tolerance with respect to costs. Thus, there are no system-wide mandated fault-tolerance policies. Instead, the services provide varying degrees of reliability and availability.

Avaki provides several mechanisms and defaults for detecting failures and recovering objects, which it does for several programming paradigms and environments. Developers can encapsulate fault-tolerance functionality into reusable software components and incorporate them transparently into user objects.

The default policy for core objects such as schedulers, classes, contexts, hosts, vaults, and files is to periodically and atomically save state updates. In the event of a crash failure, an object can be recovered based on its previously saved state. An extension of this policy is to replicate state onto multiple storage devices for higher availability. Yet another policy is to replicate critical classes. If a service or an object becomes unavailable, users' requests can be rerouted to an equivalent service. Thus, replication is used for both improved performance as well as fault-tolerance. The location of the replicated object is platform-independent. An Avaki object state can be recovered on any architecture. For example, an object running on a crashed IBM RS6000 workstation may be restarted on an Intel machine running Microsoft Windows.

With respect to resource management, host and vault objects are monitored by their respective class objects and by Collection objects. Crashed hosts and vaults are automatically removed from scheduling consideration by removing them from the appropriate collections.

Avaki allows users to incorporate their own fault-tolerance policies or use the default policies that are provided.

The Globus Toolkit's Meta Directory Service (MDS), discussed in Chapter 7, also provides a framework for addressing issues relating to intermittent presence and failure. In particular, the registration protocol allows a monitoring entity (e.g., a user or index server) to detect when a resource becomes unreachable or is otherwise unavailable. Time-to-live information associated with registration messages, and the recipient's own policies, can then be used to determine how to deal with this apparent failure. For example, the monitoring entity might decide to hand over responsibility for a task to another processor, generate additional replicas of files held by that system, wait for further news, or simply ignore the failed entity from then on.

Content Coherency and Synchronization

One of the major tasks of some P2P platforms is to ensure that messages are delivered and all peers access the same content. Here we have two solutions, from Groove and Escher, respectively:

- Groove addresses the issue for a small group setting
- Escher deals with transaction within a large organization with many locations of subgroups of peers

First, let's review the "small group" solution:

In Groove, intermittent connectivity is assumed. Members of a shared business space frequently are disconnected from the local network or the Internet. Groove allows disconnected members to continue working in a shared space, propagating all the changes made by all members when they reconnect. This keeps all members up to date even when they are not online at the same time. Groove manages this by using the Groove relay service. When members are offline, the online "sending" Groove members automatically forward their changes to a designated Groove relay service for the offline "receivers." The relay service queues the changes to forward later. When offline users reconnect to the network and establish their presence, the Groove relay service transmits all changes. All activity and content is delivered directly to the receiving user's computer and cleared from the Groove relay service queue.

In Groove, the user never has to explicitly save work in progress. Every change made in Groove – every keystroke, drawn line, activity, and gesture – is stored immediately in Groove's XML storage system. Even if the system crashes, all content is saved. There is no "save" command in Groove. In general, each peer has all the content all the time, subject to synchronization after being disconnected.

Escher delivers messages reliably to a very large and dispersed organization.

WebRiposte is installed for some large customers. The UK Post Office uses the application on about 40,000 seats, and the German postal service runs it on about 20,000. These seats are organized into hundreds of scattered branches.

Fault-tolerance in a distributed environment must be built into the architecture of the system. The system needs to manage the following:

- Temporary loss of network connectivity
- Temporary unavailability of a peer
- And the permanent loss of one or more peers

Indeed, intermittent availability of communications and peer presence is assumed to be the rule, not the exception. As an extreme example, one of the largest WebRiposte networks operates almost entirely on a transient communications infrastructure, with less than 10% of the peers connected at the same time.

In order to communicate efficiently in an environment where network connectivity may be intermittent, the communications are based on a connection-less, message-oriented protocol built on UDP. This has the advantage of providing a clear model for explicitly handling communication failures, in a best-effort message delivery fashion.

It means that WebRiposte must support the ability to detect and recover lost messages, and it must be able to handle duplicate or out-of-sequence messages. It should be noted that these issues are present even if TCP is used, although they may be more cumbersome to handle.

Another advantage to taking a message-oriented approach is recovery. If communications are interrupted while a large document or other piece of content is being transmitted from one peer to another, this transmission will be automatically resumed once communications have been reestablished, and it will restart where it left off. This is accomplished by dividing all content into reasonably small messages, which are used as the unit of transmission over the network.

In addition to handling network failures, WebRiposte must also be able to recover from the permanent loss of a peer. Such a loss can occur at any time due to hardware failure or to operational changes in the configuration of the system. In a WebRiposte network, there should always be at least one other peer who has the ability to effectively replace and recover from the loss of a peer.

This is accomplished via replication. All of the messages created by a peer are replicated to a subset of other peers in the network. This subset of peers is referred to as a replication group. A replication group is typically made up of 3 to 100 members. Each member of the replication group holds all the necessary information required to reconstitute any other member of the replication group. In order for this to work, it is necessary to replicate the transaction history, as well as any local content that the peer needs.

Thus, whenever a transaction takes place or an element of content is created or updated on a given peer, the relevant information is replicated to all members of the replication group. This replication is done via message-based communication between individual peers. A given peer does not need to know the location or identity of all members of the replication group. The replication group simply needs to be a connected sub-set of the peer topology. When a peer fails, any other peer in the replication group has the ability to take over that peer's function. And once a replacement piece of hardware becomes available, the lost peer can be recovered from any peer in the replication group. In fact, this recovery process is automatically distributed among the available peers in the replication group in order to speed recovery and to reduce the impact on any one peer.

Availability of Resources

The need to deal with the availability of resources is common to all P2P applications. It is, however, most direct for those who perform distributed computations on the Internet. Therefore, let us review how Entropia handles the uncertainties of the net.

One of the challenges in wide-area Internet computing is dealing with intermittent connectivity. A peer's machine may become disconnected from the Internet and from the Entropia servers for many reasons – the user manually disconnects the internet connection, the user shuts down or turns off the machine, or network congestion may block communication temporarily.

Internet connectivity is automatically addressed in the Entropia system. Entropia does nothing that would change the user's ability to control his or her machine. Entropia peers typically execute tasks that can last from minutes to hours. If the connectivity is restored before the job is complete, there is no disruption in job processing. If the disruption lasts longer, then the end-to-end fault-tolerance mechanism eventually will detect that the job has not been completed, and it will restart the relevant job or jobs at a different peer host.

For jobs that require a greater guarantee of completion, they may be replicated and executed on multiple peers simultaneously. The results of the redundant executions may also be aggregated or compared for security purposes.

Connecting to the Entropia system presents no problems. When a peer has started, or the connectivity of a peer machine initiated, the peer automatically contacts an Entropia server that adds its resources to the pool of available resources. When a peer disconnects for a long time, the peer is removed from the list of available resources. Because the peer initiates the connection to the server to receive tasks, this is not a problem.

In general, the P2P infrastructure strives to hide the complexity of the environment from the user. The user does not need to know (nor care) where the application is running or where the data resides. Indeed, as we see with Avaki, the infrastructure can provide recovery even when participating peers fail. Avaki will automatically migrate the execution and the data to other hosts, when such resources are available.

Availability of Content

A general problem that intermittent communications raises is the availability of content that is stored at a remote location, which may not even be part of the peer network (a web site, for example).

Escher offers a content distribution solution in their WebRiposte product. Content distribution is provided to:

- Improve availability by ensuring critical content is still available, even if the network isn't.
- Improve performance by moving content closer to where it is being used.

To improve availability, WebRiposte employs two features:

- Distributing content ahead of time to those peers who require access to the content.
- "Subscription Group." This is a special type of replication group, which is used to distribute content to a large number of peers. Content is retrieved via a standard HTTP interface. It is built into WebRiposte in a way that makes the location of the content transparent to the application.

To improve performance, WebRiposte supports dynamic caching of content as it is requested via the standard HTTP Proxy Server protocol. In this environment, WebRiposte acts as an intermediary between a local web browser and an HTTP server. The application manages a multi-level replicated cache that may be shared by multiple peers. The advantage of this is that if one peer in a replication group requests an item of content, it is immediately made available to other peers.

Intermediation – With Fault-tolerance and Performance

We saw how Groove uses the relay server to mediate the transmission of messages when peers are not connected. Here is another approach, one that is suitable for the WebRiposte application. The mechanism described here eliminates the possibility that any server is a potential single point of failure.

Each peer has a list of "virtual neighbors." Virtual neighbor definitions are used to provide both fault-tolerance and load-balancing. This is how the list is created:

You may remember, from Chapter 5, that each message server (the peer's software) is aware of correspondence servers that maintain a single cache of all the content. The message server sends an initial broadcast to all IP addresses, which have been listed under the virtual neighbor definition. This typically includes at least one IP address for each correspondence server. All of the correspondence servers that receive this initial broadcast will respond, and the message server will select one of these responses to "instantiate" the virtual neighbor definition. From this point on, until a failure or disconnect occurs, all traffic will be sent only to the instantiated address.

A "virtual neighbor" definition is used to allow any of the correspondence servers to act as the neighbor, but the protocol assures that only one correspondence server will be in this role at a time. This arrangement reduces network traffic. If that correspondence server should fail for any reason, the remote message server will automatically attempt to reestablish communications with its "virtual neighbor." This will result in one of the other correspondence servers being selected to fill this role. Thus, in general, the remote message server is not dependent on the availability of any one correspondence server; it can automatically "fail-over" to another available correspondence server if a failure occurs.

The correspondence servers, defined as virtual neighbors, often serve this function for many peers. Through random assignment of servers to peers, the connections will usually be load-balanced across the set of available correspondence servers.

System Management

The Avaki people, like most other P2P developers, put some serious thought into system management issues in a P2P network. Some of their thoughts are captured here.

System management for P2P computing is significantly different from traditional systems because there is not necessarily a single system administrator that is universally trusted. Instead, there are a large number of different administrators who manage a portion of the overall environment. Often, this system administrator is just a regular user at home.

Those who need to manage domains with multiple systems need a number of tools – to add user identities, add hosts, add vaults, shutdown hosts and vaults, set access control lists, list attributes, update attributes, check system status, analyze why a particular object is not responding, perform group management for users, and so on.

Avaki has created a number of such tools that help give a quick view of what's going on in the system. Such a status monitor can be very helpful in improving availability and optimizing resource utilization in very large networks.

P2P networks that are geographically fragmented can be organized into *domains*. These domains can operate independently, or they can be linked together. The domains can be linked to allow for communications, and they can transfer information and responsibilities at relatively high levels. For example, domains in different time zones may transfer an application from one domain to another, so the resources will be used when systems are likely to be otherwise idle. At times, it will make sense to join domains together to form a larger domain.

Avaki has some tools that facilitate this level of system management. This is an area that will surely receive more attention as P2P networks become larger, and as more complex applications are attempted.

Lessons, Observations

A number of the solutions described in this chapter advance the idea that the more transparencies we have, the more usable the P2P network is. Users, content, and objects move around. When we need a resource, we don't care where it is located, or if it is the original or a replica. Avaki summarized these desired transparencies in the architecture overview submitted to the P2P Working Group. Since most have to do with availability and fault-tolerance, it is worth repeating here:

- *Access*. The mechanism used for a local call is the same as for a remote call.
- *Location*. The caller does not need to know where the object is located.
- *Failure*. If the object fails, the caller is unaware. Somehow the requested service or function recovers and the request is performed.
- *Heterogeneity*. Architecture and OS boundaries are invisible. At a bare minimum, communication with objects on other architectures requires no data coercion.
- *Migration*. The caller does not need to know whether an object has moved since they last communicated with it.
- *Replication*. Is there one object or many objects behind the name? The caller does not need to know or deal with coherence issues.
- *Concurrency*. Are there other concurrent users of an object? The caller does not need to be aware of them.
- *Scaling*. An increase or decrease in the number of servers requires no change in the software. Naturally, performance may vary.
- *Behavioral*. Whether an actual object or a simulation of the object is used is irrelevant. For example, am I talking to a host object, or a virtual host object?

The manner in which companies address the issue of changing presence and availability is more dependent on the application's setting than on the application itself.

It is prudent to take preventive action, as a number of companies are doing. Content is being replicated and cached. And a number of solutions establish a third-party presence, which will always be connected, and where messages can be queued.

Most P2P networks, if not all of them, share the issue of keeping content persistent. They share the issue of gracefully continuing when peers disconnect, and updating their states when they re-join.

It is interesting to note that a few solutions to the intermittent presence of peers have led to setups that improve performance. When data is replicated, network traffic can be further optimized by selecting alternate routes. Multiple copies allow for load balancing of processing and communications.

And even though a P2P network is a fairly loose organization, the issues of fault-tolerance and availability require a system-wide view. The interplay between the peers' local autonomy and the desire to offer a reliable setting for applications will continue to be challenging. And it will certainly require more attention.

Chapter 9
Security – The Big Concern

"The three little pigs have a lot to teach us about security. The successful pig didn't have a core competency in wolf detection, he had one in house building. When the wolf is at the door, it's too late to start building a sturdy house."

Frank Prince, Forrester Research

Security issues and lack of trust are the highest ranked concerns with regard to P2P computing. Opening up your system for access by others can be disconcerting.

P2P infrastructure spans large collections of heterogeneous computing resources. With P2P technologies, users can access resources on other systems, share data and computing power, and run applications across the network. While these possibilities are attractive, users will only adopt P2P if they feel confident that it will protect the privacy and integrity of their existing resources, as well as any new resources they create through the P2P applications. Solid security is essential if P2P is to become widespread.

The security that users demand boils down to these statements:

- I need to be sure that the person I am communicating with is who he or she claims to be.
- I need to control when and how people access resources on my system.
- I need to have confidence that my messages are not read or modified en route.

In this chapter, you will read about how P2P developers address these issues with the focus on the technical aspects of the security requirements.

The more social factor, and a very important one, is that of trust between peers. Some interesting technical work is being done in the area of reputation on the net. Reputation is captured through metrics and tools for measuring and recording various behavioral characteristics of users. Access to the appropriate reputation record will help peers determine the level of trust they have in a given environment.

Why Security is such a Big Deal for P2P

Security has become a major concern on the Internet, with or without P2P. Users are connected for long periods of time – some are always connected, as is common with users of broadband. This makes them more vulnerable to attacks. Web browsers make it very easy to download and execute applications that cannot be trusted. Online commerce involves transmissions of confidential and private information.

Peer-to-peer computing adds other risk factors:

- Peers act as servers, and their systems offer services. They are available to requests made by other entities, which aren't always known.
- Peers offer resources on their systems for use by others. They need to shield that which isn't shared. They need to manage the level and mode of access.
- Most of the owners of the peer systems have no prior experience in managing a server or a service. Exposing your system to access and communications by others can have undesirable side effects, whether malicious or unintentional. Servers on the web have full-time administrators who monitor security advisories, so they can immediately patch their servers when new vulnerabilities are discovered.

The P2P infrastructure or application must address these issues to create a secure computing environment for the participating peers.

The potential risk is very real – here are some of the actions that can occur around P2P:

- Direct communications that include general file sharing may result in peers installing new applications on their host machines, before you realize what is happening. When you get an application from another domain, you don't know what side effects this new application may have on your system, nor whether it may damage your local network.
- P2P communication schemes often provide a way to tunnel through a firewall. Once a port is open to direct communication, the content that's passing through may not be monitored by the organization's firewall software.
- Without carefully constructed safeguards, you risk exposing content and files to others outside your local network and external to your organization.

- When you request and download a file from another peer, you often do it based on blind faith – you are simply assuming that the file that you receive really is the file you want.
- Some of the popular file-swapping networks don't offer sufficient protection against "guests" snooping around your system. When someone can access your browser's cookies, then they can steal your online identity.
- Instant messaging applications are, in general, an insecure communication mechanism. Messages can be easily intercepted. Despite this risk, people often use IM to exchange sensitive information. Of course, the same security risk exists in our regular email system. But IM allows us to imagine the exchange is a private conversation.

These scenarios, among others, raise concerns and alarm within the IT ranks, and justifiably so. The security risks should be a concern to the home user, too, and for the same reasons. See also (Phillips, 2001).

So, what are the basic security features that will make us feel safe in the P2P world? The bare minimum a peer needs is:

- **Authentication:** Be certain of the identity of the peer communicating with you
- **Authorization:** Control what others can do on your system
- **Data Integrity:** Have confidence that data you send or receive was not tampered with[1]

Along with the technical aspects listed above, there are social factors that can add to, or detract from, our sense of security. Trust and reputation are central to building online relationships, just as they are in our "real" world.

---

[1] Some users will make the no-tampering requirement stronger by insisting that no one can read the communication between peers; i.e., that messages are not intercepted. This is referred to as "communication security."

What is expected of a P2P security solution?

- Integrate with local security measures, and adapt to local policies. Do not compromise what's there.
- Provide a framework for access control. This is the utility through which authorization policies are exercised.
- Do not expose information on identities and data of others to unauthorized users. Delegation of tasks and authority has to respect the rules set by the owners of the identities involved. Secure data has to be protected on-the-wire if sent to another location.

Authentication: Know who you're talking to

What is authentication? Authentication is the process of verifying the identity of an entity. An authentication process consists of two steps:

- First, the *identification* step is where an identifier is presented by the entity to the security system. The shape and form of an identifier depends on the security mechanism that is used. Once authenticated, these identifiers are the basis for other services where security is important, such as access control.
- The second step is the *verification* step. This is when the entity presents evidence that the identity is correct and this evidence is validated.

Authentication makes it possible to ensure that only authorized users have access to data and applications. Authentication also enables us to check who did what (if and when the need for that arises).

There are different levels of authentication that can be performed. Of course, the more demanding the verification, the more confidence we have in the process. But a stricter authentication comes with a cost of higher overhead and added complexity. The method used for authentication should match the value of the data being accessed, and it should correspond to the type and level of access you are providing.

Another important consideration is the nature of the network environment you are in. If both you and the user wishing to be authenticated belong to a "trusting" network, then the process of authentication can be somewhat relaxed. A trusting network might be the local network at work: made up of your colleagues and safely operating behind a firewall. Of course, more caution should be exercised (and a stricter test administered) when authenticating a user who joins your network from over the Internet.

The most common way of categorizing authentication methods is by the concepts of "something you know," "something you have," and "something you are."

- Something you know is a password and a user identifier. This is a one-element method, and is considered to be a weak one. It is a particularly poor choice for a peer-to-peer application, because you must either use a different password for every peer you want to access, or you must give some peers a password they can use to impersonate you elsewhere.
- In the next level you add "something you have." In our physical world this might be a card, accompanied by a Personal Identification Number, or PIN (which is the "something you know"). In the cyber world, you might have a digital certificate and know a key, and the object you have might have a limited "time to live."
- Last, you can add "something you are." Here you get into biometrics. The something you are – that nobody else can be – may be a voice or a hand print, an iris scan, or a fingerprint. Of course, this requires equipment and greater amount of processing.

We find that the second category ("something you know" and "something you have," also called two-part authentication) is the most commonly used in P2P security systems.

Very often in P2P networks, both ends of the exchange wish to authenticate the other. Therefore, it is useful to define a process of *mutual authentication.* We describe a public key security handshake (there are others). In a highly simplified form, this is how it works:[2]

We assume the two parties have digital certificates, and both trust the Certificate Authorities (CA) that signed each other's certificates. In practice, trusting the CA means that they must have copies of the CA's certificates (which contain the CA's public keys), and that they must trust these certificates really belong to the CA.

To mutually authenticate each other, the first person (Alice) establishes a connection with the second person (Bob). To start the authentication process, Alice gives Bob her certificate. The certificate tells Bob who Alice

[2] The procedure presented here is described in (Globus, 2001).

is claiming to be (the identity), what Alice's public key is, and what CA is being used to certify the certificate. Bob will first ensure that the certificate is valid by checking the CA's digital signature to verify that the CA actually signed the certificate and that the certificate hasn't been tampered with. This is where Bob must trust the CA that signed Alice's certificate.

Once Bob has checked out Alice's certificate, Bob must make sure that Alice really is the person identified in the certificate. Bob generates a random message and sends it to Alice, asking her to encrypt it. Alice encrypts the message using her private key, and sends it back to Bob. He decrypts the message using Alice's public key. If this results in the original random message, then Bob knows that Alice is who she says she is.

Now that Bob trusts Alice's identity, the same operation must happen in reverse. Bob sends Alice his certificate; Alice validates the certificate and sends a challenge message to be encrypted. Bob encrypts the message and sends it back to Alice, and she decrypts it and compares it with the original. If it matches, then Alice knows that Bob is who he says he is.

At this point, Alice and Bob have established a connection to each other and are certain that they know each other's identities.[3]

Authorization: You Control what is Allowed on Your System

Authorization is the step that follows authentication. Authorization is the process of giving someone permission to do or to have something. That "someone" may be an object, in the P2P world.

The authorization process is less tricky than authentication, because it doesn't need to involve communications over the network. Generally, the peer who is granting the access has an *access control list* (ACL) that contains the permissions granted to other users on that system.

The function of authorization is to check the current request against the ACL. If the request falls within the parameters of permissions granted, then it may proceed. If it does not, the request is denied. When a request is denied, it is a function of the application or the environment. A denial

[3] A security-minded reader will notice that this procedure, as described above, is not secure. I have omitted the subtleties that make the SSL mutual authentication secure.

may be as simple as sending a polite notification to the requestor, or it may be as serious as calling on the security system to investigate a potential intruder.

Another mechanism for tracking permissions is by placing them within the resources themselves. This is particularly natural when all the resources are treated as objects. The object contains information on users, other objects, and groups, and whether or not they may ask it.

Authorization, in this case, will be a part of the call to that object-resource.

Access Control

We see that authorization is very closely linked to access control, though the two are not the same. Authorization, in the context of this discussion, is a specific operation. It is the act of granting or denying access in response to a specific request.

Access control, the mechanisms and policies that restrict access to computer resources, is a process. In a traditional setting of multi-user computer systems there is a system administrator who defines who can access what, and at what level. For example, a user may be allowed to access a file system with only read permission.

In our P2P world, we all have to worry about these access issues on our systems. Who can have access to our system? Which of our resources will we make available to whom? How do we restrict the times we allow others on our systems? How do we get visitors off of our system when we choose to? And the list goes on.

The users, the permissions granted to them, the resources and what we allow, are constantly changing. Someone (or something) has to manage the changes.

The P2P infrastructure or application must take care of the access issues for us. It will determine who belongs to the community and can make requests of us. The application defines the files that are shared, and what a user can do with them. And if you allow another program to run on your system, a single keystroke transfers control back to you.

Of course, this works fine in a trusting environment. It assumes that the authentication and the authorization assure good behavior by bona fide users. This is a big assumption to make, given that some P2P networks are open and huge.

What users are looking for, even in a trusting network, is a clear divide between shared resources, and their private space.

Sandboxing

One metaphor for this separation between private and shared space is a *sandbox*. As the name implies, this kind of tool defines boundaries that enclose a "sandbox," where the shared resources are. The sandbox is where others can "play," and the rest of the system is off limits.

However, the sandbox metaphor goes only so far. There are no physical boundaries placed upon a guest program, such as assigning it specific sectors on the hard drive. Sandbox software checks for adherence to rules. The main items monitored are:

- Files access, including network-connected drives. The sandbox software will verify permissions to access the files, and the operations allowed there (read, write, copy, delete).
- Operating system calls. The application, in general, is prevented from modifying any settings, including the registry.

There are different ways to implement the sandbox concept.

One way is to define the sandbox boundaries within the context of the application. The behavior of the application is intrinsically constrained (or is encapsulated somehow). For example, the application may be limited to access a set of pre-defined files. There are similar programs, referred to as *wrappers*, which play the sandbox role with Common Gateway Interface[4] (CGI) scripts.

The old Virtual Machine (VM) from the days of IBM mainframes was another mechanism that provided a general-purpose sandbox. The VM was a complete set of the software components that make up an operating system (OS) and its utilities. The sandbox, in this case, is a complete operating system sitting on top of another. We still haven't seen an implementation like that for a P2P infrastructure, but it's a way to have a secure divide between participating in a P2P network and a private desktop environment. The P2P software can occupy the secondary OS. The downside is that we can only be in one mode or the other at any given time. Switching between the two modes involves a re-boot, judging by the way this idea was done in the past. With this

---

[4] The common gateway interface (CGI) is a standard way for a Web server to pass a Web user's request to an application program and to receive data back to forward to the user.

technique for separation, applications can make system calls and modify OS settings, since a version of the OS is within its "sandbox."

The third type of sandboxing is akin to the capability provided for Java programs via the Java Virtual machine (JVM). JVM is the layer that interprets Java bytecode for a given computer platform. In Java, the sandbox is the program area and set of rules that programmers must use when creating Java code. This is done so Java applets, when sent to users with web pages, are prevented from unlimited access to resources on the system they are visiting. The programmer has to write code that conforms to the limitations set by the rules that govern this type of a sandbox. JVM mediates access to system resources and ensures that the sandbox is restricted. Recent versions of the Java Development Kit (JDK) allow for several levels of trust for programs that run in the sandbox. The more trust bestowed on the code, the more capability it has to play outside the original sandbox.

There are a few commercial products of software sandboxes. See, for example, references in (Vamosi, 2001).

In the Security Models and Practices section (see below), you will see that some sandbox-type implementations already exist. Entropia employs an application-level sandbox, like the first type described above. And Groove's shared space confines its peers in a way that isolates them from resources that are not shared. Its sandbox functionality is close to that of the JVM sandbox.

Data Integrity: No One Modified Your Transmissions

By *data integrity* we mean that the data has not been changed, destroyed, or lost in an unauthorized or accidental manner. Or, that the information has not been modified or destroyed in an unauthorized manner. Data integrity deals with the constancy of data values, not with the quality of the information that the values represent.

In the context of P2P, we are interested in two types of data integrity issues. The first (and the one applicable to all P2P applications) deals with data tampering. The second type of data integrity applies to the distributed computing applications. It deals with the confidence in returned results, and, in general, the content of the results file.

Digital signatures (see Glossary) provide a way to detect any tampering with the data. When a message is "signed" using the public key method, the recipient will know if the body of the message was modified en route. The digital signature of the received message will not verify if the latter was tampered with.

A message can be encrypted and not digitally signed.[5] If strongly encrypted, with DES for example (see Glossary), it is highly unlikely that it can be read by anyone if intercepted. If an encrypted message is intercepted and tampered with, it is unlikely the decryption will produce anything but a meaningless stream of bits and characters[6].

A data integrity service can be linked to authentication. In particular, in systems that identify both users and objects, the transmitted objects carry an identifier of their origin. When signed, the identity can only be verified if the message was not tampered with.

Recovery is not always easy, even if we can detect tampering. It is unlikely we can fix a message that was modified. We can alert the sender, and request a resend, but only if we can tell who the sender was. This might be possible if the signature part of the message remained intact (assuming public key encryption). However, once one message is intercepted, who's to say the next one will arrive untouched?

In distributed computing, there is another aspect of data integrity, which has nothing to do with what happens over the network: we ask unknown machines to perform calculations for us. How do we know we can trust the results?

The application can ensure the user cannot write or modify the file into which the computed results are written. The developer of the application will certainly not make any modifiable parts of the application visible to the user. But this is not the issue, usually. The users who volunteer, or sell time on their systems, have no reason or motivation to produce faulty results. But mischievous people, sadly, can be a huge menace.

---

[5] When speed is important, you may not want to use digital signatures, because public key encryption is very slow.

[6] At the packet level we can use IPSec to authenticate packets by the sender to ensure that the data has not been altered during transmission.

Another potential risk to the quality of the results arises from the unknown hardware on which the computations are running. Old libraries and strange floating point rounding settings may, potentially, affect some results. Such discrepancies may be crucial to the final outcome of the computation.

There are two main ways to deal with the risk of incorrect results:

- Duplicate computations. Perform the same task at least twice, for tasks sensitive to hardware and software settings.
- Attach tests to the task sent over to the peer machine. If the tests do not produce the expected results, do not use the machine.

Security Models and Practices

There are a number of specific solutions for implementing security within the P2P context. The first two represent comprehensive security frameworks built firmly into the P2P infrastructure. These are the security models from Avaki and Groove.

Security for an Object-Based Infrastructure

The Avaki developers learned from their past experience with distributed computing, that adding security to an already existing system is problematic. As a result, they have built security into the base design of the software.

Avaki, and P2P in general, allows users to access remote resources and to share content and computing power. At the same time, they make these resources available to others. Generally, the relationships with other entities on the Internet are ones of distrust. Users must feel secure and fully in control of their systems before they join a P2P activity, and this where security features and capabilities come in.

Recognizing the distrust in the environment and the need to be in control over one's system, the infrastructure must:

- **Do no harm.** The installation of Avaki at a site should not compromise that site's security policies and goals.
- **Adapt to local policies.** In concert with the first requirement, Avaki must be configurable to the security needs of different organizations.
- **Provide an access control framework.** Objects must have flexible access control mechanisms for authorizing and denying method calls.

- **Maintain and protect identities.** Avaki should not only protect identities from theft and spoofing, but also minimize the dispersion of authority that delegation causes.
- **Protect communication.** Objects must be able to communicate with guaranteed integrity and privacy as needed. Message replay must be detected and prevented, as it might indicate an attempt to intrude.

The security model for Avaki differs significantly from that of conventional systems. An Avaki "system" is really a federation of resources from multiple administrative domains; each with its own separately evaluated and enforced security policies. As such, there is no central kernel or trusted code base that can monitor and control all interactions between users and resources. Nor is there the concept of a super–user: no one person or entity controls all of the resources in a Avaki system.

Avaki programs and objects run on top of host operating systems, in user space. Therefore, they are subject to the policies and administrative control of the local OS. However, there is no requirement for the objects to trust other objects. A critical aspect of Avaki security is that the security of the overall system does not rely on every host being trustworthy. A large Avaki system will include multiple trust domains, and even within one trust domain, some of the hosts may be compromised or may even be malicious. For example, two organizations might use Avaki to share certain resources in specifically constrained ways. You wouldn't want one organization to be able subvert the other's objects through its ownership of some part of an Avaki system.

These aspects of Avaki provide the foundation for satisfying the first two security requirements (do no harm, respect local policies). For example, local policy may require Kerberos authentication, audit logs, resource usage accounting, encapsulation of critical security functionality in small, easily vetted programs, etc. Any of these features can be implemented without departing from the overall model and the minimal assumptions that are made between Avaki objects.

Access control for Avaki objects first requires that the user determine the security policy for an object by defining the object's rights and the method calls they allow. Access control is then supported via a special member function present in every object. This access control layer is Avaki's traffic cop: all method calls[7] to an object must first pass through the access control layer before the target member function is invoked. Only if the caller has the appropriate rights for the target method will the access control layer allow that method invocation to proceed.

This is how it works:

The owner of an object gives it a non-forgeable credential that lists the rights granted. When a caller invokes a method on the object, it presents the appropriate credential to the access control layer, which then checks the scope and authenticity of the credential. Alternatively, the owner of an object can semi-permanently assign a set of rights to a particular caller or group.[8] The access control layer then confirms the identity of the caller and its membership in one of the allowed groups and compares the rights authorized with the rights required for the method call. The caller can access the object if he passes these checks.

To accomplish these tasks, we need some tools.

The means for establishing identity in Avaki also address the requirement for protecting communications between objects. Every Avaki object has a public key pair. This public key is part of the object's name. Objects can use the public key of a target object to encrypt their communications to it. Likewise, an object's private key can be used to sign messages, providing authentication and non-repudiation. The integration of public keys into object names allows Avaki to avoid the need for a certification authority (although such an authority is still useful for establishing user identities). If an intruder tries to tamper with the public key of a known object, it will create a new name that is unknown.

The combined components of the security model can foster the creation of a large-scale Avaki system with multiple overlapping trust domains. Each domain can be separately defined and controlled by the users it affects. When difficult problems arise, such as merging two trust domains, Avaki provides a common and flexible context in which they can be resolved.

---

[7] In object-oriented programming, a method is a programmed procedure that is defined as part of a class and included in any object of that class. A method in an object can only have access to the data known to that object, which ensures data integrity among the set of objects in an application.

[8] We have been advocating the idea of a group as an identity. This is an example of how the notion may be applied.

We saw how security is embedded in the way objects interact. This is how it looks from the viewpoint of the triplet of authentication, authorization, and data integrity:

- Authentication is based on a single sign-on with strong authentication using public key technology and signed certificates. Users may possess multiple certificates, one for each "identity" or role they assume. The result is role-based access control. Users can create new "groups" rapidly and add and remove members from the group at their discretion without system's administrative support. A user may be a member of an arbitrary number of groups. Group membership revocation is immediate.
- Authorization and access control is based on identities and group membership. The access control module may be tailored for different object types and organizational requirements. The security modes propagate through the calls – if one call asks for encryption, for example, all the calls that follow will comply with the demand automatically.
- Data integrity is achieved through public-key cryptography based on RSA (see Glossary), and using the Open Secure Sockets Layer (OpenSSL).

So, how is the model is currently implemented?

Avaki's security model has two layers. The message layer is responsible for ensuring that communications between Avaki objects are secure. The access control layer is responsible for access control, and it determines what objects (or users) are allowed to call a particular object's methods. It also relies on the message layer for some services, such as encrypting rights certificates. The relationship between the object, the message layer, and the access control layer is depicted in Figure 9.1.

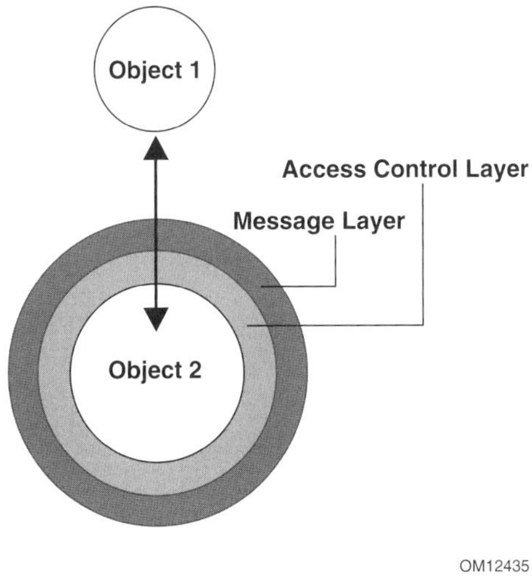

Figure 9.1 Avaki security layers

The message layer intercepts every message that is sent from or received by an object. For outgoing messages, the layer uses the implicit parameters associated with the message to determine what security measures to apply.

An outgoing message can be sent three ways: in the clear, in protected mode, or in private mode. When a message is sent in the clear, no encryption or other security processing is applied to the body of the message. An eavesdropper can extract any information from the message, and if certificates are included it can use them in constructing fraudulent method calls.

In protected mode, the body of the message is not encrypted. However, any certificates sent with the message are encrypted, as are the tags uniquely identifying the method call with which this message is associated. The body of the message is cryptographically digested. These transformations yield several guarantees. First, the certificates cannot be extracted and used by an attacker in another message. Second, the attacker cannot modify the message in any way, although he can copy it and replay it. Third, the attacker cannot forge a reply message because he cannot access the tags.

Private mode encrypts the entire message. Full encryption provides the same features as protected mode, as well as privacy. The attacker cannot read the message.

The choice of message security mode is stored in the current implicit parameters. These parameters are inherited through call chains, so if one object calls another object in private mode, the called object will use private mode for any messages it sends on behalf of the original caller. There is also a special implicit parameter for message security that is not inherited; it can be used to send an encrypted message and receive an unencrypted reply.

The basis for all these security mechanisms is public key encryption. When an object's identifier is created, typically by a class object, it is given a newly generated public key pair. The public part of the key becomes part of the object's identifier, and it can be used by others to encrypt their communications to that object. They can also verify that received messages were actually generated by the object, because the private key of the object is never revealed. The object's class, host, and vault all could potentially access it, although in the default Avaki implementation they do not. In Avaki, an object implicitly trusts its class, host, and vault.

Because public key encryption is expensive, caching is used so that objects engaged in repeated communications can reuse a Data Encryption Standard (DES) session key. These cached keys eventually time out and are refreshed.

Next, let's look at a security model for a different setting and architecture. You will see that the same basic security-enabling technologies are used in both cases. The same is true for most other implementations.

Security in Shared Spaces

This is an overview of the Groove security model.

The essence of Groove is that two or more people can interact with complete personal control over the content, function, and duration of a shared space. A user can invite others into a shared space across organizational boundaries. Users interact in these shared spaces, perhaps sharing sensitive information and conducting confidential business in the process.

The Groove security design set out to reconcile two somewhat opposing factors:

- Complete end user control, and
- The need for security in and around the content and activities of a shared space.

More specifically, the Groove security model addresses these challenges:

- Protect the confidentiality of content and activity in a shared space.
- Allow users to authenticate the identity of other users.
- Lock the shared space from access by unauthorized users.
- Protect the shared space from inadvertent or malicious spread of viruses.

Here is how Groove deals with these security issues within its shared spaces architecture:

First, Groove encrypts all content on disks and over the network.

Groove automatically encrypts the user's account, all shared spaces, and the local content on the user's device. Groove uses strong, 192-bit encryption. Users create a passphrase to encrypt their account and shared spaces. A passphrase (a collection of words) makes it more difficult for someone with malicious intent to make an educated guess at a user's secret code. Even if an intruder gained access to the file system in which Groove spaces are listed, the contents of those spaces would remain encrypted and impossible to compromise without the user's passphrase.

As described in earlier chapters, all content and activity within a shared space is sent across the network to all recipients. This traffic is also encrypted, and only members of the shared space can decrypt it. Each change or addition to a Groove shared space is sent as a discrete "delta" across the network to all other members of the space. Even in the unlikely event that a packet of data is intercepted and decrypted, only that small amount of content would be compromised. The shared space and the rest of its contents would be safe from unauthorized access.

Content is encrypted on the systems and on the wire.

Second, Groove authenticates users automatically. This is how it works:

In Groove's peer-to-peer architecture, there is no server-based administration of security. Therefore, all security function and management is relegated directly to the peer devices themselves. For this approach to be effective, the peer-computing environment must not only provide robust security, but must do so in a way that is effectively transparent to the user.

Groove users establish trusted relationships via the exchange of contact information in the form of "vCards." vCards include the user's public key. There are a number of convenient ways that this exchange can occur between two or more people.

In a trusting environment, I may email you an invitation to a shared space. When you accept the invitation, you automatically have accepted my Groove vCard. Your reply, via Groove, sends me your vCard in return.

This peer distribution of keys ensures security without requiring centralized certificate and key management.

There are two additional methods available to users to ensure that an invitation does indeed come from the person who sent it. This is important, since an invitation sent via email, for example, depends in part on how much the user trusts the email system itself. The two methods are:

- **Voice annotation.** Groove uses an approach that emulates the way people authenticate one another in real life. This approach uses human forms of recognition, as opposed to the typical methods used by public key infrastructure-based systems, in which you always trust that someone "notarizes" that you are who you claim to be.
  Groove invitations include the ability to record a person's voice. When I receive an invitation from you, I authenticate you because I recognize your voice. We can take further precaution by referencing a "personal shared secret."
  From a technology standpoint, this "recognition" process only needs to occur once. Groove provides mechanisms when people rendezvous so they can recognize one another. After that, the recognized person will be forever recognized, and nobody else can pretend to be him or her.
- **Digital fingerprints.** Your vCard includes your public key. When you first send me a message, Groove uses that public key to compute, on my machine, your digital fingerprint. It is a long, alphanumeric string of characters. The fingerprint is stored as part of the your vCard. When I receive a subsequent invitation, I can check the digital fingerprint in the invitation against the fingerprint in the stored vCard. If they match, I can be assured that you are indeed you.

Third, only invited members can participate in a Groove shared space.

After you have accepted my invitation and we have authenticated each other, Groove then sends to you a set of keys and the shared space itself, as well as a set of keys that allow you to decrypt the content.

This exchange of keys for the space itself provides an easy mechanism for managing membership for the duration of a space. Throughout the normal lifecycle of a shared space, it is likely that new members will be invited and other members will have their invitations rescinded. This presents a security challenge, since the ejected member still retains the keys to the shared space. Whenever a member is evicted from a shared space, Groove automatically issues a new shared-space key to all members so that subsequent data is protected and kept private from all past members. As far as the evicted member is concerned, the "old" shared space is still on his or her local device(s), and he or she can still review the content and history of that space. However, he or she can no longer look at new content and activity.

Finally, Groove includes safeguards against rogue components.

The issue is this: it is all too easy to add a component to your system. How do you maintain this flexibility without letting undesirable components in?

As a peer-computing platform, Groove provides users with extraordinary control over the functionality of a space itself. If any member decides the shared space needs new or additional functionality, he or she can add new components or tools on the fly. When a user adds a tool, Groove sends a command to all other users to do the same. If the other members already have the tool installed, Groove automatically adds the tool to the shared space. If any member does not have the tool installed yet, Groove – *transparently to the user* – locates and downloads the tool from any recognized Groove component server. Groove installs the tool locally and adds it to the shared space.

Business users find this flexibility one of the defining characteristics of Groove. On the other hand, most IT managers view it as cause for alarm. Strict guidelines often forbid the random downloading of executable code, some of which may have bugs or viruses, or which may violate standard desktop configurations. For this reason, Groove includes administrative controls that allow IT staff to "lock down" Groove desktops so that they may only download components that have been digitally signed by trusted authority, and/or that are found on approved server sites. This continues to allow users a great degree of freedom while balancing necessary IT protection against viruses.

You can read more about Groove and security in (Oram, 2001).

Grid Security Infrastructure

The Grid Security Infrastructure (GSI) is the name of security services from Globus Toolkit. GSI enables secure authentication and communication over an open network.

There are several factors in the Grid computing environment that affect security:

- Large and changing user population.
- Large and changing pool of resources.
- The set of processes that make up the computation is dynamic.
- The processes may communicate through a variety of mechanisms.
- Resources may require different authentication and authorization mechanisms.
- An individual user may have different credentials at different sites.

These characteristics of the Grid dictate the following requirements from a security service that supports that environment:

- Secure communication, authenticated and perhaps confidential, between elements of a computational Grid.
- Support of security measures across organizational boundaries. This requirement prohibits a centrally-managed security system. It mandates integration with various local security solutions and policies.
- Support of "single sign-on" for users of the Grid, including the ability to delegate credentials for computations that involve multiple resources and/or sites.

So, what is the solution?

A central concept in GSI authentication is the *certificate.* Every user and service on the Grid is identified by a certificate, which contains information vital to identifying and authenticating the user or service.

A GSI certificate includes four primary pieces of information:

- A subject name, which identifies the person or object that the certificate represents.
- The public key belonging to the subject.
- The identity of the Certificate Authority (CA), which certified that the public key and the identity both belong to the subject.
- The digital signature of the CA.

Note that a third party (a CA) is used to certify the link between the public key and the subject in the certificate. In order to trust the certificate and its contents, the CA's certificate must be trusted. GSI certificates are encoded in the X.509 certificate format, a standard data format for certificates established by the Internet Engineering Task Force (IETF). These certificates can be shared with other public key-based software, including commercial web browsers from Microsoft and Netscape.

The GSI uses the Secure Sockets Layer (SSL) for its mutual authentication protocol, which was described above.[9]

Here is an example of how GSI allows the security to be dialed up or down:

By default, the GSI does not establish *confidential* (encrypted) communication between parties. Once mutual authentication is performed, the GSI gets out of the way so that communication can occur without the overhead of constant encryption and decryption.

However, the GSI can easily be used to establish a shared key for encryption if confidential communication is desired. United States export laws were recently relaxed, allowing encrypted communication as a standard optional feature of the GSI.

Looking at data integrity, though, the GSI does provide communication integrity by default, and it can be turned off if desired. Communication integrity introduces some communication overhead, but it is not as large as encryption overhead.

GSI provides two ways to secure private keys:

- The private key is stored in a file on the local computer, encrypted via a passphrase.
- The GSI developers have also prototyped the use of cryptographic smartcard. The use of a smartcard makes it even more difficult for others to gain access to the key.

Let us see how delegation and "single sign-on" work in GSI.

The GSI provides a *delegation* capability. It is built as an extension of the standard SSL protocol, and reduces the number of times the user must enter his passphrase. This is useful when a Grid computation requires that several Grid resources be used, each requiring mutual

[9] SSL is also known by a new, IETF standard name: Transport Layer Security, or TLS.

authentication, or if there is a need to have agents (local or remote) requesting services on behalf of a user.

The need to re-enter the user's pass phrase can be avoided by creating a *proxy*. A proxy consists of a new certificate, with a new public key in it, and a new private key. The new certificate contains the owner's identity, modified slightly to indicate that it is a proxy. The new certificate is signed by the owner rather than a CA. The certificate also includes a time notation, after which the proxy should no longer be accepted by others. Proxies have limited lifetimes.

The proxy's private key must be kept secure, but because the proxy isn't valid for very long, it doesn't have to be kept quite as secure as the owner's private key. It is thus possible to store the proxy's private key in a local storage system without being encrypted, as long as the permissions on the file prevent anyone else from easily looking at it. Once a proxy is created and stored, the user can use the proxy certificate and private key for mutual authentication without entering a password.

When proxies are used, the mutual authentication process differs slightly. The remote party receives the proxy's certificate, signed by the owner, as well as the owner's certificate. During mutual authentication, the owner's public key, obtained from the certificate, is used to validate the signature on the proxy certificate. The CA's public key is then used to validate the signature on the owner's certificate. This establishes a chain of trust from the CA to the proxy through the owner.

The Globus developers believe that, as of mid-2001, their GSI and the software based upon it is the only software that supports the delegation extensions to TLS (a.k.a. SSL). The Globus Project is actively working with the Grid Forum and the IETF to establish proxies as a standard extension to TLS, so that GSI proxies may be used with other TLS software.

It is fitting to close this section with the call for greater interoperability through protocols. For further reading about security in Globus see (Globus, 2001; Foster et al, 1998; and Butler et al, 2000).

Globus represents Grid Computing. Now, let's look at the security settings for its related discipline: distributed Internet computing.

Securing Distributed Internet Computing

The discussion on distributed computations is demonstrated through the Entropia system.

The security measures need to provide a system that is:

- Non-intrusive towards the user
- Tamper-resistant against attempts to affect the application
- Network-friendly to minimize impact on existing IT infrastructure

In order to guarantee non-intrusiveness, the Entropia system executes the task application within a proprietary sandbox that monitors the application and ensures that the application is well behaved. File access is strictly controlled: the application may read and write to files, but not arbitrarily. The application may not open user files or write to files in arbitrary locations. The application may not spawn arbitrary programs and may not generate a GUI's elements. In addition, memory and disk usage is strictly monitored. If the limits are ever exceeded, the job is terminated and a notification is sent to the Entropia servers. The job may be re-executed on a machine with greater resources, or a notification may be sent to the user who submitted the task.

The Entropia system also guarantees that the user cannot tamper with the application. To provide this, the Entropia system uses strong encryption for all communication that occurs between the Entropia client and the Entropia servers. The encryption scheme is based on the Intel® P2P Trusted Library that is described below. All the files associated with the application are transparently encrypted. Therefore, it is very unlikely that a user could interfere with the correct execution of an application. The user may, of course, terminate the job, but will not be able to tamper with any results. In addition, task replication can be used to further guarantee that results were not tampered with.

The third item is not a strict security measure; it is one exhibiting "good citizenship."

For enterprise networks, it is especially important that the Entropia system not interfere in any way with the existing corporate environment. This means that network bandwidth is maintained at a reasonable level and that the applications running on behalf of Entropia do not interfere with existing applications on the host machine. Entropia's sandbox is used to monitor the application's network bandwidth consumption, and it can be used to restrict the amount of bandwidth used if needed. The sandbox also ensures that the application does not interfere with any existing software running on the user's behalf.

Applying Security Basics in P2P Networks

All the platforms we examined address security concerns very seriously. I will conclude the section on security practices with a few short takes on variants in applying the fundamental security aspects of:

- Authentication
- Authorization
- Integrity

Note how the same protocols and techniques are universally chosen.

Security with WebRiposte from The Escher Group

User authentication and management of local security policy is based on close integration with the Windows NT/2000 security model. Correspondence servers and clients can authenticate their neighbors.

User rights and permissions can be associated with any of the objects stored in WebRiposte, and the application provides full support for access control lists at the individual object level. By using the access control list, specific users or user groups can be permitted or denied access to web content stored in the Message Store.

In addition, the Web Proxy Server supports Internet security by letting system administrators restrict user access to external Web sites, through the use of access lists that define allowed and disallowed site addresses.

The security policy is replicated among peers to ensure consistent enforcement within a peer group.

In order to secure communication, WebRiposte provides support for SSL/SET (SET stands for Secure Electronic transaction, another security-related protocol). These mechanisms secure both the communications between peers, and provide secure communications to applications via HTTPS. For example, the replication of messages between Correspondence Servers and remote Message Servers is secure.

WebRiposte protects data against tampering even in the event that the access control mechanism has been bypassed. It does so through the application of digital signatures to any object stored in its content repository. The application verifies these signatures automatically when the content is retrieved. This applies not just to software components, but to any HTML page as well. This provides a much higher level of protection than is usually afforded in a web environment. Certificates are typically managed centrally and distributed to peers via replication.

Data encryption is supported via integration with the Windows CryptoAPI; however, WebRiposte does not include any built-in encryption technology. It is left to the customers to integrate encryption based on local requirements.

It is interesting to note that not including encryption was primarily due to export restrictions – the same ones that were recently relaxed.

Engenia's Collaborative Services Platform

For a collaboration platform to be truly successful, all stakeholders must have faith that the collaboration around information is secure, and only the people meant to see the information have access.

Security within the Engenia platform starts with user credentialing. All users are required to identify themselves and enter a password before a connection is permitted.

The application secures transactions between desktops and servers using secured sockets (SSL). This ensures that information transferred between systems stays private. Server administrators may obtain a server certificate from Verisign. The SSL system is secured by RSA (see Glossary).

Engenia implements object and user level security. Each entity (an object) in the system is capable of maintaining its own security policy. It can grant access to others, and it can delegate its security policy to another entity, which acts as its proxy.

Within the infrastructure, the objects are protected with access control lists and ticket-based handles. With this extensive system, users can be prevented from accessing certain objects as well as grant permissions to those who require it.

Group rights are managed through relationships between entities. A group may be granted privileges to access or manipulate another entity in the system. Users related to that group would be told what those privileges are. The notion of a group in the platform, however, is abstract. Any entity can be a group for the purposes of conveying security privileges, provided that the platform has been informed that the particular entity or type of entity may serve that function.

All permissions granted are issued through a ticket. Within the Engenia platform, access can be controlled beyond the typical access control specification; a ticket can included time-based restrictions as well as a punch count.

Security Between Magi Peers

Security between Magi peers employs a combination of Public Key Infrastructure (PKI), HTTP content encryption, Secure Sockets Layer (SSL), and Access Control Lists.

The PKI is governed by a Magi Certificate Authority (CA). During initialization each Magi peer generates its own RSA key pair, and sends the public key along with a username and password to the Magi CA. The password is used as an "out of band" verification for who may apply, as well as subsequent authentication in case of a compromised key. If accepted, the CA then binds the username to the public key with a digital certificate. In this way a given deployment of Magi peers may be configured to only recognize other peers of the given Magi CA's choosing. This defines a unique name space that can not only use standard human readable names, but also correspond to an existing name space (such as that in a corporate environment). Finally, if a peer becomes compromised the Magi CA issues periodic certificate revocation lists.

There are times when secure communication between peers does not need a protocol as heavy weight as SSL. In other cases such as store-and-forward SSL simply won't work. In these cases, Magi uses an SSL-like encryption method they call HTTP Content Encryption. With this encryption method, the symmetric key is negotiated between the two peers using a specific symmetric key negotiation protocol. By negotiating a unique symmetric key for each message, the source of the message is non-refutable, and the message can be tested against being replayed.

Magi also includes a full SSL implementation which utilizes their existing PKI as well as the strongest encryption level allowable for a given deployment.

We have addressed how Magi communicates but not who gets access to what. This is control by the Access Control List. All peers maintain an access control list (ACL) stating what resources they make available, who is allowed to execute them, and with what requirements in terms of authentication and encryption. In a controlled Magi environments this list is remotely configurable by the Magi CA. In this way a central authority can make sure that the peers in its domain are not exposing any sensitive material to the wrong peers. In an open environment this is left entirely up the end user.

Security in Mangosoft's Mangomind

We will finish the short survey of security in P2P platforms with a short note about what Mangomind does for its network file system.

Mangomind offers complete file-level and directory-level permission settings for both individual users and groups of users. This lets users specify privileges to allow or deny other Mangomind drive users access to specific files. For example, you may have a document that you want to be able to both read and change, but ensure it is read-only for everyone else. Using the Mangomind permissions, you can easily configure this type of access to the file.

Mangomind allows users to set access permissions for files and folders on a Mangomind drive. These mechanisms provide fine-grained security settings among the authorized users of a drive. For protection against unauthorized users, Mangomind employs a layer of encryption at the client-to-client level (i.e., P2P). Data encryption at the client-level ensures that all files are securely transmitted and stored at the server.

Mangomind possesses a client-side, 128-bit RSA encryption scheme that meets mission-critical business requirements for data confidentiality. With Mangomind, data is encrypted on your PC before transfer and storage, so even people managing the Mangomind service cannot access the information you store on Mangomind drives.

The security services for every platform covered in this book have not been explained, but that does not mean these platforms do not have such services. Check with each vendor for their application's security services.

The Peer-to-Peer Trusted Library

This overview on security capability clearly demonstrates that the same basic security measures are required by practically all P2P applications. This is clearly an area where a common facility should be most welcome, and there is a modest start in this direction: Intel has produced the Peer-to-Peer Trusted Library (PtPTL).

P2P has security aspects that are unique from other Internet applications. For example, existing public key infrastructures (PKIs) are often inappropriate for use with P2P. Digital certificates available from commercial vendors cost money, involve paperwork and time, and often provide only limited assurance of identity. Certificates that are generated and signed by individuals are sufficient for many P2P applications, especially when accompanied by additional identifying information like an attached voice message. Application developers need a security toolkit that fits the specific needs of P2P.

What is the PtPTL? The Peer-to-Peer Trusted Library (PtPTL) is a software toolkit providing security components tailored for the creation of P2P applications. It allows for the establishment of trust between individual P2P clients and the organization of secure groups of trusted peers. Ultimately, the PtPTL allows users to share information and collaborate securely across the Internet. The goal of this project is to spur open innovation in the P2P security space. P2P is not a new technology but many questions remain unanswered, especially in the area of security. The PtPTL project allows developers and users to experiment and prototype a variety of approaches and solutions to security in P2P applications. To this end, the library serves as the basis for an open-source project for investigating the security aspects of P2P. It is hosted on SourceForge (http://www.sourceforge.net/projects/ptptl).

Why PtPTL? Good security is costly and difficult to achieve. Because of the cost, many P2P applications lack security support entirely, leaving users vulnerable to attack. Other developers have assembled their own security implementation, which usually requires a team of engineers knowledgeable in computer security, not to mention many hours of testing. The PtPTL project seeks to lower the bar to security for small and large commercial software vendors and open-source developers alike.

Why open-source for PtPTL? The open-source software development model is ideally suited to the development of security software. It speeds the location and repair of bugs and security holes and ensures a stable product. Open-source also motivates the development of lasting security components and not encourage security through obscurity. Developers have the ultimate flexibility in removing unnecessary components, as when implementing for embedded devices, or integrating entirely new components like support for smart cards or biometric devices. As apparent from the success of Linux, there is definite value in letting the open-source community guide a project's architecture. Often, the result is a more stable and lightweight product than is available commercially. Through open-source development, the PtPTL should be more secure and certainly more widely usable than toolkits developed in isolation.

Some of the capabilities and features of the peer-to-peer Trusted Library:

The PtPTL includes a wide variety of cryptographic features through uniform and easy-to-use object-oriented interfaces. It supports digital certificates, public and private key encryption, and various secure-storage formats. It conforms to existing cryptography standards like the widely used X.509 digital certificate format and most of the public key cryptography standards (PKCS). The PtPTL can use digital certificates and public key encryption to authenticate and verify the identity of a remote user over the Internet. It can be used to digitally sign data, allowing a recipient of a message to identify the sender, or to create digital envelopes (private envelopes of data that can only be opened by an intended recipient). The library also includes simple support for networking and operating system primitives – like threads and locks – to allow the creation of complete but simple secure applications.

Portability was a major consideration in the design of the PtPTL. It currently supports Win32, the 32-bit Windows operating systems, and Linux, but minimal effort would be required to port to any other modern operating system. The PtPTL is portable in part because it is built on the open-source OpenSSL toolkit (http://www.openssl.org), which provides some of the PtPTL's low-level cryptographic support. The library can also be built on top of Intel's Common Data Security Architecture (CDSA) in place of OpenSSL.

The PtPTL allows developers to secure insecure P2P applications. One of the sample applications included in the release shows how security can be added transparently to the Gnutella protocol. Developers can also produce new secure applications from the ground up using the PtPTL.

These applications would be immediately interoperable with existing standards, have stable security components, and would be portable. The PtPTL is also useful for producing tests for other secure applications. Certificates, signatures, and digital envelopes can be easily generated for import into applications undergoing testing.

These are only the early days for the PtPTL. What should you expect in the future? Ultimately, the PtPTL will be headed in the direction that contributors and the open-source community take it. There are, however, some high-level issues that will certainly be addressed in the future, such as better integration with modern operating systems and existing PKIs, and support for all types of Internet connections, including firewall negotiation and proxy support. The PtPTL will provide the tools necessary to create all manner of secure P2P resource sharing, search, and messaging applications.

Concluding Remarks

We see that all the security solutions address the same basic needs of authentication, authorization, and data integrity. These are the items that matter to P2P users. Implicit in *authorization* is the concern about virus protection. Limitations on which external programs can be installed and what they can do are the key to protecting your system from malicious programs.

The need of all the P2P frameworks to follow the same basic functionality presents an opportunity for agreement on a set of common security services or common library.

P2P computing faces the need for coexistence between its infrastructure policies and the hosts' local policies. The consensus is that the P2P policies cannot be allowed to relax the local ones. The P2P application may, of course, employ more restrictive policies in its own domain. In general, the solutions we describe strive to accommodate the local settings, and certainly should not act in conflict with the host's security.

Strong security is needed; there is no doubt about that. But users are also looking to establish relationships of trust with other peers and within online communities. There is much work to be done in order to provide the users with tools that will assist in creating trustful communities. A promising direction for such tools is the emphasis on reputation. Reputation may measure a number of metrics. Trust, fundamentally, is based on behavioral patterns. It is also based on shared interests. We saw one such application in OpenCola's search strategy. The similarity metric used in that application can be used for creating trusting relationships between users.

So, first comes security. Then, reputation and trust.

The bottom line of the security issues is this: without increasing the comfort level of users in the P2P space (by individuals and by IT managers), there can be no mainstream, broad-adoption of P2P computing.

Chapter 10
Cooperative Management of Shared Resources

Peer-to-peer computing is about two things – direct communications between peers, and sharing resources at the edges of the net. This chapter is about managing these resources, which are scattered all over, come in many shapes and forms, and are owned by thousands of different individuals and institutions.

What are these resources that we can share through the magic of P2P technologies?

- **Computational power.** This is the resource that is central to distributed computing. It is also referred to as *cycle sharing*.
- **Storage and files.** Peers store files that are shared with others – envision an application where unused storage is used to store files that are not shared with the owner of host system. An IT organization may use such space for backup or the replication of files belonging to members of the organization.
- **Network bandwidth.** P2P infrastructure can be applied to route network traffic of messages and file transfers. The peers then share the bandwidth of connections emanating from their systems.

These three items represent shared hardware elements. They will be the focus of this chapter. Indirectly, we will also refer to two other resources that are shared in the P2P world. They are:

- **Content.** Content uses storage. But sharing storage does not necessarily imply that the content of these files is shared although that might be the case. Similarly, you can share content with your peers in a way that does not involve sharing storage. The shared content may be somewhere on a server, or it might be moving between locations. The item that is shared is the *content*, not the physical medium.
- **People.** Well, we don't share people. But the direct exchanges and real-time interaction with people in a collaborative setting is a shared resource.

Not all P2P implementations deal with every resource type listed above. Some focus entirely on cycle sharing, with the run-time files needed, of course. Others focus on content sharing and manage file sharing. And those solutions that address all the aspects of P2P need to create mechanisms for managing all the resource types.

There are a few steps in using resources in P2P computing that are independent of the type of resource:

- The peer or the application needs to be able to discover the resource. The discovery includes learning about the resource's state and structure.
- The P2P application needs to establish access to the resource. This includes ensuring it can abide by the resource's local policies. And, for some applications, scheduling is also necessary.
- The host where the resource resides has the ability to authenticate the requesting entity. And it can enforce its local policies on the application that asks for use of the resource.

Managing Distributed Resources

In this section, we will take a look at the approaches to the management of distributed resources taken by the general-purpose architectures Globus and Avaki. These are well on their way towards providing a comprehensive set of service for managing distributed resources.

The Globus approach

Globus is a toolkit, but its architects describe its current direction in terms of layers, as we saw in Chapter 5. In this scheme, the resources are managed within the Resource layer, which builds its functionality on top of the Connectivity layer. It uses the communication and authentication protocols to define protocols for the secure initiation, monitoring, and control of sharing operations on individual resources. Resource layer implementations of these protocols call Fabric layer functions to access and control local resources. Resource layer protocols are concerned entirely with individual resources; they ignore issues of global state and atomic actions across distributed collections. Such issues are the concern of the Collective layer and are discussed below.

There are two primary classes of Resource layer protocols:

- *Information protocols* are used to obtain information about the structure and state of a resource; its configuration, current load, and usage policy, for example.
- *Management protocols* are used to negotiate access to a shared resource. For example, they will find out the resource requirements, including advanced reservation and quality of service and the operations to be performed. Since management protocols are responsible for instantiating sharing relationships, they must serve as a "policy application point." They ensure that the requested protocol operations are consistent with the policy under which the resource is to be shared. Issues that must be considered include accounting and payment. A protocol may also support monitoring the status of an operation and controlling the operation, and terminating it, if necessary.

These information and management protocols must be chosen so as to capture the fundamental mechanisms of sharing across many different resource types and management systems. They need to do so without overly constraining the types or performance of higher-level protocols.

The Globus toolkit uses a standards-based set of protocols:

- The Lightweight Directory Access Protocol (LDAP) is used to define a standard resource information protocol and associated information model. An associated soft-state resource registration protocol is used to register resources with Grid Index Information Servers, which are discussed below.
- An HTTP-based Grid Resource Access and Management (GRAM) protocol is used for allocation of computational resources, and for monitoring and control of computation on those resources.
- An extended version of the File Transfer Protocol, called GridFTP, is used for data access. Extensions include use of security protocols, partial file access, and management of parallelism for high-speed transfers. FTP is adopted as a base data-transfer protocol because of its support for third-party transfers and because its separate control and data channels facilitate the implementation of sophisticated servers.

The Globus Toolkit defines client-side C and Java APIs and SDKs for each of these protocols. Server-side SDKs and servers are also provided for each protocol. The SDKs facilitate the integration of various resources, such as computational, storage, and network into the Grid.

The Resource layer is focused on interactions with a single resource. The next layer in the architecture contains protocols and services that are not associated with any one specific resource, but rather are global in nature and capture interactions across collections of resources. For this reason, that layer of the architecture is called the *Collective* layer. The Collective components can implement a wide variety of sharing behaviors. For example:

- *Directory services* allow participants to discover the existence and/or properties of resources. A directory service may allow its users to query for resources by name and/or by attributes such as type, availability, or load.
- *Co-allocation, scheduling, and brokering services* allow participants to request the allocation of one or more resources for a specific purpose and the scheduling of tasks on the appropriate resources.
- *Monitoring and diagnostics services* support the monitoring of resources for failure, adversarial attack, overload, and so forth.
- *Data replication services* support the management of storage resources to maximize data access performance with respect to metrics such as response time, reliability, and cost.
- *Community authorization servers* enforce community policies governing resource access, generating capabilities that community members can use to access community resources. These servers provide a global policy enforcement service by building on resource information, resource management protocols, and security protocols in the Connectivity layer.

There are more possibilities of collective services (see Foster et al, 2001).

Notice that while Resource layer protocols must be general in nature and are widely deployed, Collective layer protocols span the spectrum from general purpose to highly application- or domain-specific. Collective functions can be implemented as persistent services, with associated protocols, or as SDKs (with associated APIs) designed to be linked with applications.

Collective components may be tailored to the requirements of a specific user community or application domain, like an SDK that implements an application-specific coherency protocol, or a co-reservation service for a specific set of network resources, for example. Other Collective components can be more general-purpose, like a replication service that manages an international collection of storage systems for multiple communities, for instance. Generally, the larger the targeted user community, the more important it is that a Collective component's protocols and APIs be standards-based.

In addition to the example services listed earlier in this section, Globus has a Meta Directory Service, which introduces Grid Information Index Servers (GIIS) to support arbitrary views on resource subsets. Other services include replica catalog to support replication of datasets on the Grid. An online certificate repository service provides secure storage for proxy credentials.

Let's look at the direction taken by Avaki.

Managing Resources in Avaki

Avaki provides two types of resources:

- Hosts, that are computational resources
- Vaults, the storage resources

There are plans for network resources to be incorporated. Information about these resources is stored in databases called Collections to enable scheduling and resource discovery.

Encapsulating resources as objects provides a tremendous degree of autonomy. For example, if system administrators want to enforce a specialized access control policy for local hosts, they can extend or replace the implementation of the host object to enforce that policy. For example, some hosts in an Avaki network may require access through a local queue system. In these cases, resource providers simply use extended, queue-aware host objects. Yet another example is to allow access to hosts via a screen-saver model, i.e., using host resources only when they are idle. Likewise, if a resource provider makes storage in a local file system available to Avaki, yet wants to continue using local Unix-based accounting and quota tools, he uses a Vault object implementation that allocates storage under the appropriate local Unix user-id for Avaki services.

The Avaki scheduling philosophy is based on negotiation between resource providers and resource consumers. Ensuring autonomy is the single most crucial aspect of this process.

Autonomy is vital in attracting resource providers. In particular, resource providers must be assured that their local policies will be respected. For example, a set of resource providers may wish to allow access to their resources only when they are idle, or between midnight and 6 am, or they may allow access only to a specified community of users.

Autonomy with respect to the scheduling policy is also crucial in achieving maximum performance. A single scheduling policy is not the best answer for all problems and programs; rather, users should be able to choose from scheduling policies and select one that solves their problem, or they should be able to provide their own schedulers.

The scheduling process typically consists of four major components:

- A run-time Collection which can be queried or resource state information database
- A Scheduler/Enactor that maps scheduling requests to a set of hosts and vault resources
- An application or tool that issues a scheduling request
- A Class object that is responsible for instantiating objects on a specified set of resources

Information kept at the Collection includes time-sensitive information, such as current load or memory used, as well as more static information, such as the host type, the host operating system, and the number of processors. When an application or tool issues a scheduling request, the scheduler/enactor queries the collection to obtain status information. An example query would be "retrieve all hosts whose operating system is Windows 2000 and whose current load is below 2.0." Based on the returned candidate set of hosts and vaults, a scheduler can return to the tool or application a set of hosts and vaults on which to schedule an application. The tool or application can then request that the class instantiates the application with the computed schedule.

If they are not satisfied with the default schedulers provided by Avaki, users can develop their own schedulers or use schedulers provided by third-party providers. To date, Avaki supports the following scheduling policies:

- Random placement
- Round-robin
- Least-loaded
- Adaptive scheduling via queuing objects

Avaki also supports the development of additional policies via a flexible query language on Collections.

Computational Resources

We saw examples of large projects that harness many thousands (sometimes hundreds of thousands) of computers to jointly perform a large computational task. More examples will follow in the next chapter. We refer to this activity as *cycle sharing*. Of course, in addition to using CPU cycles for processing while being hosted by the peer computer, the application also uses memory and disk space.

Grid computing has its origins in distributed computing, where the computational resources came from a relatively small number of powerful computer systems in computer centers that are distant from each other. Each such center is likely to have multiple computers, supercomputers and other parallel systems that are dedicated to providing computational services to its users. These centers are also likely to be connected via high bandwidth connections.

This is not the distributed computing that is typical to P2P. And we saw that Globus, too, offers services for a P2P network that relies on many individually owned computers.

Cycle sharing in P2P falls into two major categories:

- Internet computing
- Intranet computing

Internet computing is represented by applications like SETI@home, for example. The cycle providers are likely to be users on home PCs with dialup connections. Intranet computing is distributed computing that is confined to a single IT infrastructure. The service providers and the enterprise desktops share a local network. It is likely to be a high-bandwidth network, and the equipment usually belongs to the organization. Intranet computing is easier to schedule. The application coordinator knows what software runs on the peer systems, and what their hardware features are. Security is not a major concern, since all the computations and communications are done behind the firewall or other security measures.

Internet computing is harder to manage. Its rate of computations is less predictable, and its network connections less reliable. Yet it has the potential to attract millions of participants to its projects. Compare this to the hundreds that may join an intranet computation.

So far, we have seen large-scale, voluntary Internet computing projects in search of extra-terrestrial beings and looking for a cure for AIDS, or cancer. The computational problems themselves can be broken into tasks that can be computed by individual peers without communicating with any other peer. Indeed, the only communication needed is to download the dataset to work on, and to return the results to the central control of the application.

An application where the tasks depend on each other and they need to communicate will rely on synchronization and scheduling of the participants. This is more readily done with an enterprise or an organization. We see examples of intranet computing within financial institutions and engineering companies (more on that in Chapter 11).

As an example of how resources are managed in Internet computing, let us look at what Entropia does. In previous chapters, we described the security aspects, language support, sandboxing, and so on (and it is unobtrusive).

Once installed, the Entropia Client first contacts the Entropia Network Manager and registers itself as a computation resource. The characteristics of the resource, such as CPU speed, processor type, and available memory, are relayed to the central server at that time. This server maintains "pools" of resources that can be used for different applications depending on resource characteristics. For example, one application may require a pool of resources that are well connected to the network, while another may require large amounts of memory. The system provides a central management interface that allows an administrator to create and manage these pools of resources and assign them to specific applications. At any time, the Network Manager has the capability to preempt the application and reassign the client resources to another application, perhaps one with higher priority.

After the client has registered or after it is started, it contacts the Entropia Network Manager and is assigned to a specific application. It then downloads the appropriate Application Package and contacts an application Job Manager for further instructions, parameters, or data files. These Managers use client resource characteristics, job priorities, and even geographic location to schedule tasks on the client. Different applications may require different scheduling algorithms, hence the need for differentiating between client pool management and application scheduling. There may be many Job Managers present, one for each application or class of applications. Once the application execution is complete, the results are transferred to a staging area on the Entropia servers. Lack of connectivity is dealt with by simply batching the results until connectivity is restored.

When running, the application executes within the proprietary Entropia Sandbox, described in a previous chapter, that ensures the application executes unobtrusively to the end user. Briefly, the application runs at low priority, replacing the idle process on Windows machines. Its memory usage, disk usage, and networking usage is strictly controlled by the sandbox. If its usage exceeds a certain threshold, the job is canceled and a status message sent to the Entropia servers.

Overall, the system is capable of harvesting useful work off a variety of systems, from mobile laptops, to PCs with dialup connectivity, to powerful desktops with broadband communications.

The premise of Internet computing is that the average PC connected to the Internet is idle as much as 95% of the time. Between mouse clicks, keystrokes, and spikes of routine software activity, these PCs are just waiting to work. The millions of PCs on the Internet represent an enormous amount of processing cycles that are literally going to waste while the clock ticks.

The Entropia client software, which the users download when they join the network, checks for availability of processor cycles every $1/100^{th}$ of a second, even between keystrokes. Using the idle cycles, it only takes a few thousand machines on the grid to provide more processing power than the most powerful supercomputers in existence.

Shared Storage

Just as there are plenty of idle cycles for computations on our desktop computers, there is also a big reservoir of underutilized disk space.

It is not easy to manage a reliable backup service for files on systems scattered around and characterized by intermittent connectivity.

While there is development and research done in distributed storage, caching and edge services are more typical of storage-related P2P applications. An interesting example is the Mangosoft Distributed Storage Engine.

The caching and virtual memory techniques, which are part of the Pooling technology, are made possible by a complex piece of software that creates the notion of *virtual storage*. Virtual storage refers to the unification of memory and storage resources of all the systems on the network into a single, dynamic pool. The technology that makes this possible is the Distributed Storage Engine.

The Distributed Storage Engine manages both memory and disk resources across the systems as a unified shared virtual memory, which is treated as a large, coherent cache. The global memory and disk managers are integrated so that both access data using the same set of global shared addresses. Each address comprises a unique, universal 128-bit quantity. Each address refers to a 4K byte page, which is the unit of allocation and administration.

There are two broad types of pages, *volatile* and *persistent*. Volatile pages are transient, memory cache creations. When a volatile page is no longer needed, it is dropped from the system. Volatile pages are only stored on disk when they are paged out, due to memory consumption. In contrast, persistent pages are stored on disk. They are permanent and are typically used for valuable data storage, such as directory structures and the contents of files.

The unification of disk and memory provides many benefits to the end user. For example, when a client's main memory becomes full, regions of the shared virtual memory space can be cached on the local disk, thereby eliminating the need to travel across the network for frequently accessed files. This improves network performance. Data cached on local disks is kept consistent using the same mechanisms that keep data cached in local memory.

In addition, this design provides a mechanism for making the shared data highly available and persistent. File system techniques such as logging, replication, and quorum management are used to ensure that undeleted regions of the global virtual memory remain available when a machine crashes, despite the fact that regions of data can be cached in any number of local memories or disks. Because the design exploits replication in clients' memories and disks as well as replication of servers, it is more fault-tolerant than a conventional server-based replicated file system. Simply put, a user's machine can fail and he or she can still access their data in the Pool from another machine.

One of the novel aspects of the Distributed Storage Engine is the elimination of one fixed home for data in the system. Data migrates to the most appropriate location based on access patterns and availability requirements. The cache is also implemented this way, meaning that many of the control structures exhibit the same homeless behavior. The benefits of this homeless design for a distributed system is similar to the effect cache memories have for a processor. Frequently referenced data is stored close to where it is used, dramatically improving performance of the entire system. This means that users access their data faster than they would if the data was statically stored on another computer.

Even persistent data stored on disk is managed as a cache. All network storage is treated as a highly dynamic cache and data is being moved, on demand, to where it is most frequently used. The steady state, and dynamic, behavior of such a system is one that will use the network much more efficiently than a client-server design. The majority of data that an individual system fetches over the network from a server will become a local reference. A Pool makes more efficient use of available bandwidth and demands less of its physical network components!

It might be interesting to look at how storage is handled in an object-based architecture. Let's examine Avaki.

In Avaki, context space is where content is stored. Users can map portions of their local file system into the context space. This action will make these files shared resources. Avaki provides both command line interface and a GUI for manipulating context spaces, storing, sharing and retrieving files, etc.

The user may set access control lists for the exported directory. The user can build and maintain his or her own groups and may explicitly add additional users to the allow list, or explicitly deny particular users or groups from access.

Network Bandwidth

Capacity for communications, or network bandwidth, is the third major type of resource that can be shared through P2P technologies. We often think of the network bandwidth as just being there. But, of course, you need to get to a gateway or a port to gain access to the network, and you may have to pass through other systems in order to find a less congested route for your transmissions.

P2P infrastructures that are concerned with the movement of large amounts of data all take steps to use the network efficiently.

Some seem very simple – that is, the explanation is simple (as is the case with Groove). In Groove, only the "deltas" (or the changes) to the files are sent out. That being said, the complexities of keeping track of what parts of what file have changed since the last time a user had access to it are all hidden from the user. In addition, even the method for sending these deltas takes the network into account. Remember, Groove uses a relay server. Depending on the size of the message and the bandwidth available to the peers, the delta may be sent directly, or it may be sent to the relay server and later fetched by the peer.

Similarly, Escher uses the Correspondence Server of WebRiposte for minimizing WAN traffic. Only one copy is sent to a branch location. Copies to individual peers travel over the (free) local network. During a recovery from a failure, each node will pass on queued requests that arrive from other nodes. The recovery transmissions are routed and balanced according to the response from the recipients and their availability.

Another technique used by WebRiposte is the employment of distributed persistent caching, which is based on polling by the peers. Updates are sent back only when there is a change, and the cache is set to be refreshed every ten minutes or so.

WebRiposte's biggest customer, the UK Postal Services, acknowledges that the network optimization measures described above have resulted in a very significant cost savings.

So far, we saw techniques for reducing the network traffic. Now, let's examine an application that takes advantage of unused bandwidth, spreading the transmissions over otherwise unused paths.

Swarmcast, from OpenCola, is a large file-distribution system for content and network providers, which serves large files faster and uses less bandwidth. This results in a better user experience and significant bandwidth cost savings.

Swarmcast accomplishes this by leveraging the computers and bandwidth of its users. Swarmcast breaks large files (> 1 MB) into multiple, easily transferred chunks. These chunks are served simultaneously from multiple nodes in the Swarmcast network that have previously downloaded them.

A Swarmcast download begins with a large file from a content provider's server. When a large group of users requests this file, Swarmcast cycles through the file, breaking it into packets which are encoded using Forward Error Correction (FEC), a mathematical system of error control that Swarmcast uses to make it easy to reconstruct the file. The encoded packets are then distributed randomly amongst the users who have requested the file. These users' computers become nodes in the mesh (a temporary network) that Swarmcast creates for this download.

Each node receives only a portion of the original packets. But each node is also aware of some of the other nodes are receiving packets. Even as a node receives a packet, it also rebroadcasts it to other nodes, so packets are rapidly swapped back and forth. Speed is enhanced because Swarmcast distributes the work of downloading.

As each packet is received, the receiving node checks to see if it is useful in rebuilding the file. As soon as a receiving node receives enough useful packets, it reconstructs the file. Once it has reassembled the file, a node is free to leave the mesh.

Not all nodes will do so, though. Many users will keep their computers as part of the mesh for some time after they've finished downloading. By staying in the mesh, users make it easier for others to complete the download.

The implication of Swarmcast is that the available bandwidth to serve a large file scales in lockstep with the popularity of that file. Currently, a server whose files are under constant high demand is more poorly equipped to serve those files than an identically equipped server whose files are desired by no one. With Swarmcast, the availability of any file is a function of the number of the users who've requested it. The more times someone requests a file, the easier it becomes to get a copy of one's own.

The benefit to the user is faster downloads. The benefit to providers is that they can serve more users with fewer resources.

There are a number of ways by which cooperating peers can achieve better performance out of existing networks.

Control of Resource Usage

Below are some more techniques that are used by some of the P2P developers whose work we examine in this book.

One of the general concerns of IT operators is that undesirable components will sneak in. Viewing the shared applications as a shared resource, this becomes an issue of managing a resource. Groove deals with shared components by borrowing from communication and security services. First, before a tool or an application is added, a message is sent to the candidate recipient. This gives the peer an opportunity to refuse the component. Secondly, the software is digitally signed. So its source can be verified, and the receiver can decide whether or not to allow the component, depending on the level of trust in that source.

United Devices uses a scheduler in its Global MetaProcessor service for what we called Internet computing. Each application has a defined service level that can indicate the amount of work needed, the time allotted, and the level of processor, memory, disk, and bandwidth resources required. The scheduler uses this information together with the MetaProcessor's knowledge of the community's available resources. The scheduler attempts to maximize the utilization of resources while minimizing the impact to the members.

United devices are working on methods to improve scheduling and resource utilization, such as statistical modeling, redundancy, and metric for reputation.

Engenia uses access control lists (ACL) and ticket-based handles for granting permissions. Their platform has the capability to add time-based restrictions or punch count. The latter restricts use by number of times the object is called, rather than a time period.

The platform also includes a job scheduling capability, enabling scheduled function calls or even more complex event-driven behavior.

Endeavors' Magi resource can be any entity that can be defined in a web-sense by an identifier (an URL, for example). A typical Magi resource is a file, a script, access to a database, or mapping to a file system. All requests for resources go through access control manager. Using XML, the requestor's identity is authenticated, and access is authorized if the permissions that are granted match the request made.

Magi also allows for mediated services (to a database, for example). The goal of the access control manager is to grant "trusted access." The trusted access is based on symmetry, in the sense that what is shared, and the permissions, are both defined within the group (whose membership is a subset of the peer's buddy list).

In conclusion, what have we learned? Resource management is an area where each implementation does something different. The tools for managing the resources are specific to the application and the settings in which it runs. This is certainly an area where more work can be done to find commonalities, and perhaps recycle existing capabilities.

PART III
SUCCESSES AND CHALLENGES

Applying the P2P technologies, the technical and social challenges, and the opportunities that lay ahead

> *"It is not the strongest of the species that survives. Nor the most intelligent. But the ones most responsive to change."*
>
> Charles Darwin

Chapter 11
Applying Peer-to-Peer Technologies

"P2P is how we do it, not what we do."

Chris Williams, president and CEO,
Oculus Technologies Corporation

We cannot do justice, in a single chapter, to the wealth of possibilities and actual application of P2P technologies to real-life cases. All I hope to achieve here is to provide a taste of some of the innovative usages of P2P computing. To get an appreciation of the breadth of activity, check out the sites listed under General References, in particular those of O'Reilly and PeerProfit.

The P2P architectures described in this book are grouped into three categories (in addition to general-purpose ones):

- Collaborative
- Content sharing
- Distributed computing

The same categories are applied here to examples of applications and usages of P2P technologies. In most cases, the descriptions of the applications are short. The purpose of this chapter is to give an impression of the kind of applications people are developing for use in P2P computing; this is certainly not meant to be an in-depth survey of P2P applications.

Interactive Collaborations

Collaboration happens between people. At least, this is how we differentiate the P2P collaborative application from others. And, as you will see, collaborative applications may well include sharing of content and (perhaps) joint computations, too.

The small sample includes several types of cooperative P2P settings:

- Creation of online communities
- Development projects
- Gaming communities
- Computing communities
- Joint virus protection

The first item is more general in nature compared to the others. You will see that these approaches may apply to a number of activities. The latter types of communities are more specific.

Collaboration and Communities

There are three types and approaches to the creation of peer communities:

- Marketplace
- Common interests
- Communities within the enterprise

P2P Marketplace

FirstPeer (http://www.firstpeer.com/) created an online marketplace that enables sellers, suppliers, and vendors to be integrated into the FirstPeer framework with their existing technologies and business models. The application employs a P2P architecture to distribute the marketplace functions to its participants, eliminating the need to replace the tools they currently use.

The FirstPeer marketplace is based on standard protocols, such as XML and DNS. The environment is showing the first signs of integration at the application level, as FirstPeer users have access to Jabber instant messaging.

A key difference between FirstPeer's marketplace and similar e_Commerce offerings is that the information about products and providers is kept on the peer computers. The P2P approach allows scaling to the range of hundreds of thousands of users.

Buyers and sellers meet online in a virtual marketplace, which is organized by three business forums:

- The Market Gateway allows suppliers can expose up-to-date, dynamic product inventory directly.
- The Publisher Gateway allows providers to advertise products, and it provides the means for subscribers to find what is available.
- The Retail Center is where buyers and sellers find the tools for conducting trade.

Building a Shared-Interest Community

We have described aspects of OpenCola Folders in previous chapters. Here we focus on features that help form communities based on shared interests. The idea is that human-machine collaboration is central to the creation of shared interest-based community.

OpenCola Folders are never fully autonomous. Meaningful documents can only be found reliably when a software agent regularly brings results back for human evaluation.

OpenCola assumes that somewhere on the Internet, there are people who share common interests with you. The participation of any of those people in the training of the Folders application will benefit your own searches. Folders constantly searches the Internet for new buddies – people who have similar Folders. OpenCola uses reputation as a measure of the similarity.

The reputation measure is what closes the loop of positive reinforcement between the user and the content. The user indicates how a file is valued by grading the results of the search. Folders increases the reputation of the user by becoming buddies with other people's Folders. Users can opt out of training Smart Folders, and simply use their buddies to do searches. Selfishness is not punished in this economy, and those who use the system in a simple manner benefit from the learning process that other people's Folders undergo.

If your Smart Folder becomes a buddy, it means you have become a "recommender" of resources for someone. People who actively strive to make their Folders stellar performers receive greater and greater positive reputation. They become *super-recommenders*.

Super-recommenders can be seen as central nodes on small, focused networks: communities of interest. Because Folders seek out similar buddies, the OpenCola network crystallizes in such communities. OpenCola automatically routes information seekers toward one another, creating a network on top of the Internet that only contains the resources its members want.

Shared Space Collaboration

One of the early corporations to try the Groove collaborative platform is GlaxoSmithKline, a pharmaceutical company. They started with a pilot program, and asked their employees to suggest ways in which Groove could be used for online collaboration.

The range of ideas and opportunities is impressive. Staff members from the Legal department wanted to review and edit documents with other parties. A development team suggested a test of new software. Scientists and Researchers wished to exchange information with external colleagues. The Operations department wished to share documents with contractors and suppliers.

A good sign for the acceptance of P2P collaboration was in some of the requests GlaxoSmithKline made of Groove: we need more integration with other popular productivity tools, and the Relay server has to be local to the customer, not just at the Groove facility. GlaxoSmithKline worries about the same things that worry IT managers elsewhere – they need to be assured that their security isn't compromised, and they need to be sure that data stored locally can be recovered, even if an employee leaves the company. See also (Harrison, 2001).

P2P and Online Development Projects

The following case is from a P2P application developer: Oculus Technologies Corporation focuses on integration between applications. We will see here what the Ford Motor Company plans to do with CO, the Oculus application.

Ford will use Oculus CO to design more fuel-efficient automobiles by allowing design teams to collaborate more efficiently and to evaluate design options quickly.

The Ford team will utilize Oculus CO to connect members of a geographically-dispersed design team working with different software applications on different operating systems. The company chose Oculus CO because the P2P collaboration promises to improve the design process. It will allow Ford engineers to evaluate many more design iterations in a much shorter period of time.

The functional groups that are involved with the project each represent a vehicle attribute such as weight, transmission, electrical, etc. The specific scenario that CO is applied to looks at how data flows from other vehicle attribute groups to the fuel economy group. The fuel economy group receives as inputs the various data points from these groups. They then aggregate the data and integrate it into the fuel economy models they were working on. Next, they need to run analyses to understand the impact on fuel economy of the individual attributes, and send those results back to the vehicle attribute group (so they could understand if they met design specifications). What used to take on average 2-3 days (and sometimes 2 weeks), Oculus CO is able to analyze in 23 seconds. This is how the team was able to evaluate more trade-off scenarios and explore more design options to save them money overall.

P2P makes the process efficient, since the engineers know who shares what data. And, although the data stays local to its source, it is accessible to the other designers who have been notified and authorized to use the data for their evaluations.

The significance of this type of collaboration is that the design process becomes less centralized. Engineers communicate directly across organizational boundaries, without needing constant coordination by management. P2P computing allows companies to improve the (ever more complex) design process by enabling the designers to explore more solutions faster.

Online Gaming Communities

An online group game is a natural candidate for a P2P application. Indeed, Pocit Labs announced such a platform for PDAs and handheld gaming devices.

The solution, BlueTalk† Game Engine, is a gaming API for short-range wireless P2P network. The application is an integral part of BlueTalk, Pocit Labs' network client for local wireless P2P communication. BlueTalk Game Engine makes it possible to develop a new generation of computer games that utilize the benefits of local ad hoc P2P networking. Regardless of whether they use handheld gaming devices, PDAs or Smartphones, users can meet and seamlessly create a wireless virtual playground without any external infrastructure. Participants can compete in teams, and individual players can join or drop out at any time.

With BlueTalk, developers can develop and deploy short-range P2P applications for handhelds, Smartphones and embedded devices, without having to access the underlying support for creating dynamic wireless P2P ad hoc networks.

This is an example of the promising combination of entertainment applications, wireless technology, and P2P computing.

Computing Communities

Grid computing has evolved over the last few years. During that time, communities of collaborators have been formed around a variety of projects. Here is a taste of what's out there (see also http://www.gridforum.org).

- **European DataGrid** is a European Union-sponsored project for the development of a computational and data-intensive grid for High Energy Physics, Earth Observation and Biology applications.
- **Grid Physics Network (GriPhyN)** is a US National Science Foundation-funded team of experimental physicists and IT researchers who plan to implement the first Petabyte-scale computational environments for data intensive science in the 21st century.
- **Network for Earthquake Engineering and Simulation** (NEESgrid) is a US National Science Foundation-funded team developing a national-scale virtual laboratory for the earthquake engineering community.

- **The DREAM Project** is funded to design, build, and use software to allow automated sharing of computing resources for Evolutionary Computing and Evolving Agent Applications.
- **The Particle Physics Data Grid (PPDG)** is a US Department of Energy-funded collaboration between High Energy and Nuclear Physics experiment teams and Computer Science groups active in grid services development. PPDG focuses on developing and deploying end-to-end applications utilizing and extending existing Grid software, together with the initial deployment of these applications into production for the participating experiments.
- **The UK eScience Grid Support Center** was created for UK application users interested in beginning to develop and use grid technologies.
- **The U.S. Grid Research Integration Development and Support (GRIDS) Center** (www.grids-center.org) was created to support the creation and deployment of a "national middleware infrastructure" for the university research and education communities.
- **The National Virtual Observatory** (www.srl.caltech.edu/nvo) is a collaborative project focused on the analysis of data from a network of astronomical observatories.
- **The Access Grid** (www.mcs.anl.gov/FL/accessgrid) is an advanced collaboration environment that supports collaborative work and communication among hundreds of people at dozens of sites around the world.

Some of the many projects that are run by these communities (and others like them) are listed later in this chapter under "grid computing."

As you read about the large-scale computational tasks organized by Entropia and United Devices, you will see that their users really are members of a new kind of a community.

Join Forces for Virus Protection

Another kind of a community can be set up for protection against digital virus attacks. A demonstration of such a capability was conducted at the Sandia National Laboratory. Here are some excerpts from a Sandia Lab news release (Sandia, 2000):

A coalition of software agents successfully protected five network-linked computers over two full working days of concentrated attack by a four-person hacker force.

The agent actually functions as a multi-agent collective, a distributed program that runs on multiple computers in a network. The program reacts with suspicion to "port scans" that scan all network ports, even if the scan takes place over a long period of time, like a year. The agent program works by setting up a collective that constantly compares notes to determine what unusual requests or commands have been received from external or internal sources. Because of this, the system response is not limited to waiting for someone to figure out a defense and put it into a virus checker.

This new software will recognize odd attacks. It will turn off services, close ports, go to alternate means of communication, and tighten firewalls. What distinguishes the Sandia agent programs from others is that they integrate security functions with normal services, such as FTP and browsers. This provides intrinsic security to each user. The program can shut down computer where it detected a "Trojan Horse,"[1] or remove from the network a computer that was taken over.

The example presented here shows peers collaborating through software agents, and without a central authority. The agents are cooperative, yet autonomous. Therefore, the collective is not vulnerable to a single-point attack or a single-point failure. These are some of the more special and valued attributes of P2P computing.

P2P can be used for virus protection in other ways, too.

---

[1] A program is called a "Trojan Horse" if it is a secret program and programmed to be operated at a later date by external hostile control.

MyCIO developed a product, called Rumor, which uses peers to deliver anti-virus updates. With Rumor, the first five users in a network who log on retrieve anti-virus updates from MyCIO. Then, those users turn into servers for everyone else on the network. Every time a system gets the latest file, it has the capability to serve that file to someone else that needs it. Rumor has such features as token-based authentication so the only files that can be shared by Rumor are legitimate, anti-virus update files.

Relevant Content through P2P

Sharing content in the P2P context deals with the techniques and technologies for effective ways to discover content's existence, its locations, and to get it delivered. When it comes to usages and applications that rely on content sharing, you cannot avoid getting involved with information- and knowledge-management. The filtering of data so that only meaningful data comes to you, and associating it with related information, becomes an integral part of the application. The power of direct exchanges and discovery searches between peers can be used to enhance the effectiveness of content management.

Network-Wide File Sharing

P2P file sharing extends traditional LAN-based file sharing to the Internet. This is a powerful technology for enabling cooperation across organizations and between companies.

Mangomind, from Mangosoft (described in Chapter 5) is one such application. How does a Mangomind community start?

The first person to join a Mangomind drive invites other users to join the drive, and he sets access permissions for files and folders. Invited users then link to the Mangosoft Web page, where they download client software and install it on their PC. Invited Mangomind drive users who join the drive can then access and share files on the drive. Once people have joined your drive, they can create, read, modify, and delete files located on the drive. They have access to this shared drive and the information on it. Information is kept up-to-date, and each user's latest changes are available to other users.

P2P and Knowledge Management

Finding the right document with just a set of key words can be time-consuming. When the organization is scattered, the problem becomes that much more complex. This was the problem facing Baker & McKenzie, the large law firm that is spread throughout 61 offices in 35 different countries.

Baker & McKenzie chose NXT from NextPage for nearly 2,800 of its attorneys. Attorneys at Baker & McKenzie can use NextPage to search throughout the firm's network for a document containing a certain word or name. With peer-to-peer technology, computers can share information without going through a central repository. This helps in getting most recent information, and reduces the burden of keeping a central repository.

Baker & McKenzie attorneys using NextPage will have access to all relevant documents residing on the firm's computers around the world, as well as those of select customers.

NextPage's unique content network technology enables continuous electronic links to connect separate content servers, allowing users to simultaneously access Internet sites, databases, intranets and document repositories, as if the data existed in a single location. See also (Barliant, 2001).

Another example of content management involves integration of applications. NextPage and Interwoven teamed to provide a content management platform to ABN AMRO Bank.

From an October 2000 press release:[2]

The first phase of the solution consists of providing internal content to 19,000 North American employees. With the NextPage-Interwoven solution, employees can simultaneously access bank policy and procedures manuals, management reports, and marketing materials. The integration will enable ABN AMRO to connect other departmental Interwoven TeamSite servers and other remote sites to provide employees with integrated access to content contained in those repositories. Employees use these materials to improve quality of service to customers and discover cross-selling opportunities.

[2] San Francisco, October 3, 2000. (http://www.nextpage.com/news/pressroom/pr_100300.html)

The benefit from the integrated product is having accurate and up-to-date information available to the employees, and, in particular, to those who are maintaining customer relationships.

With NextPage software, content can be created and maintained in its original location by its original author. Users can search, navigate, categorize, and personalize information in their content network in real time.

Distribution of Content the P2P-Way

Groove is a platform on which specific, collaborative P2P applications can be built. The partnership between eLiberation (the Internet micro-transaction software company) and Groove is an example of one such application area.

eLiberation has integrated its Financial Transaction Management (FTM) software within Groove's business-to-business environment to enable Groove Networks' customers and partners to monetize any type of P2P transaction. In particular, eLiberation is supplying Groove Networks with an FTM prototype to enable the sale of in-house pay-per-view training videos.

The prototype provides Groove users with a training account that can be used to pay for video streams. As Groove users view each stream, they are tracked and their account is "charged" according to usage; account holders can replenish their accounts using their credit card.

eLiberation believes that the combination of their experience and presence on rational micro-transaction will help establish that application within the P2P space.

You have read earlier (Chapter 10) about how OpenCola's Swarmcast makes use of network bandwidth. A prime example of Swarmcast in action occurred when Mandrake† 8 was recently released. The Mandrake community became aware of the beta Swarmcast demo and people started downloading the two Mandrake 8 images with Swarmcast. The results were quite amazing and very positive. There were (on average) between 20 and 60 people in the mesh of the files at all times. That means 20 to 60 computers available to serve the next download request simultaneously.

In a three-day period, Swarmcast helped serve up over 200 Mandrake images, which is over 130 GB of data (and it was done without any advertising or promotion – just a small leak)!

There are other applications that use this idea: that a file requested by many people also exists in many places. So a request for that file can be satisfied from many sources. BitTorrent presented their P2P-like copy product at the July 2001 DefCon conference. BitTorrent uses a browser interface. The users direct their downloads requests to "torrent://" followed by the URL from which they wish to download. The application will find an alternative source, thus allowing for faster delivery than possible when all the requests go to a single server.

Usages of Edge Services

Mangosoft's Cachelink is an example of using storage near the edges of the net. It was described in Chapter 5. Below is another example of how the idea is applied in delivering online training.

A simple definition of edge services is placing the content close to where it is to be used. This is mostly located by the edge of the network, where the users are with their desktops. Clearly, if the content is near where it is to be used, then we may end up with multiple copies, or replicas, of the content. Depending on the circumstances, you might need to worry about coherency and synchronization.

Taking the content to the edges is beneficial not just for the home users. It is a very useful technique within the enterprise, too. An example of such an application is the Intel® Share and Learn Software (SLS).

The SLS application uses a directory-mediated approach to identify the closest client containing the latest revision of the requested material. The material is then copied to the requesting machine.

The project that resulted in SLS was conceived as a tool for understanding the technical performance and economic impact of P2P file sharing capability. The chosen application was the delivery of multimedia training material to a worldwide audience.

For the pilot project, the aim was to generate a large user base, so that traffic patterns could be observed. About 2,000 users participated over a period of 12 weeks. The content consisted of 60 modules, ranging in size from 5MB to 25MB. It included different file types – video, PowerPoint†, and HTML.

This is how it works:

The client's request for a file goes to a directory server, who, by tracking the users' IP addresses, tells the client who has the file and which neighbor is closest. If that client is unavailable, the requesting client will be directed to the next closest source for the file. Tracking users by IP addresses is crucial, as 77% of them use mobile laptops.

Soon after this application got started, the primary distribution method of the files became peer-to-peer. The algorithm for finding the best "neighbor" does not look for the physically closest host with the desired file. The search also takes into account the topology and bandwidth of the network. If the file is not found on the client or its LAN, then the search will follow the "fatter" pipes in the network.

What was learned from the enterprise-wide SLS pilot?

- A significant percentage (80%) of the load is removed from the original host of the content. The requests for copies are satisfied by files distributed intelligently across the client base. As a result, the load on the WAN is reduced by over 50%, with the P2P application optimizing the use of the LAN. This comes with no extra burden on the LAN.
- Download times (as far as the user is concerned) improved three to four times. All this was delivered with no additional investment.

In short, a P2P application like SLS results in improved service to the user, while optimizing IT infrastructure.

Applying P2P to Search and Discovery

An interesting twist in applying P2P technologies is taking a distributed resource and making it look as if it were centrally located. This is exactly what NextPage is doing for the federal government.

The federal government is using Next Page's P2P enterprise content platform for its fedstats.net site that gives the public a single point from which to access statistics, like census data and economic reports, from around 70 agencies. Instead of having to build an all-inclusive database to be stored on a central server, the NextPage search technology retrieves data from wherever it resides.

Clearly, the ease of use and convenience for the users has improved, while the collection and storage of the data remains distributed, making it convenient for the content providers.

Relevancy is an important factor when developing strategies for search applications. We discussed it in Chapter 7, and in relation to OpenCola's Folders product. Even though it is not quite an application, strategies for a "relevance engine" affect the actual search results. Here is how OpenCola approaches this:

We saw that OpenCola Folders can be trained, with interaction with their human users, to bring more relevant documents. But the underlying software is also crucial. OpenCola uses multiple relevance engines to determine which set of found documents might be useful to the user.

The *Bayesian*[3] *relevance engine* provides excellent results for text-based documents. While the algorithms used by relevance engines vary, they tend to present themselves to the user in a manner similar to the Bayesian engine. Typically, the user will be provided with candidate documents that need to be rated. The relevance engine compares the candidate document against an ideal document and a junk document, and a numerical rating is given to the user. The user can then intervene by manually rating the document as junk, good, very good, or excellent. The user's rating changes the engine's internal model, nudging it in the direction of finding documents that are more relevant by the criteria of the user.

Other relevance engines are being explored. They are based on principles such as:

- Distributional clustering
- Relevancy signatures
- Latent semantic indexing

[3] The term Bayesian comes from Bayesian statistics, a method created by Thomas Bayes. It is based on the idea that present probability should take into account past experience.

Distributed Computing

This is a very active area in P2P computing. There are quite a number of companies that are engaged in some form of distributed computations. Here are examples in three flavors of computations:

- Distributed computing on the Internet
- Distributed computing within the intranet
- Grid computing applications

Distributed Computing on the Internet

By now you know what it takes to share resources in a P2P network of computers, and the infrastructure that a few companies have built to facilitate large-scale challenging computational projects on the Internet. Below are a couple of examples of great things that can be done with these tools.

Looking for a cure for cancer

Intel and United Devices joined forces with the American Cancer Society, the National Foundation for Cancer Research (NFCR), and the University of Oxford to advance cancer research with the help of distributed Internet computing. The first application involves leukemia drug-optimization research.

Here are some details as reported in the press:

To participate in the research effort, PC owners first download a small computer program. After running the downloaded file, the program is installed on the user's computer and automatically begins computing; it runs whenever computation resources are available. The program is similar to a "screensaver" that operates during normal computer use, without intervention by the user. Once processing is complete (typically a day later), the program sends the results back to the United Devices' data center and requests a new packet of data the next time the user connects to the Internet. The program incorporates a comprehensive system of security and privacy technologies to protect user privacy.

NFCR scientists estimate that this task will require a minimum 24 million hours of number crunching, which was previously unimaginable. This particular drug-optimization program evaluates four proteins. One of the four proteins has been identified as critical to the growth of leukemia, and shutting it down may lead to a potential cure.

The application was named THINK. This is how the project works and where it stands (about two months after its launch):

The THINK application has performed virtual screening of drug candidate molecules using over 600,000 unique hosts for an aggregate total computing effort exceeding 100 million compute hours.

The THINK application investigates the potential interaction between drug-like molecules and target proteins known to be critical to the growth and function of certain cancers. During its calculation, THINK considers many different conformations or different 3-D structures of the same base molecule in an attempt to find the most natural "fit" or docking between the drug-like molecule and an active site in the targeted protein. If a fit can be found, then THINK calculates various chemical properties of the interaction between the molecule and protein to help determine if the molecule will interfere with the normal function of the protein, thereby interfering with the cancer's ability to grow and spread. THINK also calculates minor chemical mutations of the drug-like molecule, potentially capable of enhancing the desirable interaction between drug-like molecule and protein.

Researchers at the University of Oxford are already using findings from early results in the project; they are refining later parts of the study and suggesting further experiments. With the overwhelming member response to this project, the University of Oxford is in the fortunate position of being able to expand the scope of their research project. They are taking the opportunity to further investigate promising discoveries almost as soon as they are uncovered in the course of this virtual drug-screening project. Because the number of operations performed in a given THINK execution is not known beforehand, accurate prediction of the total number of compute hours required for this increased scope of study is difficult, but at current estimates it may exceed one billion compute hours. Over the duration of this project, over 3.1 billion drug-like molecules will be studied by THINK to find potentially fruitful chemical interactions with as many as 16 different target proteins. Because of the multiple stages of this research project, many of these drug-like molecules will be revisited and studied further in conjunction with the same or different proteins, guided by results and findings earlier in the study. To date, more than 50% of the drug-like molecules have already been screened by THINK.

The ability of the THINK application to make efficient use of the United Devices distributed computing platform is perhaps the most dramatic demonstration to date of the extraordinary promise and scalability of molecular modeling and virtual drug screening methods on large scale distributed parallel computing platforms.

Fight AIDS at Home

Another distributed computing project that is looking for a cure is a joint cause-computing project between Entropia and the Olson Laboratory at the Scripps Research Institute, called "Fight AIDS at Home".

Here are some details reported by the researchers of the Olson Lab at the Scripps Research Institute in a recent volume of the FightAIDSatHome members newsletter:

At the end of July 2001 there were 32,000 machines computing on behalf of the FightAIDSatHome project, with a combined power of almost 15 Tera-Flops. This virtual supercomputer has about 4.5 million MB of RAM and about 50 million MB of disk space. FightAIDSatHome has already clocked up a staggering total of about 2,000 years of computation, as measured by what a fast workstation can compute in a year, making it probably the biggest anti-HIV drug-design calculation performed in history.

How does it work?

The Olson Laboratory provides both the computer program and the input data for each calculation. The Entropia software then allows FightAIDSatHome member computers to run AutoDock, the automated molecular docking software developed over the last 10 years in the Olson Laboratory. The Entropia software is instructed to download the molecular structures of an important HIV target, namely HIV-1 protease (an enzyme, or protein, essential to the replication of the HIV-1 virus), and candidate HIV-1 protease inhibitors the Olson Lab is currently evaluating. The Entropia software manages the computer's resources so that AutoDock can perform its tasks in the background without affecting the performance of FightAIDSatHome members' computers. The program incorporates a comprehensive system of security and privacy technology to protect both the user and the research. When a task is completed, the computer connects to Entropia to return its results. Since the file is very compact, the transfer does not take long. Then the next task is downloaded, and the process begins again with a new drug candidate.

As an example of what can be accomplished, consider this:

Over the December 2000 holiday season, FightAIDSatHome helped the Olson Laboratory complete over 500,000 molecular dockings of anti-HIV drug candidates with its AutoDock software in just *two days*, a feat that would otherwise have taken *years* on the most powerful workstations. The project also screened the 1,980 compounds of the National Cancer Institute's (NCI) so-called "Diversity Set." This group of molecules is supposed to represent the chemical diversity or uniqueness of the roughly 400,000 compounds held by the NCI. The NCI has at least one gram of material of each of these nearly half-a-million potential medicines, so if a good hit is found, it will be possible to obtain a real sample to test predictions made by researchers.

To learn more about the FightAIDSatHome project, see http://www.fightaidsathome.com/

Distributed Computing on the Intranet

Administration of resources within the intranet is different than on the Internet. The resources on the intranet are managed by a single entity, the local IT operations. The resources are known, and scheduling is simpler.

It is so much simpler, in fact, that DataSynapse (a provider of distributing computing) has created two platforms – one for the Internet, the other for an intranet. Here, we're going to present the latter.

The DataSynapse (http://www.datasynapse.com) Intranet platform leverages existing resources in a non-intrusive manner. The platform, called LiveCluster†, can be deployed across dedicated and non-dedicated PCs, Servers, or SMP machines across multiple operating systems. They support Java, CORBA, and Java Beans. They also support C++, COM, and XML.

DataSynapse focuses on financial institutions and their applications. The computational needs of a financial institution offer a number of computationally-intensive applications that can be parsed out into smaller tasks, which can be executed in parallel. In other words, the large computation can be divided among underutilized PCs scattered around the organization.

The solution integrates easily with the corporation's existing network environment. Employees never notice LiveCluster is working because it only takes control of a desktop PC when that PC is idle. Should a worker return to his desk during a computation, LiveCluster immediately interrupts the processing task and reroutes it to another idle system.

With some modification to the original application a retail bank, a customer of DataSynapse saw significant performance benefits. In one case, computing complex derivatives contracts performance improved by a factor of 80. Baseline time to process 200 trades on an existing server was 44 minutes. By distributing those computations across about 100 PCs, the job finished in 33 seconds.

Completing such jobs faster is invaluable to a financial services company. It can boost the productivity of traders, allow a bank to react more swiftly to abrupt economic changes, and generally increase the number of trades a company can conduct. What's more, scaling such a system to handle more and more complex calculations is easy.

For more on distributed computing in the financial sector see (Intel, 2001).

Within a number of corporations, the use of idle cycles of workstations at the workplace has been commonplace for several years. One of them is Intel, whose NetBatch facility distributes circuit simulation runs to idle workstations. Being a global corporation, Intel's NetBatch moves the jobs around the world following the sunset, thus using the workstations at night. The savings in equipment and its administration resulting from NetBatch is estimated to be around $500 million.

Grid Computing

Grid computing is a field rich in applications and projects. We have mentioned some of the Grid computing communities in the first part of this chapter. This section contains a short description of the types of applications that are amenable to Grid computing, and a very short synopsis of some of the ongoing projects.

First, it will be useful to describe how we differentiate Grid Computing from the Distributed Computing that was presented above.

Consider these two aspects – Scope and architecture:

- **Scope.** We saw that Globus and Avaki, both general-purpose infrastructures, offer a comprehensive set of capabilities for P2P and Grid computing. Whereas the distributed computing companies – Entropia, United Devices, and DataSynapse – offer platforms for computations only. Grid computing supports collaborations between nodes at different locations, distributed storage, data visualization, and more. Its scope is broader than that which we associate with distributed computing on the Internet or on intranets.
- **Architecture.** The term Grid comes from the utility Power Grid. This provides us with a suitable metaphor. While Globus can be applied to computations distributed over desktops, the current Grid projects, with a few exceptions, distribute computations between data centers. These data centers are like the power grid's power stations. They provide the power to some nodes at the edge of the network. Continuing with the metaphor, in Internet computing the nodes at the edge are the providers of power. It would be as if the utility company collected power produced by windmills or waterwheels that belong to the nodes at the edges of the Net.

At this time, Grid Computing and Internet/intranet Distributed Computing are not the same. In time, they probably will look more and more like the same type of platform.

The purpose for constructing the computational grid is to deliver better performance to the users. There are two ways to achieve this:

- Run the application at a site that has a powerful computer, or find a site where the workload is low.
- Apply multiple computer systems, or, in other words, parallelize the application. Not every application can be easily divided for parallel execution. And even when it can, it has to be divided into big enough chunks of work that can be done independent of each other.

Several types of applications are good candidates for Grid Computing:

- **Parametric Studies.** There is a class of applications where the same computation is performed on a set of parameters. For example, when NASA or Boeing simulates a design of an aircraft, they need to run the computations for many "angles of attack." The computation with each angle can be given to a different computer on the grid.
  This is similar to running the same application on a different data set, such as the case of SETI@home and FightAIDSatHome. Only, in these

cases there are millions of data sets, and each computation can be completed on a PC in a reasonable amount of time.

- **Parallel Applications.** Applications that can be broken up to parts that can work independently of each other for a time much longer than the time to communicate between any two nodes. For example, a numerical weather model is represented by a three-dimensional grid around the globe. This mathematical grid can be divided into slices that don't have much to communicate to each other in each time step of the simulation. Analyses of large amounts of data (e.g., climate or medical) can have a similar structure.
- **Multi-discipline and cross-organizations.** A grid is useful when a multi-discipline application is shared between organizations that cannot share accounts. This is a complex setup, with some of the data migrating to the grid component of the other organization, before computation commences there. For example, NASA may run a fluid dynamics simulation for a Boeing aircraft design, with the results fed into a structural analysis at Boeing.

Let's look briefly at some of the Grid projects.

- **Department of Energy (DOE) Science Grid.** Its goal is to provide Grid middleware and tools needed within DOE for a wide variety of collaborative science projects concerned with data analysis, scientific simulation, and computer-enhanced instrumentation.
- **NASA Information Power Grid (IPG).** A project to integrate computing systems, data storage, networks, and analysis software, providing reliable source of computing power for NASA aeronautics applications.
- **Tera-Grid** by the National Computational Science Alliance (NCSA) and the National Partnership for Advanced Computational Infrastructure (NPACI), both funded by the National Science Foundation (NSF). The goal of this Globus-based project is to construct an integrated computational and collaborative environment, comprised of a computational grid (infrastructure oriented) and an access grid (people oriented).

There are more projects associated with Grid computing than we can list here. They include use of data centers, clusters of desktops and workstations, and distributed resources within organizations and on the Internet. The Grid computing community also produced a rich set of tools and libraries. Those come mostly from universities and research labs. You can find pointers to all this information at the Global Grid Forum site (http://www.gridforum.org).

Web Testing

There is an interesting by-product of platforms for network-based computations. They provide the ability to test performance aspects on the web in ways that are not otherwise possible. Distributed computing companies, such as United Devices and Entropia, have realized the opportunity and the need, and will be offering tools for measurements on the net. The beneficiaries from web testing are likely to be various network service providers and IT organizations within the enterprise.

Let's first examine how United Devices address web testing by using their MetaProcessor† platform:

United Devices teamed with Exodus Communications to devise two types of tests, which answer two questions:

- Stress load testing answers the following question: "How many users can my website serve before performance degrades to an unacceptable service level?"
- Performance monitoring answers the following question: "How does my website perform for users on an ongoing basis?"

Stress load-testing measures the peak capacity of e_Business applications, and accurately predicts how they will respond to spikes in visitor traffic.

Performance monitoring is done, typically, with a small set of sensors or monitors that are placed strategically throughout the Internet to deliver ongoing measurements of a website's performance.

Factors such as location and bandwidth can dramatically impact the general performance of a website, and the measurement taking is typically complemented with root cause analysis of website performance slowdowns.

Using the thousands of volunteer PC users, who make up the United Devices Member Community, the resulting stress load testing can be done with a one-to-one user to machine ratio (instead of simulating some 20 to 200 virtual users per machine).

With the membership mentioned above, performance-monitoring can be targeted to any demographic and geographic vicinity and mix of users.

Entropia can also apply its user community to performance measurements of the Internet.

Whereas current methods employ servers at hubs across the Internet, Entropia brings to bear actual user machines at the edge of the network. In addition, instead of simulated loads, the measurements now can reflect actual performance at the "last mile."

The Entropia Grid contains thousands of real live users at the edge of the last mile, in nearly one hundred countries around the globe. The software agents that collect the data for the performance testing can be deployed on any number of machines, in any location, and at any time.

The sample sizes are fully scaleable. Entropia will locate the available resources that meet the test's criteria and automatically download and install the software agent on those additional machines.

A single API handles job scheduling and management. The API initiates communication directly with the Entropia server and its registered member PCs. There is no need for system administrators, manual or remote installations, or hardware maintenance.

The worldwide Internet user community is quite heterogeneous. Using server nodes to simulate the differences among user machines, including geographical distribution, operating systems, network connection types, and competing ISPs, is impractical.

From a simple machine-query API, the Entropia Grid Services can create sample pools of nearly every permutation of machine criteria possible. Factors that can be selected include geographic location, network connection types, the operating system, CPU model, available memory, disk space, etc. The pool can also be connected to a specific ISP.

Web testing may turn out to be one of the unexpected popular P2P applications. Any Internet service provider and IT organization may want to utilize such an accurate way of measuring performance on the network.

A potential issue of concern is privacy. The users who volunteer their resources for doing computations need to agree to participate in the testing. These users will want assurances that information about their system is not disclosed to others. And it does not need to be, since the testers do not need to disclose who participated.

Concluding Remarks

The purpose of this chapter is to show you how diverse P2P applications can be. This is not a comprehensive survey of P2P applications; there are so many more that deserve to be mentioned, and the field and scope of applications is changing in a very rapid pace.

Similarly, I did not tell you how these applications were constructed. only what they do (and even that is very brief.)

Again, P2P is *how* we do it, not *what* we do, and the "what" covers a wide spectrum of applications.

Chapter 12
Challenges and Outlook

As we come to the end of this book, it behooves us to consider the challenges still ahead for wide adoption of P2P computing. And, to finish on a more positive note, let's also speculate on what the future holds for P2P computing. The challenges in front of P2P are concluded from the technology discussion. The outlook is based on some of the research and developments we observe. In any event, the opportunities are plentiful.

Though the lines get blurred at times, I will separate technical barriers from social, cultural, and attitudinal resistance to P2P. The mindset and the technical challenges do feed on each other, and addressing an issue in one class often resolves an obstacle in the other.

Technical Challenges

The technical discussion in Part II highlighted the important technical issues that need to be dealt with in order to make P2P computing work. We saw that there are solutions that, in general, address a specific computing environment or application. A couple of challenges were not addressed directly, but they should be mentioned here. I break down the technical challenges of P2P into these areas:

- Connectivity
- Security and Privacy
- Fault-tolerance and availability
- Performance and Bandwidth
- Scalability
- Self-management of systems
- Interoperability
- Complexity

Connectivity

The Internet has evolved and changed from its early days and its original design. The direct connection between two client devices has been replaced by a connection mediated by a server. Another change in the networks we use is the pervasive employment of firewalls and NATs.

The consequences of the current environment is that P2P services need to include mechanisms for locating peers that don't have public IP addresses. And they need to include mechanisms for communicating through firewalls.

The problem is aggravated by the fact that there different types of NATs and firewalls.

There is no universal solution to naming and mapping of names to network addresses. There is no general-purpose solution to the traversal of firewalls. Each infrastructure developer, and sometimes an individual application, came up with their own answer to connectivity.

P2P computing will benefit from a consensus on how to make direct peer-to-peer communications transparent to the users. It will be a great bonus if it is also transparent to the application developers.

Security and Privacy

The security discussion in this book focused on authentication, authorization, and data integrity. We have extended the data integrity topic to include the issue of confidence in results obtained by distributed computing applications.

Security is a big concern. Home users and corporate desktop users become providers of services, without the experience and administrative attention that is given to traditional central servers. These users are concerned about who accesses their systems, and what others can do while having the access.

IT administrators and managers worry about opening direct communication channels between external users and their own users, tunneling through (or bypassing) the corporate security. The IT personnel are concerned about:

- The risk of spreading viruses
- Unauthorized access to confidential and private information
- Installation of new applications on desktops that might have unknown and undesirable side-effects on the local network and policies

We saw that there are a number of security frameworks that provide effective techniques for authentication and authorization. Encryption and digital signatures assure privacy and detection of tampering with transmissions.

The level of security within the solutions varies. It depends on the nature of the application and the environment in which it is run. In some P2P infrastructures, security is deeply embedded in the naming and identity schemes. In others, security measures are added to supplement the communication mechanisms. A consequence of the disparate security schemes is that some level of security is given up when two applications are integrated.

In many ways, the security issues for P2P are similar to those of any Internet user. The commonality applies to what happens while the messages move between locations. The added risks to the P2P user arise from allowing access to the peer's system.

In the P2P setting, the security role of a gatekeeper, be it the ISP or the corporate firewall, becomes more complicated, or impossible. A plausible direction for P2P-style security is not to rely only on a gatekeeper, but to bring security to each client system.

The security challenges, then, are:

- Provide strong security at the client's device
- Maintain security across namespaces created by different P2P applications

Fault-tolerance and Availability

The central idea behind P2P is the sharing of resources that are otherwise idle. The two big factors that challenge the reliable provision of a P2P service are:

- Intermittent connectivity of resource providers
- Finding the required resources available when needed

Intermittent connectivity does not affect us only during the phase of discovering the resources, but also while using them. A peer we use for a computation or content may be disconnected in the middle of the task we're performing. A file stored or found on another host one day, may not be available the next time we're looking for it, and so on.

The challenge of recovering from a fault or assuring availability of resources will not go away. The P2P services and applications can take steps to mitigate some of the risks. As with fault-tolerance and availability in general, a part of the solution involves redundancy and replication.

The larger the pool of resources we have, the bigger the chance is that the requested resources will be found. The more copies there are of content items the more we're likely to always find one of them. The more repeated computations we perform, the more certain we'll be in getting a complete, and verifiable, set of results. The answer to availability and fault-tolerance is in:

- Large pool of resources we don't control, or policies that govern provision of resources by members of the P2P community
- Redundancy of operations
- Replication and caching and frequent synchronization of content

This issue will remain with us, however, and will continue to add complexity to P2P solutions.

Performance and Bandwidth

In this book, I have not discussed performance issues. First, we need to get the basic functionality and features in place. Of course, even while building the foundations we need to keep performance in mind, lest the outcome is not usable because it is too slow or incapable of handling the required volume.

Most people agree that the mitigating factor for P2P performance is the network. There are two elements to network performance:

- Latency
- Bandwidth

Latency is important when we're trying to communicate in real-time. Examples of applications that rely on low latency are Instant Messaging, and, more acutely, online Gaming. When the network has sufficient capacity, latency is actually helped by the direct node-to-node routing of the P2P model.

Bandwidth presents a different problem. Some, who look at file swapping (a la Napster), are concerned that popular P2P applications may saturate networks and bring them to a halt. Some colleges experienced network bandwidth saturation due to music file sharing, and had to restrict such usage. Of course, not all P2P applications move large amounts of data all the time. But bandwidth capacity is still a potential problem.

P2P introduces a twist to the network bandwidth problem. It is possible that more data will be passed around on the net. But that is not the only issue. More significantly, the source of large amounts of data shifts from servers to nodes on the edge of networks. There are several ways to address the P2P bandwidth issue:

- Network developers have to focus on routing algorithms from node-to-node, and not only from servers to nodes.
- P2P increases the demand for broadband at the edges of the net. Currently, in many circumstances it is faster to send a file to another person via a server (source node to server, server to destination node), than letting the network route directly between nodes.
- Use peer cooperation to spread the transmissions between peers and along many paths. We saw some an example of this in OpenCola's Swarmcast.
- Apply caching and updates of "deltas" to minimize network traffic. This technique is employed by Groove, Escher, Mangosoft, and others.
- Find the nearest node that can be the source of a transmission, as is done by Escher and Intel's SLS application, among others.

Scalability

Scalability is assumed to be a problem whenever we talk about the Internet and connecting peers. The fact is that there are classes of P2P applications and environments where scaling is not an issue. Frameworks for small groups, such as Groove, and applications for corporate intranets, are not faced with scaling issues that arise from P2P.

That being said, we do expect a general-purpose P2P infrastructure to scale with the growth of the number of participating peers. What are the elements that can face scalability issues?

- **Central naming scheme.** The DNS is replaced by P2P naming schemes. The new schemes have many advantages, but some rely on a central computer where the name-to-address mapping takes place. Scaling this approach to many millions of users will bring us back to the old DNS system with its inability to synch up changes of addresses fast enough.
- **Distributed naming schemes.** The scaling problem here is one of finding efficient ways to update lists and details of names and attributes. Hierarchies and "neighborhood" approaches may be employed.
- **Directories, discovery, searches.** Just as in naming schemes, the mediated services are vulnerable to the same scaling difficulties faced by a central naming service. And, when distributed, these services need to consider the same approached the distributed naming schemes might use.

In general, any architecture with a flat structure is susceptible to stalling when it reaches certain size, in terms of number of peers. Either hierarchies or "neighbor" relationships may be necessary for the environment to scale.

There is some talk in the P2P community about "super-peers." These are peers that have a special role, and they are expected to be (always) available. That special role might be acting as a hub for communication, or being the keeper of a directory, and some such functions. These super-peers can serve as a foundation for scaling the space of the peers. The caution here is that if we rely too heavily on super-peers, we'll essentially end up with the client-server model.

The P2P computing model needs to find a way to scale while preserving the unique attributes of P2P.

Self-Managed Systems

In P2P, individual users provide services to others. They act in a limited capacity of servers. Many of these users do not have the experience or the tools to manage a server.

Users are not comfortable in making their resources available to others without a sense of control and monitoring. IT managers are nervous about loss of control over the network and exposing enterprise resources.

The challenge here is how to provide the users with the tools for allowing the sharing of their resources while maintaining control over their private information and flexibility in revoking access. At the same time central bodies within the enterprise wish to centrally manage these resources that are being shared, for distributing computing, for example.

Another way of putting this challenge is this: How to implement the right balance between global (enterprise) and local (user) policies, while maintaining secure and autonomous environment.

Interoperability – Standards, Protocols

The P2P infrastructures described in this book, and all others, are not interoperable with each other. They share a small set of communication protocols, and most use XML and SOAP. Yet, the end result is that we don't have the interoperability or the bridges for crossing over from one P2P framework to another.

The P2P developers, who already created their infrastructure services, their applications, and their peer communities, may not feel the urgency in interoperability, even though future growth may favor interoperability with other solutions.

The main beneficiaries of interoperability are the application developers who wish to migrate (or develop new) applications for P2P computing. The assumption here is that interoperability will precipitate the availability of the basic services. This will save much development time.

Following this argument all will benefit in the long run. There will be more P2P applications, and they can talk to each other. Users will have more reasons to join a P2P environment, and applications will have more chance at being used – because they interoperate with others.

- Use of the same standard does not always means interoperability:

  "The devil is in the details," as the saying goes. And this is true for standards and P2P, too. It is easy to get complacent and assume all is well when two services use something like XML. By itself, it does not provide the level of interoperability that we may wish to experience. XML describes data. But XML also allows the developers to define their own schema or to use DTD (Document Type Definition[1]). So, for interoperability in the sense of reading each other's description of documents and content, we also have to agree on the syntax and the semantics of these descriptions. Alternatively, we need to find a way to describe our schema to others.

- The need for application-level interoperability.

  One of the scenarios where interoperability is needed is between applications that do similar things. For example, say there are members from two groups who wish to videoconference, but use two different video conferencing applications. Some companies (one of them is Endeavors) are developing plugins to accomplish exactly this kind of interoperability.

What are the challenges around interoperability between P2P services and applications?

- **Variety of computing models.** From pure P2P, to varying degrees of server mediation.
- **Variety of network settings.** Behind the firewall intranets, Internet, a mix of the two, between a number of separate intranets. One of the implications here is the necessity to support a wide range of security measures. And allowing them to coexist.
- **A wide range of application types.** Different shades of sharing resources, content, and collaborative interaction.
- **Different population sizes.** From small groups of less than 10 peers to networks of millions.
- **Balance between the P2P community and the peer's local autonomy.** Maintaining interoperability in the face of allowing flexibility in setting local policies.

---

[1] See, for example, http://www.xml101.com/dtd/dtd_intro.asp

At this time, it is not clear if interoperability is needed, or to what extent. Even when assuming we agree on its benefit, implementing interoperability is a complex task.

Dealing with Complexity

The enormity and the variety found in the space where P2P belongs (global networked computing) can be intimidating. Complexity has become an attribute of the P2P infrastructure. Without dismissing the numerous factors you have read about, it may be comforting to take a more abstract view on what we mean by complexity. On an intuitive level, we think of environments as complex when one of two things happens: We observe unexpected results of some activity that occurs, or there are so many parts and elements that we cannot begin to guess what the outcome might be. Though both facets are applicable to P2P computing, the "many parts" aspect dominates our concerns.

In the world of mathematics, complexity is often mentioned together with non-linear, dynamic systems and with chaos theory. One interesting differentiation between complexity and chaos is that complexity is the study of how complicated systems can generate simple behavior, while chaos deals with complicated behavior that simple systems can generate.[2] With this understanding, the surprising results we see sometimes correspond to chaos, and are almost always associated with non-linear relationship between variables. In the context of P2P, we are more interested in how a complex system can exhibit a "simple" behavior such as self-organizing into a well-regulated entity. I have mentioned Resnick's "Beyond the centralized mindset" (Resnick, 1996). The essence of his thesis is that simple rules governing the interactions between immediate neighbors and nearby objects can lead to a simple and desirable global structure. Resnick gives the example of a flock of migrating geese. It has been found that no one special goose is the leader. The leadership alternates among the geese, and its rotation can be demonstrated through simple rules that affect a goose and its neighbors on either side.[3] The beauty of this explanation is that we don't need to make 'strange' assumptions to explain the group dynamics of geese migration. Similar simple rules can demonstrate how ants "decide" where to create the pile of all the seeds they collect.

---

[2] http://www.vanderbilt.edu/AnS/psychology/cogsci/chaos/workshop/Glossary.html

[3] See, for example, *Complexity: The Emerging Science at the Edge of Order and Chaos*, by M. Mitchell Waldrop.

How is all this relevant to P2P computing? It is quite possible that an infrastructure that allows a community of peers to set simple rules for interactions between neighboring peers is all that is needed for the formation of large self-organizing and effective online communities with shared values and objectives.

Complexity is a good term to wrap around the technical challenges that are barriers to a wide acceptance of P2P. Complexity, and the technical issues that bring it about, are a result of taking the computing action to the edges of the net. We now have multiple autonomous entities, multiple points of entry into a network, and distributed resources. Security, monitoring, and administration seem much more complex. At least, they will as long as we examine the new environment from the centralized mindset vantage point.

Merging P2P with the existing centralized infrastructure is possible with placing more responsibilities (and tools) in the hands of the computers at the edge of the net. These responsibilities will include security, and reporting to the central authority. And the current IT structures will have to integrate existing solutions with distributed processing and distributed resource management.

Large P2P communities will seem less complex when the self-organizing and dynamic community is defined in terms of the relationships each peer has with a small number of physical and logical neighbors.

Social and Mindset Challenges

Let's go over the aspects of P2P computing that are not strictly technical. You will see that some technical solutions resolve social and attitude objections. In other cases, a change in attitudinal approach help see technical issues in a different light, and a new direction for a solution offers itself.

I won't offer solutions (at least, not complete and definitive) to the social and cultural challenges that face P2P computing. The intent in the following passages is to provoke thought about these topics.

Self-Organization and the Centralized Mindset

The concept of self-organized online communities is central to quite a few P2P applications. We saw that intermittent presence and moving the control of resources to the edges cause a number of technical challenges.

The loss of central control is also difficult for IT organizations, where the administration and monitoring of resources is centralized. Indeed, all shared resources are central or controlled by a central authority.

Changing a mindset from a static center providing resources to the nodes on the edge, to that of a dynamically changing reservoir of resources at the edge is a difficult one. First, one needs to think "distributed." Then, one needs to be comfortable with resources moving around and switching irregularly from being connected to being disconnected.

To see where the difficulties are, let's consider the types of networks that can make up a P2P network:

- **Internet users.** Assume all connected via an ISP. A group of online gamers, for example.
- **Intranet.** All the peers belong to a single intranet, as in a typical enterprise setting.
- **Multiple intranets.** Peers belong to one in a number of intranets, which may not have full trust in each other. It's a typical setting for a B2B (Business to Business) connection.
- **Internet and intranet.** Peers may either be a part of an intranet, behind a firewall and a NAT, or an individual on the Internet. This configuration applies to a B2C (Business to Customer) interaction.

The top two categories are the easy ones.

The gamers on the Internet, or the family sharing vacation photos, will not be concerned with resource administration issues. Their security concerns are not as consequential as those of the enterprise IT managers.

The P2P network that is contained within a single intranet, and protected by a gateway from the outside world, feels secure and comfortable to its users. All the peers are subject to the same local policies. Authentication and confidentiality are not big issues. Connectivity is easy.

The mixed networks, the bottom two categories, represent the areas of least comfort and most distrust.

A good starting point for P2P in business is to limit it to applications on the local intranet. Once used to managing distributed resources within the enterprise, extend to applications involving cooperation with a business partner. Move on from there to customers on the Internet, once security measures and adequate monitoring of access are in place.

Concerns of IT Managers

There are several levels of concerns that IT managers have with regard to P2P operating in their domain:

- **Security.** Direct 2-way communications between users in the intranet and users from outside the firewall. We saw that such connections can be established through tunneling or initiated via a third party. These communications may pose a security risk by bypassing filtering and other checks.
- **Unknown components.** Some P2P networks allow sharing of software components between the peers. New applications may thus be installed on peers' desktops without clearance from IT. Apart from licensing issues, such applications may have side effects on the normal operation of that user or others.
- **Distributed resources.** It is more difficult to manage distributed resources, especially when the systems are not always connected. And their users have certain amount of control and autonomy over the use of their resources.
- **Integration with existing applications.** The collaborative P2P frameworks are expected to make use of existing commonly used tools, so that there is no need to create a parallel suite of productivity tools, for example.

All these concerns can be addressed, and at least some of the P2P infrastructures do accommodate some of the issues raised by IT. It is clear that P2P within the enterprise requires a lot more monitoring and resource management capabilities, and will not tolerate anonymity mechanisms, compared to some P2P applications on the Internet.

In general, we find some amount of skepticism among IT managers regarding the effectiveness of P2P technologies in the enterprise. This attitude is by no means universal. You saw in the previous chapter that P2P applications are welcome in a growing number of businesses.

Creation of Online Communities

Online communities are depicted as one of the more interesting outcomes of applying P2P technologies. There are online groups, or communities, on the Internet today. The members meet in chat rooms, or exchange views on a "list" or a weblog. The existing forums are managed centrally, and a server serves out the content.

P2P technologies can extend the concept of grouping by interest. They can allow exchanges in multiple media. The content being shared can be distributed. The community can be self-organized, its policies defined and enforceable. Members can join and leave, perhaps without a trace. Members can easily create specialized forums for a subset of the whole membership.

And what is the challenge here? The cultural challenge is in creating atmosphere that will be welcoming to non-expert users who wish to step forward and start an online forum with others.

What such users need is an easy access to the basic facilities that are needed for the formation of communities. These include services such as naming, authentication, authorization, and others.

Trust Between Remote Users

The topic of trust between peers should be at the top of the list of issues that carry with them a lot of emotional content. You know P2P has a major hurdle in front of it when you hear stories about security lapses on home computers even before peering is pervasive. In late March 2001, I heard a news story on national radio. The message of the story was: Compromising your home PC privacy and the risks of someone accessing your files and the likelihood of virus infections will only get worse as more people install broadband internet connections. An interview with a security expert revealed that some 10 million PC users reported unwanted intrusions onto their computers in the year 2000. And these were only the *reported* cases. The expert was confident the real number was much higher. Businesses will not be happy to learn that, in addition to malicious hacking for gathering information in the pursuit of identity thefts for financial gains, many of the intrusions are used for acquiring business login and passwords from the many people who frequently dial in from home. Given this (quite justified) perception of threatening and unsafe existence while connected to the net, we all understand the reluctance to open up one's computer to unknown people who just happened to join the same online community. And, in the P2P spirit, we also expect peers to stay connected longer.

You can see why it is imperative to increase the comfort level of the potential peers while collaborating and sharing the computer resources. Beyond the security measures you read about in Chapter 9, much more needs to be done in the area establishing peers' reputation through attestation and other means of validating people's credentials.

Trust and Reputation

Users wish to feel safe when sharing resources of their systems with others. They wish to have confidence that no damage can happen to that which they own. They want to be absolutely sure that their privacy is not violated, and that their confidential information remains so.

Security services address the technical aspects of making users comfortable with sharing their resources with others, sometimes strangers. Security and trust are, in some sense, opposing concepts. You need security when there is no trust. But security measures can create a foundation on which trust can be built, in time.

There is another concept that is useful for developing trust in what starts as an untrusting environment: Reputation. It turns out that reputation online plays as big a role as it does in our physical world. There are also ways in which it can be measured, given some specific criteria (see Oram, 2001).

Reputation is a means for establishing the level of trust bestowed onto a peer. It is a dynamically changing attribute, a measure for assigning positive marks as well as negative marks. Reputation is a measure of behavior in relation to expectations in the environment.

You can apply reputation in a transitive manner, much like we do in real life. If someone you trust tells you that another person is knowledgeable about a certain subject, and a source for reliable information, you may well assign a high reputation level to that other person. You'd do so without first-hand acquaintance with that person, and, probably, with regard to the subject at hand.

We can differentiate between "objective" and "subjective" reputation attributes. The objective ones can be applied to you by everyone else. For example, an online marketplace can rank you by your diligence in performing to your commitments, be it as a buyer or as a seller. It is fair to assume that we all agree on what is a positive reputation and what is a negative reputation, in such cases. Other reputation measures are more subjective. They are built upon personal taste and shared interests. We tend to trust those who have similar opinions and interests to ours.

In a previous chapter we saw how OpenCola builds reputation-like metrics based on "similarity" in content of interest. Mojo Nation uses reputation as a currency. In their system, you build up reputation by availability of your system and the time it takes to download a file you have. The idea is that people will pay more for better service. Each person keeps a database of the reputations of others. The Google search engine ranks web pages by some measure of reputation. The pages are ranked by how many others sites list and mention that page.

Reputation will become an important attribute for building trust among stranger peers, and for like-minded users. We need a set of objective and a method for subjective metrics on which to base reputation. And the P2P services, or the application, will need to include a mechanism for monitoring and synchronizing the reputation values as they change in time.

Protection from Undesirable Content

One of the disturbing phenomena of P2P is that file swapping applications bypass the traditional filters that parents and institutions use against undesirable content from the web, including that which comes from search queries.

To many, the loss of filtering control is a deterrent against joining the application. The P2P communication mechanism must take into account the presence of other software components intended for use in external communications. P2P services have to integrate into the existing policies.

How to Create the "P2P Groundswell"

With over 60 million users, Napster has been a most popular application of P2P file swapping. Similarly, AOL Instant Messaging, with some 100 million subscribers, is hugely successful. Neither is a "killer app," in the sense that they have not substantially changed our lives.

Consider the first spreadsheet program that brought about the popularization of the PC, and what that did to our lives. And, later, the arrival of the graphical interface browser caused the explosive success of the Internet, which changed how we conduct our business and social lives.

It is not clear that P2P needs a Mosaic-like application in order to become a success. But it does need some more Napster-like successes in the broader range of P2P application. A wide-ranging acceptance of P2P requires a demonstrated success of collaborative P2P, peer communities paradigm, content sharing and discovery that bring the use of the net to new levels, or some such application.

P2P may not experience an explosive overnight adoption. It hasn't yet. Its adoption may be gradual, maybe as client-server computing model has. And, in that case, we need to see a continuing flow of new applications, and regularly hear about new customers of P2P applications.

The challenge facing the P2P developers is to keep the momentum going for new releases, new features, addressing the technical hurdles, and signing up new customers.

About Business Models

This book is not about the business aspects of P2P. The reason I have included a section with the word Business in its title is that the question of business viability presents a non-technical challenge, be it a perceived or real one.

On April 4, 2001, the Wall Street Journal published an article about the state of P2P computing with this opening sentence: "It's starting to look as if the end may be near for the 'peer-to-peer' fad." The reasons given for this premature end-of-era prediction revolved around the closure of a number of small new start-up companies, and the tendency of some of the surviving companies to position themselves by the applications they support, rather than as "P2P company."

Another perspective to take is this: Did you ever hear about a "client/server company"? No. Then why should there be a segment of P2P companies? P2P computing is a computing model. P2P represents a set of technologies. If, or when, mainstream software developers adopt the model and technologies to achieve their goals, then we will not need companies who specialize in P2P. We used to talk about Internet companies, and now every company is. So, perhaps we are heading in the right direction, and what the WSJ interprets as the demise of P2P is anything but.

Having said that, there are two reasons for the creation of P2P-specific entities. And even these reasons hold only for the initial period of introducing a new technology and a new mindset. The first motivation arises from the need to provide the infrastructure on which to build. Combined with that are early experiments and proof-of-concept kinds of projects. Freenet and Gnutella and InfraSearch come to mind as examples for these early companies. The second reason we might continue to observe new P2P companies come into being is related to the first. The new mindset, of decentralization and pushing computing to the edges of the net and of peer collaboration, opens the doors to completely new applications. Existing vendors do not cover these new applications; they involve higher risks because they are based on new ideas, and many will fail. Therefore, it is natural to see these new applications developed by startups. Later, they may be absorbed into existing mainstream companies, just as InfraSearch was acquired by Sun Microsystems. Or, in some cases, we may see new "industries" developed around the new types of applications. But what is important to note is that it is the application that is the *reason for being*, not the underlying technology.

In short, we should look for signs of P2P adoption in the mainstream of applications for business and the home, and not be too alarmed that many newly created companies that focused on P2P fade away, one way or another.

Looking Ahead

This book attempts to provide a snapshot of a segment of the activities around P2P computing. It is not a summary of a completed task. We tracked the solutions and issues faced by a representative group of developers who focus on P2P within an organizational structure of corporations and laboratories, and we made a number of detours to discuss the participation of individual home users of the Internet.

Not only is the story not finished, but we are probably only in the very early phase of learning what can be done with P2P technologies. Even the technologies themselves are still evolving. Just consider what there is still to accomplish in such areas as search, software agents, metadata usages, and all the challenge areas described above.

So, we close the book not with a summary of all that was done, but with some mentions of all that is happening.

The section about the industry initiatives gives us an idea of who might be involved in setting practices and services for the P2P infrastructure. The commentary about research projects provides hints of advancing the future scope of P2P applications.

Industry Initiatives and Research

There are numerous industry-wide projects and initiatives that aim at promoting and advancing P2P computing. Some have been mentioned in this book, others have not.

One of the topics not discussed in this book is about P2P infrastructure-related projects that have been started by some large corporations.

- **Sun Microsystems' JXTA (http://www.jxta.org/)**
  JXTA is an open source project that provides services for writing P2P applications. With JXTA the user can find other peers, share files, find content on remote sites, create a group of peers, monitor activities, and communicate securely.
- **Microsoft .NET (http://www.microsoft.com/net/)**
  .NET is a framework for web services. As such, it can also serve as a platform on which P2P applications can be built.

Hewlett-Packard and IBM have projects to investigate P2P computing.

In addition, IBM is investing in about 50 server farms all over the world, from where they will offer computing services through the Globus middleware (see Globus in chapters 6 to 10, and below).

Intel is involved with the P2P Working Group, Internet computing philanthropy projects, and some internal P2P pilot projects.

At the beginning of the book I mentioned the P2P Working Group (P2PWG, http://www.p2pwg.org/). As of August 2001, it has almost 40 member companies. The group is engaged with infrastructure topics such as Security, NAT/Firewall traversal, and File Systems. The working group also promotes the Peer-to-Peer Trusted Library (PtPTL), which was described in Chapter 9.

Another industry association is the New Productivity Initiative (NPi, http://www.newproductivity.org/). The group has about a dozen members, as of August 2001. It is specifically committed to Distributed Resource Management (DRM). NPi has published a Reference Model for DRM in the summer of 2001 (New Productivity Initiative, 2001).

NPi and P2PWG collaborate and have established reciprocal membership in each other's organization.

I have discussed the Grid Forum and Globus at length earlier in the book. A recent meeting of the Global Grid Forum (GGF) attracted 340 participants from some 20 countries, and 180 organizations. At present, the GGF gatherings are more popular than their equivalent P2P events. Grid computing, as a particular brand of distributed computing, is a very active and productive field. There is an impressive list of ongoing projects, most of which represent specialized computing communities, as listed in Chapter 11.

It is yet to be seen if the various activities around infrastructure, services, and standards for P2P will converge. We may end up with commonality at some levels and not in others. Or, there may be defined interfaces that will serve to create bridges between different infrastructures. Time and the Market will tell.

We are beginning to see research projects that are closely related to P2P topics and applications. There are many projects that carry the P2P label in their title, but nonetheless will be advancing the state of P2P applications. I am referring to projects that involve intelligent agents, distributed storage, metadata, cluster computing, and many more.

Let's take two projects of distributed storage, for example.

IBM and UC-Berkeley work jointly on project called OceanStore (http://oceanstore.cs.berkeley.edu/). OceanStore is designed to scale to users in the billions. Users join the infrastructure, and become contributors of storage space and consumers of files. The architecture uses promiscuous caching and redundant replication in order to deliver performance and fault-tolerance. The data is encrypted to protect from untrusted hosts.

Another project aimed at huge amounts of distributed storage is Microsoft's FarSite (http://research.microsoft.com/sn/Farsite/). FarSite's broad objective is to figure out how to build highly available, reliable, and secure systems on a collection of cooperating but mutually distrusting hosts. FarSite is designed to be adaptive and self-configuring, resistant to attacks, reliable, and available.

One of challenges listed above is about performance. It is gratifying to see proposals for measuring performance of different types of P2P networks. Analyzing the application-based networks will provide the basic data for improving both the design of the application and the configuration and routing of the networks.

Outlook

"P2P is how we do it, not what we do." --Chris Williams, CEO of Oculus.

This apt quote nicely captures what P2P computing is about. P2P is a tool, a set of technologies; a way of doing things. What people do with the P2P technologies covers the gamut of applications.

P2P came on the (mainstream) scene with a bang. Now the dust has settled, and we can clearly see all the work that is still to be done. There are technical and social challenges that need to be overcome. And there is great promise of the wonderful ideas people have for applications, which, in many ways, bridge the gap between the real world and the cyber-world. They are about interacting and sharing at the edges, where the people are.

What we have now are the pieces. The early P2P pioneers showed us what could be done, and they will tell us what else they can do. Startup developers and corporate architects are getting together, finding unifying principles, common standards, and fundamental services on which to build a P2P structure. It is a comprehensive and complete model for computing; a model that coexists with, and enhances, the Internet models of today.

When P2P "grows up" there will be no need to identify a company as a "P2P company." The infrastructure, even if multiple flavors of it survive, will be a part of our "standard" software. The developers of novel applications will become just another ISV (Independent Solutions Vendor). And many existing ISVs will have versions of their application that is adapted to the P2P model of computing.

What can we expect to see along the way when P2P is used as casually as "client-server" is used today?

- P2P will become an integral part of the solution to security on the Internet, an issue that exists independently of the arrival of P2P.
- P2P will present new ways to address the growing issue of extracting meaning and relevance from the information glut presented by the Web.
- We will witness huge populations of users participating in solving computational problems too large to solve before: problems that will advance our understanding of diseases, our environment, and our climate changes.
- We will witness an acceleration of breaking down geographical and cultural boundaries through the formation of online communities based on shared values and shared interests.

And, there will probably be much more.

This is not the end of the Peer-to-Peer story. It is barely the beginning.

References

Chapter 1:

Christensen, Clayton M. *The Innovator's Dilemma.* Harvard Business School Press, 1997.

Oram, Andy. O'Reilly Network: *Peer-to-Peer Makes the Internet Interesting Again.*
URL: http://www.oreillynet.com/pub/a/linux/2000/09/22/p2psummit.html

Hayes, Brian. *Collective Wisdom.* American Scientist, Volume 86, Number 2, March-April 1998, pages 118-122.

Resnick, Mitchel. *Beyond the Centralized Mindset.* Journal of Learning Sciences, vol. 5, no. 1, 1996, pp.1-22.
URL: http://el.www.media.mit.edu/groups/el/Papers/mres/JLS/JLS-1.0.html

Sandia National Laboratories. *Intelligent agents challenge computer intruders.* New Release, May 18, 2000.
URL: http://www.sandia.gov/media/NewsRel/NR2000/agent.htm

Chapter 3:

Museum of Science and Industry, Chicago. *History of the Internet.*
URL: http://www.msichicago.org/exhibit/commex/history.html
1997.

Shoch, John F.; Hupp Jon A. *The "Worm" Programs - Early Experience with a Distributed Computation.* Communications of the ACM (CACM), Volume 25, Number 3, March 1982, pages 172-180.

Hauben, Michael. *History of the ARPANET*.
URL: http://www.dei.isep.ipp.pt/docs/arpa.html

Sample of Groupware and Instant Messaging references:

Instant Messaging 101
(http://netconference.about.com/internet/netconference/library/weekly/aa042098.htm?once=true&)

RootsWorks: Instant Messaging
(http://www.ancestry.com/library/view/news/articles/2763.asp)

History of Notes and Domino (http://www.notes.net/history.nsf/)

Groupware, Workflow, Email, Calendar, Collaborative Software
(http://www.compinfo-center.com/email.htm)

Chapter 4:

AVAKI / (Applied MetaComputing). *Legion – An Integrated Architecture for Secure Resource Sharing*. Proposal submitted to the Peer-to-Peer Working Group, December 2000.

Endeavors Technology, Inc. *Peer-to-Peer Architecture and the Magi† Open-Source Infrastructure*. Proposal submitted to the Peer-to-Peer Working Group, December 2000.
URL: http://www.endtech.com/html/Architecture.html

Catlett, Charlie; Foster, Ian. *Grid Forum*. March 2000.
URL: http://www-fp.mcs.anl.gov/~catlett/GF/GridForum-Overview.pdf

Foster, Ian; Kesselman, Carl; Tuecke, Steven. *The Anatomy of the Grid*. To be published Intl. J. Supercomputer Applications, 2001.
http://www.globus.org/research/papers/anatomy.pdf

Foster, Ian; Kesselman, Carl, eds. *The Grid: Blueprint for a New Computing Infrastructure*. Morgan Kaufmann Publishers, 1999.

Foundation for Intelligent Physical Agents (FIPA). *FIPA Abstract Architecture Specification*. Proposal submitted to the Peer-to-Peer Working Group, November 2000.

Proksim Software. *Peer-to-Peer Architecture Proposal*. Proposal submitted to the Peer-to-Peer Working Group, December 2000.

The Globus Project. *Grid Research*. URL: http://www.globus.org/research/papers.html

Chapter 5:

The links to companies and products described in Part II:

Entropia: http://www.entropia.com
United Devices: http://www.ud.com/home.htm
OpenCola: http://www.opencola.com/ and http://www.opencola.org:8080/
Mangosoft: http://www.mangosoft.com
NextPage: http://www.nextpage.com/nextpage2.asp
Escher Group: http://www.eschergroup.com
Groove Network: http://www.groove.net and http://devzone.groove.net/
Endeavors Technology: http://www.endeavors.com/ and http://www.endeavors.org/
Engenia: http://www.engenia.com/indexfl.html
AVAKI: http://www.avaki.com/home.html
Globus: http://www.globus.org/ and http://www.gridforum.org/

Oram, Andy, ed. *Peer-to-Peer: Harnessing the Power of Disruptive Technologies*. O'Reilly & Associates, 2001.

United Devices. *MetaProcessor™ Platform Architectural Overview*. 2001. http://www.uniteddevices.com/products/mp_platform.htm

Chapter 6:

Davidson, John. *An Introduction to TCP/IP*. Springer-Verlag (ISBN 0-387-96651-X),1988.

Comer, Douglas E. *Internetworking with TCP/IP*. Prentice-Hall (ISBN 0-13-468505-9), 1991.

PC Network Advisor. *Understanding TCP/IP Tutorial*. 2001. http://www.pcnetworkadvisor.com

IETF RFC2663 by Srisuresh, P. and Holdrege M. *IP Network Address Translator (NAT) Terminology and Considerations*. August, 1999. http://www.ietf.org/rfc/rfc2663.txt

IETF RFC1631 by Egevang, K. and Francis, P. *The IP Network Address Translator (NAT)*. May, 1994.
http://www.ietf.org/rfc/rfc1631.txt

IETF RFC1928 by Leech, M., Ganis, M., Lee, Y., Kuris, R., Koblas, D., Jones, L. *SOCKS Protocol Version 5*. March, 1996.

Borella, Michael; Montenegro, Gabriel. *RSIP: Address Sharing with End-to-End Security*. USENIX. March, 2000.
http://www.usenix.org/publications/library/proceedings/ine2000/full_papers/borella/borella_html/

Peer-to-Peer Working Group. *Bidirectional Peer-to-Peer Communication with Interposing Firewalls and NATs*. [http://www.p2pwg.org/.. – paper is in "members only" section.. check if public] 2001.

Chapter 7:

Shirky, Clay. The Domain Name System is Coming Apart at the Seams. October, 2000. http://www.shirky.com/writings/dns.html

Brickley, D., Dornfest, R. The Power of Metadata. January, 2001. http://www.openp2p.com/pub/a/p2p/2001/01/18/metadata.html

uddi.org. *UDDI Technical White Paper*. September, 2000. http://www.uddi.org/pubs/Iru_UDDI_Technical_White_Paper.pdf

Czajkowski, K., Fitzgerald, S., Foster, I., and Kesselman, C. *Grid Information Services for Distributed resource Sharing*. IEEE International Symposium on High Performance Distributed Computing (2001), IEEE Press. http://www.globus.org/research/papers/MDS-HPDC.pdf

Chapter 9:

Phillips, R. *Peer to Peer Networking: Communication paradigm for the transient Internet, or a catalyst for social change*. May, 2001. http://www.cs.uwa.edu.au/undergraduate/units/233.410/book2001/ritchiep/

Vamosi, R. *Alternative Protection Against Malicious Code*. May, 2001. http://www.zdnet.com/zdhelp/stories/main/0,5594,2702096,00.html

Groove Networks. *Groove Security*. July, 2001. In http://devzone.groove.net/technotes/

Globus. *Grid Security infrastructure*. July, 2001. http://www.globus.org/Security/

Foster, I.; Kesselman, C.; Tsudic, G.; Tuecke, S. A Security Architecture for Computational Grids. November, 1998. Proceedings of the 5th ACM Conference on Computer and Communication Security, and -
http://www.acm.org/pubs/articles/proceedings/commsec/288090/p83-foster/p83-foster.pdf

Butler, R.; Welch, V.; Engert, D.; Foster, I.; Tuecke, S.; Volmer, J.; Kesselman, C. A national-Scale Authentication Infrastructure. December, 2000.
http://ieeexplore.ieee.org/iel5/2/19227/00889094.pdf?isNumber=19227

Chapter 11:

Harrison, A. *Groove Customer Speaks Up*. Network World Newsletter. July, 2001.

Barliant, C. *Law Firms Begin to Understand and to Embrace 'Peer-to-Peer' Technology*. Law Technology News. January, 2001.
http://www.lawtechnews.com/january01/technology_trends_p54.html

Intel Corporation. *P2P File-Sharing at work in the Enterprise*. March, 2001. http://www.intel.com/eBusiness/products/peertopeer/

Intel Corporation. *Peer-to-Peer-Enabled Distributed Computing*. June, 2001. http://www.intel.com/eBusiness/products/peertopeer/

Chapter 12:

New Productivity Initiative. *New Productivity White Paper*. July, 2001.
http://www.newproductivity.org/White_Paper.pdf

General References for P2P:

Werbach, K. *Peering into the World of Peer-to-Peer, Parts I & II.* Release 1.0, Volume 18, No. 10 & No. 11, November & December, 2000.

Peer-to-Peer Working Group
URL: http://www.p2pwk.org

OpenP2P.com – the O'Reilly site for P2P
URL: http://www.oreillynet.com/p2p/

Ben Houston's P2P Idea Page – for technical information, resources, and papers
URL: http://www.exocortex.org/p2p/

PeerProfit – for news and company watch
URL: http:// www.whimsical.net/peerprofits/

P2PTracker – news, opinions, about companies
URL: http://www.p2ptracker.com/

PeerIntelligent – "The knowledge hub for P2P business,"
http://www.peerintelligence.com/

Peer-to-Peer File Sharing – Yahoo links
URL: http://dir.yahoo.com/Computers_and_Internet/Internet/Peer_to_Peer_File_Sharing/

Distributed Computing – Yahoo links, with a P2P bend
URL: http://dir.yahoo.com/Science/Computer_Science/Distributed_Computing/

P2P Glossary

The list was created with support from the P2P Working Group, the New Productivity Initiative, O'Reilly Network, and a number of individuals. Some definitions were found on whatis.com (http://whatis.techtarget.com) and RSA Security FAQ (http://www.rsasecurity.com/rsalabs/faq/).

.NET — .Net is a business strategy from Microsoft that is aimed at a convergence of personal computing with the Web. The goal is to provide individual and business users with a seamlessly interoperable and Web-enabled interface for applications and computing devices and to make computing activities increasingly Web browser-oriented.

See http://www.microsoft.com/net/default.asp.

1-copy serializability — A consistency model where no user can observe even temporary inconsistencies caused by multiple users accessing and updating data on multiple replicas.

Access Control — Mechanism for granting controlled access to another user to one's own resources. These resources can be processors, storage, files, peripheral devices, or even bandwidth. Access control includes setting permissions and level of access, monitoring, and terminating the external access.

Example: locking of a file, to prevent simultaneous access and possible modification by multiple agents.

Access control list (ACL): A set of data associated with shared resources that defines the permissions that users and/or groups have for accessing it.

ACID — ACID (atomicity, consistency, isolation, and durability) is an acronym of the four primary attributes ensured to any transaction by a transaction manager. These attributes are:

Atomicity. In a transaction involving two or more discrete pieces of information, either all of the pieces are committed or none are.

Consistency. A transaction either creates a new and valid state of data, or, if any failure occurs, returns all data to its state before the transaction was started.

Isolation. A transaction in process and not yet committed must remain isolated from any other transaction.

Durability. Committed data is saved by the system such that, even in the event of a failure and system restart, the data is available in its correct state.

The ACID concept is described in ISO/IEC 10026-1:1992 Section 4. Each of these attributes can be measured against a benchmark. In general, however, a transaction manager or monitor is designed to realize the ACID concept. In a distributed system, one way to achieve ACID is to use a Two-Phase commit (2PC) protocol, which ensures that all involved sites must commit to transaction completion or none do (and the transaction is "rollback").

AES The Advanced Encryption Standard (AES) is an encryption algorithm for securing sensitive but unclassified material by US Government agencies and, as a likely consequence, may eventually become the de facto encryption standard for commercial transactions in the private sector.

AES replaces the Data Encryption Standard (DES, see below). The specification called for a symmetric algorithm (same **key** for encryption and decryption) using block encryption of 128 bits in size, supporting key sizes of 128, 192 and 256 bits, as a minimum. The algorithm was required to offer security of a sufficient level to protect data for the next 20 to 30 years.

An algorithm called Rijndael, (submitted by two Belgian cryptographers, Joan Daemen and Vincent Rijmen) was chosen in 1999 following an open selection process.

Agent A software entity situated within a part of an environment that senses that environment and acts on it, over time, as programmed. Agents exhibit autonomy – the ability to act without human interface, and cooperation with other agents or other software entities. An agent may be static or mobile. It can be reactive or deliberate. Agents can perform one or more functions such as collaborate, interface, collect information, watch for events, and more. When an agent can learn from its own experience it is often referred to as a smart agent.

Mobile agents are of special interest to P2P. A mobile agent is an agent that moves, or can move, through a network in order to perform a given task on behalf of a user. Example: an agent that performs a distributed search, per search parameters provided by the user.

The terms "intelligent agent" and "bot" are often used synonymously with "agent."

[alternate definition:]

An intelligent software process that can be configured to respond automatically when the circumstance it is monitoring changes.

Agent, Intelligent Used synonymously with "agent."

Anonymity
: The quality of not being identifiable.

In the context of P2P there are a number of anonymity types (from the Free Haven chapter in (Oram, 2001)):

Author anonymity: The author cannot be linked to a document.

Publisher anonymity: The publisher of a document cannot be identified

Reader anonymity: The reader of a document cannot be identified. This is a privacy attribute.

Server anonymity: The system that serves a document cannot be identified.

Document anonymity: A server does not know which document it is storing.

Query anonymity: The server cannot tell which document it is serving to satisfy a request.

Partial anonymity: When a search for an identity can be narrowed down to a "set of suspects," but no further.

Application
: A program or group of programs that performs a specific function for users. An application program is in contrast to system programs such as operating system kernels, etc.

Authentication
: Authentication is the process of determining whether someone or something is, in fact, who or what it is declared to be.

Authorization
: Authorization is the process of giving someone permission to do or have something.

Autonomy, Local
: The level of control that can be exercised by the owner of a shared resource. In many cases, the term implies being the final authority of what use is made of the resource, and when. It also implies the ability to establish and enforce local policies.

BEEP (or BXXP)
: BEEP (Blocks Extensible Exchange Protocol) is an XML-based messaging framework for building application protocols in progress at the IETF. BEEP provides a generic application protocol kernel for asynchronous interactions that is designed to permit simultaneous and independent exchanges of both textual and binary messages.

http://www.ietf.org/html.charters/beep-charter.html
http://www.bxxp.org

Binary Management
: Binary management refers to system-level management and transport of application and component executables. A system that provides binary management keeps track of executable versions, caches and transports them as necessary, and ensures that the latest version (or the appropriate version) is used. A system that does not provide binary management requires a human (end user, system administrator) to explicitly copy application executables around using tools such as FTP and to ensure that the correct versions are in place everywhere. The lack of binary management facilities significantly increases the burden on system/application administrators and greatly increases the opportunities for version skew due to human error.

Binding Naming and binding is one of the most fundamental issues in distributed systems. A binding maps a "name" to another name or to a lower level address. Binding can occur at many different times – this is called the bind time. Binding can occur when a program is written, for example, when the programmer might specify a hard-wired address. Binding can occur at compile time, at link time, at load time, or dynamically each time an invocation on some named entity is performed. Delaying binding typically provides greater flexibility at greater cost.

Bind-Time The time when a name is bound to a lower level name or an address. Examples include compile time, load time, first access, and each access.

Bot Used synonymously with "agent."

Caching Caching, in the P2P sense, is the practice of placing oft-requested data closer to the requestor. Caching is coherent if all copies of the data are updated when any individual copy is changed. Multiple caches of the same data may be created, or a single cache can serve multiple requestors.

Certifying Authority A certifying authority (CA) issues certificates (see Certificates), and can be any trusted central administration willing to vouch for the identities of those to whom it issues certificates and their association with a given key. A company may issue certificates to its employees, or a university to its students, or a town to its citizens. In order to prevent forged certificates, the CA's public key must be trustworthy: a CA must either publicize its public key (see Public Key) or provide a certificate from a higher-level CA attesting to the validity of its public key.

Certificate See Digital Certificate.

Checkpointing The creation of a persistent store of the state and volatile data of a running batch job, such that the job can be restarted later, potentially on a different host.

Cluster A collection of hosts that are configured and managed by a single resource management component – a virtual system.

Clerver Clerver (combination of terms client and server) is synonymous to a node that is peer; i.e., it has both client and server functionality.

Client A role in a network-computing task, in which a client node requests a service that can be provided by another (server) node. A client node can neither offer nor respond to requests for services. The term "client" is also sometimes applied to a node that can operate in the client role (e.g., a desktop PC).

Client-Server (or Client/Server) A computing model in which any of a collection of "client" nodes may request and obtain services from a "server" node. Clients can only consume services. Servers exist to provide services, but they can also consume services. Such nodes may have exceptional processing capacity, or specialized capabilities.

Collaboration
An application that consists of a collection of discrete capabilities, all of which support work done collaboratively by a group of individuals. Collaboration tools include the ability to distribute information and jointly modify information in a way that ensures that all participants view the same information as it is modified. Collaboration also typically includes calendaring, and real-time communication capabilities, such as voice-over-Internet and instant messaging. Collaboration is often, but not necessarily, synchronous.

Connectivity
The property through which a node is physically attached to, and having an active communication pathway into, a network. The node's physical connection may be wired or wireless. The logical connection establishes an identity for the node on the network.

There are three categories of connectivity:

A *static* connection is permanent, so that the connected node is always present and available on the network, with a permanently-assigned and valid network identity.

In an *intermittent* connection, a node may not always be attached to the network, either because of periods of physical disconnection, or because the connection is not always kept active, perhaps in spite of constant physical connection. "Roaming" notebook computers or hand-held devices exemplify this type of connectivity.

In a *limited*-connectivity connection, an attached node has access to only certain portions of an extended network. These limitations can be imposed by network gateway or address-mapping devices, such as firewalls or NATs.

Control Node or Coordinator
A network node that provides control information to a collection of peer nodes that are performing a distributed computing or resource-sharing task. That information may include directory services, task-allocation and data-distribution services, etc. The control node may not itself participate in the actual execution of the subject computing task.

Credential
A credential is data that is transferred or presented to establish either a claimed identity or the authorizations of a system entity. A credential is the information one entity presents to another to authenticate the other's identity. An authentication agent or a certification authority typically issues credentials. Depending on the model for authentication, credentials may only be valid for a session, or they may have longer validity periods.

Data Partition (also Data Decomposition)
The process of dividing the data associated with a computing task into sub-portions, which can then be distributed to a collection of peer nodes for processing. Data partitioning is normally accompanied by task partitioning, which provides participating peers with the programs needed to process the partitioned data. Various partitioning metrics and algorithms may be typically used, by a control node that performs the partitioning and task distribution.

DES

Data Encryption Standard (DES) is a widely-used method of data encryption using a private (secret) key that was judged so difficult to break by the U.S. government that it was restricted for exportation to other countries. There are 72,000,000,000,000,000 (72 quadrillion) or more possible encryption keys that can be used. For each given message, the key is chosen at random from among this enormous number of keys. Like other private key cryptographic methods, both the sender and the receiver must know and use the same private key.

DES applies a 56-bit key to each 64-bit block of data. The process can run in several modes and involves 16 rounds or operations. Although this is considered "strong" encryption, many companies use "triple DES," which applies three keys in succession. This is not to say that a DES-encrypted message cannot be "broken." But few messages sent today with DES encryption are likely to be subject to the code-breaking effort that is required.

The next standard is known as the Advanced Encryption Standard (AES, see above).

DHCP

DHCP (Dynamic Host Configuration Protocol) is an Internet protocol for automating the configuration of computers that use TCP/IP. DHCP can be used to automatically assign IP addresses, to deliver TCP/IP stack configuration parameters such as the subnet mask and default router, and to provide other configuration information such as the addresses for printer, time and news servers.

http://dhcp.org

Digital Certificate

A digital certificate is an electronic "credit card" that establishes your identity when doing business or other transactions on the Web. It is issued by a certification authority (CA). It contains your name, a serial number, expiration dates, a copy of the your public key (used for encrypting messages or for digital signatures), and the digital signature of the certificate-issuing authority so that a recipient can verify that the certificate is real. Some digital certificates conform to a standard, X.509. Digital certificates can be kept in registries so that authenticating users can look up other users' public keys.

Digital Signature — Using public key cryptography, it is possible to digitally "sign" a piece of information. Signing information essentially means assuring a recipient of the information that the information hasn't been tampered with since it left your hands.

To sign a piece of information, first compute a mathematical *hash* of the information. (A hash is a condensed version of the information. The algorithm used to compute this hash must be known to the recipient of the information, but it isn't a secret.) Using your private key, sign the hash, and attach it to the message. Make sure that the recipient has your public key.

To verify that your signed message is authentic, the recipient of the message will compute the hash of the message using the same hashing algorithm you used, and will then use your public key to verify the signature that you attached to the message. If the signature verifies, then it proves that you signed the message and that the message has not been changed since you signed it.

Dispatching — The action of sending a job to the execution host.

Distributed — Processing, computing resources or program-execution control that is delivered by a collection of multiple networked nodes.

Directory — A directory, in the P2P sense, is a software entity that maintains information about the location, attributes and accessibility-state of distributed resources, such as files or services available from each network node. It is capable of tracking the overall contents of a collection of nodes. The directory may be centralized (but with global scope), or portions of it may be distributed across multiple nodes.

Discovery — The process of finding various nodes or resources available within a network of nodes. These resources may include hardware (e.g., disk-storage space, peripheral devices), software (e.g., Web services, directory services, etc.), or users. Discovery may be local (i.e., identification of all hardware resources attached to a node), or it may be distributed (i.e., finding the resources on multiple nodes such as the set of all printers attached to a network).

Distributed Computing — A computing model where a computation or its data or both are divided into smaller pieces and distributed across multiple nodes, and is executed in parallel on these nodes.

Distributed Computation — A computation that is divided into smaller pieces and distributed across multiple nodes, and is executed in parallel on these nodes.

Distributed Resource Management (DRM) — DRM is the effective operation of computing systems to increase people productivity, improve products, and reduce IT costs. DRM enables the extraction of superior computing capabilities and performance from existing resources to do more processing faster, the automation of computing processes to easily manage enterprise workloads, and the intelligent utilization and maximization of resources to obtain greater control, reliability and availability of computing hardware, software applications, network and storage infrastructures.

DNS The domain name system (DNS) is the way that Internet domain names are located and translated into Internet Protocol addresses. A domain name is a meaningful and easy-to-remember "handle" for an Internet address.

Because maintaining a central list of domain name/IP address correspondences would be impractical, the lists of domain names and IP addresses are distributed throughout the Internet in a hierarchy of authority. There is probably a DNS server within close geographic proximity to your access provider that maps the domain names in your Internet requests or forwards them to other servers in the Internet.

DNS constitutes a global namespace for computers, but many PCs hidden behind NAT firewalls are disenfranchised because they have no IP address, making P2P communications difficult.

http://www.dns.net/dnsrd

DRM See Distributed Resource Management.

Dynamic DNS The ability to automatically update a DNS server when an IP address is automatically assigned (typically from DHCP) to a network device.

(see also DNS and DHCP)

ebXML ebXML (Electronic Business XML) is a project to use the Extensible Markup Language (XML) to standardize the secure exchange of business data. Among other purposes, ebXML would encompass and perhaps replace a familiar standard called Electronic Data Interchange (EDI). ebXML is designed to enable a global electronic marketplace in which enterprises of any size, and in any location, could safely and securely transact business through the exchange of XML-based messages. Because ebXML relies on the Internet's existing standards such as HTTP, TCP/IP, MIME, SMTP, FTP, UML, and XML, it can be implemented and deployed on virtually any computing platform. The use of existing standards gives ebXML the advantage of being relatively inexpensive and easy to use.

http://www.ebxml.org

Edge Services (also File-Staging)
A service that performs caching to nodes at the edge of the net. The facility of making data available near to a requesting node by copying the data onto a peer or a neighbor server.

[alternate definition:]

A capability for the dissemination of data to nearby point(s) of consumption. The associated data transmission is unidirectional, from data-source node to consumer node(s). This capability eliminates or reduces the need for multiple transmissions of the data, resulting in more-efficient use of network bandwidth. There are 2 types of edge-services:

"Streaming" edge-services, which involve transmission of latency-sensitive data (e.g., multimedia content streams).

Non-streaming edge-services, which involve transmission of non-time-sensitive information (e.g., large corporate training files).

Encryption (and Decryption)
Encryption is the conversion of data into a form, called a ciphertext, that cannot be easily understood by unauthorized people. *Decryption* is the process of converting encrypted data back into its original form, so it can be understood.

Modern ciphers work according to sophisticated computer algorithms that rearrange the data bits in digital signals.

In order to easily recover the contents of an encrypted signal, the correct *decryption key* is required. The key is an algorithm that "undoes" the work of the encryption algorithm. Alternatively, a computer can be used in an attempt to "break" the cipher. The more complex the encryption algorithm, the more difficult it becomes to eavesdrop on the communications without access to the key.

The stronger the cipher -- that is, the harder it is for unauthorized people to break it -- the better, in general. However, as the strength of encryption/decryption increases, so does the cost.

Entity
Any object that has an identity and is addressable without qualification. An entity (e.g., a peer or a user) may have multiple identities.

Event Notification
Mechanism that allows the detection of specified events within a node or in a network of nodes, and notification of occurrence of those events to a set of subscriber resources (e.g., exception notification to processor, presence notification of a buddy in an instant messaging system). An event notification can be distributed where the notification propagates to a resource located on a different node.

Extensibility
An extensible system can be changed to have new behaviors and semantics without heroic effort.

Failback
After a failure, a process can be resumed on the same host at an earlier point in its execution (perhaps even at the beginning).

Failover After a failure, a process can be resumed on an alternate host while fully recovering the functionality of the process previously running on the failed host – i.e., without losing any data and without having to restart the process.

Fault A failure of the system occurs when the behavior of the system deviates from its specification (system fails when it cannot provide the desired service).

An error is the part of the system state which can lead to subsequent failure. The cause of an error is a fault.

Fault Classes *Crash*; Component halts or loses its internal state (no incorrect state transitions taken).
Omission; Component does not respond to some input.
Timing out; Component responds too early or too late.
Byzantine; Arbitrary behavior.

Fault Detection Determining that a fault has occurred. Typically the first step to resolving the problem.

Fault-tolerant A system is fault-tolerant if it can mask presence of faults in the system.

In other words, a system is fault-tolerant if the system is consistent with its specification despite the failure of some of its components.

File Sharing File sharing, in the P2P sense, has come to mean the transfer of a copy of the file.

The traditional definition of file sharing is that two or more different users can access (read and/or modify) the same file – typically the same single instance of a file. This is a capability a typical shared distributed file system supports.

Note: Napster is a popular file sharing application where people share and copy MP3 files with each other.

File System, Distributed A distributed file system is an application that allows clients to access and process data stored on the server as if it were on their own computer. When a user accesses a file on the server, the server sends the user a copy of the file, which is cached on the user's computer while the data is being processed and is then returned to the server.

Ideally, a distributed file system organizes file and directory services of individual servers into a global directory in such a way that remote data access is not location-specific but is identical from any client. All files are accessible to all users of the global file system and organization is hierarchical and directory-based.

Firewall A firewall is a network device that routes or forwards packets from one network to another after first checking whether the packets meet some criteria. For example, is the packet an http request? Is it TCP or UDP? Is it an ICMP? What port range is the destination? From what IP address does it come? Does byte 42 have a "?" in it? Firewalls are used to prevent against some forms of attack.

A typical firewall allows only http traffic to/from any destination, and ssh connections from well known, and trusted IP addresses.

See http://www.soscorp.com/products/BS_FireIntro.html for more information.

Framework An application architecture in which low-level capabilities are integrated into ("buried" within) the application, without developer-accessible interfaces that allow access to those capabilities in isolation. Such an application cannot easily be extended beyond whatever specific interfaces have been provided as part of the application definition/specification. The capabilities used within such an application cannot easily be re-used in other applications. The architecture of a framework-based application contrasts with the architecture of an infrastructure-based application.

Group An entity that includes and represents a set of entities within a given name-space.

GUID GUID is short for Global Unique Identifier. The GUID is a randomized string that is used to uniquely identify a host or message on the P2P network. This prevents duplicate messages from being sent on the network.

Hailstorm Part of Microsoft's .Net initiative, Hailstorm is the company's plan to provide a single place on the Web where any individual user (who pays a fee) may securely store personal and financial information that can be shared with others when desired (for example, to pay for something at an online store). Hailstorm makes use of the Extensible Markup Language (XML) and the Simple Object Access Protocol (SOAP). http://www.microsoft.com/net/hailstorm.asp

Host See "Node"

HTTP The Hypertext Transfer Protocol (HTTP) is the set of rules for exchanging files (text, graphic images, sound, video, and other multimedia files) on the World Wide Web. Relative to the TCP/IP suite of protocols (which are the basis for information exchange on the Internet), HTTP is an application protocol. http://www.w3c.org/protocols

HTTP Tunneling The act of getting through a firewall by specifying 80 as the port number. HTTP uses port 80 to transmit web pages, and many firewalls allow port 80 traffic to go through.

Hybrid A descriptor for computing configurations or applications that use different computing models (e.g., "pure," "mediated," "client/server") in different services or service layers.

Identity	A value, globally unique within a single name-space, that is associated with (at most) one entity. Ideally, an identity is able to be generated locally, rather than only by a central "naming resource" (e.g., a Microsoft GUID).
Infrastructure	An application architecture in which low-level capabilities are built in modular fashion, with standardized, well-documented interfaces. The collection of those modular capabilities constitutes a low-level application "infrastructure" layer. This arrangement allows application developers to easily "re-use" needed elements of those low-level capabilities in other applications. The capabilities of an infrastructure-based application can be easily and relatively quickly extended beyond what is provided in current versions of that application. The architecture of an infrastructure-based application contrasts with the architecture of a framework-based application.
Interoperability	The ability of two or more hardware devices, or two or more software entities, to work together without needing to know the implementation details at each end point.
JXTA	JXTA technology is a set of open, generalized peer-to-peer protocols, initially developed by Sun Microsystems, that allow any connected device on the network to communicate and collaborate in a peer-to-peer manner. http://www.jxta.org
Location Independence	The ability of an entity (an entity here is used in the most generic sense referring to both users and software modules) to move within the network without loss of its functionality or access to its resources. As an example consider the use of commonly used e-mail systems like Yahoo and Hotmail. Access for the users e-mail (resource) is available from a variety of access points (Internet Connected Home PC, Internet Connected Airport Kiosk, Internet connected Office PC) giving the user freedom of movement. A user is the entity which has location independence in this context.

Location Transparency

The ability of accessing a resource (a resource is used here in the most generic sense, it could be an object, file etc.) at the application level using its qualified name without direct knowledge of its actual physical location within the network. The physical location here refers to the network address of the resource (example: In an IP network this could refer to the IP address and the port number for the service offering access to that resource). By definition, it implies that resources could be mobile within the network and their movement within the network still permits access to that resource using its qualified name.

On numerous occasions people use the term Location Independence for this definition of location transparency.

[alternate definition:]

Given the name of an object (file, process, stream) the user (including programmer) of the name does not necessarily know where the object is located. Often the user may find out – but the name contains no location information. Thus, the name must be bound to an actual location at some point (see “binding”).

Metadata

Metadata is "data about data." Used in the context of digital spatial data, metadata is the background information which describes the content, quality, condition, and other appropriate characteristics of the data.

Migration Transparency

Given the name of an object (file, process, stream) the user (including programmer) of the name does not necessarily know where the object is located. Further, the object may move, possibly while the name is in use.

Name

A name is a way to refer to something such as a file, a process, or a machine. A name can be an address, e.g., 0x4454 or 128.143.67.15:5432, a variable name, e.g., int X, or a string such /home/myfile. Names are abstractions and must be bound to address, either directly, or via a series of bindings via intermediate levels of names. Names are how transparencies such as location transparency are realized, for example, the string /home/myfile does not say where the file is located – what host, disk, track, or sector. That gives the system the freedom to move the file – or replicate it.

Namespace

A convention for naming resources uniquely. The namespace denotes a very large set of names of which only a subset of names are ever used. For example, the set of all possible fully qualified domain names is infinite; but only particular names within the space, such as www.ptpwg.org, are assigned to particular resources.

The scope of a namespace refers to the set of entities within which names are expected to be unique. For example, the set of possible California license-plate numbers is one namespace; Nevada's is another. The scope of each namespace is the set of vehicles registered in the state. Two cars can have the same license-plate number if they are registered in different states.

NAT

A Network Address Translator (NAT) translates multiple internal IP addresses into a single external IP address, effectively multiplexing a single IP into many other IP addresses. Addresses managed by NAT's are in the "non-routable" set, e.g., 10.X.X.X or 172.X.X.X. See also http://www.faqs.org/rfcs/rfc2663.html for more information.

Node

A computing device residing on a network. Nodes may be general-purpose computers, or they may be specialized to provide particular services or capabilities (e.g., a storage node or control node). Note the term computing device is used in the most generic sense in that a node can range from a multi-processor server to embedded systems.

Object

A self-contained module of data and its associated processing. Objects are the software building blocks of object technology.

Also, in a compound document, an independent block of data, text or graphics that was created by a separate application.

Object-based

Object-based refers to a system in which objects can be selected - that is, individually identified -- and manipulated, but does not necessarily imply object-oriented notions of encapsulation of code and data. In peer-to-peer systems, objects can include processors, files, or specific services. An object-oriented programming language can be used to build an object-based system.

[Alternative definition:]

A programming language, software architecture or other system that uses the conceptual basis of object oriented programming languages, software architectures or other software-systems. An object-based system relaxes some of the features of a full-fledged object-oriented system. An early use of the term was in references to the Ada programming language. Ada only supported a subset of the inheritance mechanisms required by a full object-oriented language, hence it was called "object-based" as opposed to object-oriented.

Object-oriented

Object-oriented is a term often used to refer to a programming methodology in which objects encapsulate code and data together. Here the methods or functions used to query, set, and manipulate the data are bundled with the data. Some methods are private and only callable by other methods in the object; some methods are public and provide interfaces into the object for external callers. In a pure approach, objects are treated as black boxes whose contents are manipulated only by the published methods. Besides encapsulation, object-oriented methodologies permit establishment of relationships between objects. For example, attribute inheritance. Objects can induce other objects to change state through method invocation, but each object is ultimately responsible for its own internal/local state changes.

[Alternative definition:]

A programming language, software architecture or other software-system based on generalizations of hierarchical abstract data types. Pragmatically, this implies a hierarchy of classes linked together through some type of inheritance tree. These classes define the potential values available to instances of the classes and all the operations that can be applied to these instances. These instances (called objects) map the potential values and operations (or methods) onto actuals thereby precisely defining the abstract data type.

Passport

A single sign-on and digital wallet service for the Web from Microsoft. The Passport Single Sign-in Service (formerly known as the Passport Authentication Service) enables users to enter their IDs and passwords once and be able to log onto all Passport Web sites without having to retype the data. The Passport Digital Wallet service stores credit card, shipping and billing information on Microsoft secure servers, which enables users to make purchases without having to retype the information. When users make a purchase on Passport sites, the merchant sends a request to the Passport server, which returns the appropriate information. This server-based wallet supersedes the client-based wallet in Microsoft Internet Explorer.

Peer A network node that can act as a client or a server, with or without centralized control, and with or without continuous connectivity. The term 'peer' can apply to a wide range of device types, including small handhelds and powerful server-class machines that are closely managed.

[alternate definition:]

A peer can be anything that will talk to another peer using some protocol that both understand. A peer could be PDA, a desktop, or a supercomputer. For some a peer is always a piece of hardware, for others it is a software component on a piece of hardware, and there may be many peers per physical hardware device.

[alternate definition:]

A device that is capable of both initiating communications and accepting communications initiated elsewhere.

Peer-to-Peer A computing model in which peer nodes collaboratively perform a computing task. In addition to that defining property, these two characteristics are typical of peer-to-peer systems in varying degrees: avoidance of central control and the use of edge resources. With reference to the first characteristic, a pure peer-to-peer system is one that completely eliminates reliance on a centralized control node. A system that uses a centralized node (for support such as directory or control services) is described by terms such as hybrid, mediated, or brokered peer-to-peer.

Persistence, Global (State-) A method for preserving given items of data or program-state for a specified lifetime. That lifetime may exceed the duration during which the subject contents remain valid and available in their node of origin.

Persona Used synonymously with "identity."

Policy Collections of operational rules that direct the behavior of a management component. Policies apply to areas such as security, resource usage, and others.

Presence Presence services or systems are typically associated with protocols or discovery processes by which state changes of an object, service, or user are exchanged. Entities of a presence service can be partitioned into those that provide state and those that receive state, usually through a registration or polling process. The most common terminology use is with respect to instant messaging systems where a presence service provides the means for users to determine the on-line (accepting IM's) or offline (not accepting IM's) status of other users.

Protocol

In information technology, a protocol (from the Greek protocollon, which was a leaf of paper glued to a manuscript volume, describing its contents) is the special set of rules that end points in a telecommunication connection use when they communicate. Protocols exist at several levels in a telecommunication connection. There are hardware telephone protocols. There are protocols between each of several functional layers and the corresponding layers at the other end of a communication. Both end points must recognize and observe a protocol. Protocols are often described in an industry or international standard.

Proxy Server

A proxy server is a server that acts as an intermediary between a user and the Internet so that the enterprise can ensure security, administrative control, and caching service. A proxy server is associated with or part of a gateway server that separates the enterprise network from the outside network and a firewall server that protects the enterprise network from outside intrusion.

A proxy receives a request for an Internet service (such as a Web page request) from a user. If it passes filtering requirements, the proxy server, assuming it is also a cache server, looks in its local cache of previously downloaded Web pages. If it finds the page, it returns it to the user without needing to forward the request to the Internet. If the page is not in the cache, the proxy server, acting as a client on behalf of the user, uses one of its own IP addresses to request the page from the server out on the Internet. When the page is returned, the proxy server relates it to the original request and forwards it on to the user.

To the user, the proxy server is invisible; all Internet requests and returned responses appear to be directly with the addressed Internet server. (The proxy is not quite invisible; its IP address has to be specified as a configuration option to the browser or other protocol program.)

Public Key

A public key is a value provided by some designated authority as a key that, combined with a private key derived from the public key, can be used to effectively encryption messages and digital signature.

The use of combined public and private keys is known as *asymmetric* cryptography. A system for using public keys is called a public key infrastructure (PKI).

Public Key Cryptography

Public key cryptography does not rely on a single key (a password or a secret "code"), but on two keys. These keys are numbers that are mathematically related in such a way that if either key is used to encrypt a message, the other key must be used to decrypt it. Also important is the fact that it is next to impossible (with our current knowledge of mathematics and available computing power) to obtain the second key from the first one and/or any messages encrypted with the first key.

A property of the RSA system (see RSA below) is that by making one of the keys available publicly (a *public key*) and keeping the other key private (a *private key*), a person can prove that he or she holds the private key simply by signing a message. If the message can be verified using the public key, the person must have used the private key to sign the message.

Note that it is critical that private keys be kept private! Anyone who has access to the private key can easily impersonate the owner.

Replication

Replication is the act of duplicating some data or computation. Replication is usually done for two reasons, availability and performance.

Replication is usually defined as either replication in space and replication in time.

Replication in space means that at any given time there are multiple copies of the object. If one copy fails, other copies may be used. Alternatively, different copies may be used to get better performance, e.g., choose a closer copy, or a copy on a lightly loaded host. A special case of this is load managed stateless web servers.

Replication in time is usually only used for computations – if a computation fails, then it can be restarted using the same input data.

Of course one can replicate both in space and time for both availability and performance reasons. For example, a client could start three copies of a computation going and take the first available result, discarding the rest.

Resource Network-resident services or capabilities. These may include hardware (e.g., CPU cycles, disk-storage space, peripheral devices) or software (e.g., Web services, directory services, etc.). Resources may be low-level (e.g., hardware access) or high-level (e.g., access to complex applications). A resource may have a global identity, or it may be addressable by qualification of the identity of its host peer (aka node).

RSA RSA is an Internet encryption and authentication system that uses an algorithm developed in 1977 by Ron Rivest, Adi Shamir, and Leonard Adleman. The RSA algorithm is one of the most commonly used encryption and authentication algorithms. The technologies are part of existing or proposed Web, Internet, and computing standards. To learn how the RSA algorithm works see http://www.rsasecurity.com/rsalabs/faq/

Scalability A scalable system or application can use one host, two hosts, a thousand hosts, or a million hosts. Scalability is best described by the distributed systems principle – a system is scalable if "the amount of work required of any particular component must not be an increasing function of the number of nodes in the system."

The bottom line is that as the system grows and adds hosts, devices, users, and files, there must be no component that becomes a bottleneck. This means that centralized schemes are not scalable.

Note: Scalability has a similar, but different meaning in the parallel processing world. There, an application is scalable if one can add processors without a loss of efficiency. There are two variants on this definition depending on whether the problem size is allowed to scale up with the number of processors.

Scheduling The resource management function by which demand is matched with supply to initiate active processing and future planning. Scheduling is under the control of policies.

Services, Aggregated A process for building large, complex Web applications by utilizing services provided by various nodes in a network. Each such node can provide its requested services by recursively obtaining services from other providers. Providers can discover available providers through registry/brokerage services; they can choose from the available providers; and they can then contract with the chosen provider(s) for delivery of the needed service(s).

Server A role in a network computing task, in which a (server) node provides a service requested by another (client) node. The term "server" is also often applied to a node that can operate in the server role (e.g., a powerful, resource-rich "server" computer), or one that is physically secured and closely managed.

Services Contracting	Capability to request delivery of a service from a selected service provider. This capability includes the ability to confirm commitment by the service provider, as well as the ability to track completion/delivery status by the service provider.
Services Registry/ Brokerage	Capability to gather information about a set of services available from various nodes across a network. This information is intended to support the selection of service providers by a service requester. The registry/brokerage is typically maintained in a centralized location (e.g., on a server). The registry/brokerage may include the ability to identify the "best" available service provider, per "goodness" metrics supplied by the requester and/or registry/brokerage.
Session	A period of time (therefore has a start and end time) in which computing resources are bound to a discrete user request.
Session, Batch	User request is statically defined and de-coupled from the actual session (job definition vs. job instance). Higher levels of de-coupling are sought e.g., I submit my job, turn off my computer and turn it back on 5 hours later to find that my work has completed somewhere in the 'system'. Resource usage may be highly repeatable and predictable.
Session, Interactive	For an interactive session, user requests are dynamic and strongly coupled to the session. Higher levels of coupling are sought -- i.e., interactive user expects work products of multiple programs (e.g., CFD engine and visualization tool) to be integrated in real time. Resource usage responds to real time user input and is not planned out ahead of time. Resource usage is usually not highly repeatable and predictable.
Sharing	This term is synonymous with "resource-sharing."

Sharing, Resource- A means by which requesters can be allotted resources provided by one or more other nodes within a network. These resources can include disk-space, peripheral-device access, access to specific data-files, etc. Resource-sharing is usually orchestrated by a centralized service registry/brokerage, which tracks resources provided by each participant node. The registry/brokerage may allocate resources based on resource characteristics, or utilization data.

Cycle sharing: An application in which requesters can be allotted (typically unused) compute capacity provided by one or more nodes within a network. A registry/brokerage may assign work to a known collection of nodes, based on node attributes such as processor architecture, available memory, utilization data, and prior execution success history.

Storage sharing: Controlled sharing of the space on a storage device by multiple networked computing nodes. Storage capacity is typically presented through a file system interface.

Peripheral sharing: Peripheral sharing typically refers to allowing multiple nodes access to resources with I/O external to the computer network (e.g., cameras, microphones, printers, CD-burners, etc.). Such I/O devices often require more extensive access control capabilities, as well as location aware discovery and scheduling services.

Bandwidth sharing: A mechanism by which available bandwidth from one or more peer nodes is applied to network communication. The most common examples are in the area of content distribution (where a node relays content) or connection sharing (where a node provides access to a network to another node).

Site Autonomy The state where the resource owner in a system determines the policies governing its use.

SOAP SOAP (Simple Object Access Protocol) is an XML-based protocol for exchanging information in a decentralized, distributed environment. It's mostly used for remote procedure calls (RPC)—causing a remote computer to execute a bit of code and return the result over the network.

SOAP has three parts: an envelope that defines a framework for describing what is in a message and how to process it, a set of encoding rules for expressing instances of application-defined data types, and a convention for representing remote procedure calls and responses.

http://www.w3.org/TR/SOAP/
http://www.develop.com/soap/

SSL (also TLS) Transport Layer Security (TLS) is based on Secure Sockets Layer (SSL), a commonly-used protocol for managing the security of a message transmission on the Internet. TLS is based on SSL. SSL uses a program layer located between the Internet's Hypertext Transfer Protocol (HTTP) and Transport Control Protocol (TCP) layers. SSL is included as part of both the Microsoft and Netscape browsers and most Web server products. SSL became the de facto standard until evolving into Transport Layer Security. SSL uses the public-and-private key encryption system from RSA, which also includes the use of a digital certificate.

TLS and SSL are an integral part of most Web browsers (clients) and Web servers. If a Web site is on a server that supports SSL, SSL can be enabled and specific Web pages can be identified as requiring SSL access.

TLS and SSL are not interoperable. However, a message sent with TLS can be handled by a client that handles SSL but not TLS.

State, Central A mechanism, often used by the gaming community, in which a file is used to give multiple nodes controlled access to shared information. Such shared information may complement private information that a given node uses to execute its tasks. Example: global graphics, sound or game-state data that is provided by a game server to all of the (distributed) users of a multi-player game.

State, Distributed Overall program state for a distributed application resides on a set of nodes. Example: state of a particular user's data, in a distributed multi-player game. In a distributed-gaming application, for example, the overall game state includes both the central state, and the distributed state information maintained by each participating player's peer-node.

Sum of Services Architecture An architecture based on a set of services that are separable from each other. The sum of these services provides the complete intended functionality.

Super Peer A peer node that preferentially provides one or more services to a collection of peers. While other peers may be capable of providing these same services, the super peer usually does so, because it has some uncommon or unique resource such as stable network connectivity and presence, unusually large memory or storage space, or high processing capacity. In this role, the super peer fills a role analogous to that of a server in a traditional client/server architecture. A common example of a super peer is a constantly connected node that serves as a persistent peer who that may offer high availability messaging services to intermittently connected peers.

Alternatively, a super peer is peer that provides additional services based on its configuration or role.

Synchronization, Distributed Mechanism(s) to keep multiple copies of a given file, residing on different nodes, consistent with one another. This is a cache-like mechanism that reflects changes to one copy of a file into all other copies. Different synchronization policies are possible.

Task Partition A facility that allows the division/partitioning of a task in such a way that the constituent parts can be executed using a collection of resources, with the overall results being acquired and assembled by the partitioning/distribution facility. The partitioning may use resources that reside across a collection of nodes (e.g., CPU cycles, memory, disk-space, peripherals, data, etc.).

Index

F

J - K

L

M

N

O

Q - R

S

T

U

V

W

X